MEDIA REGULATION

Governance and the interests of citizens and consumers

Peter Lunt and Sonia Livingstone

Los Angeles | London | New Delhi
Singapore | Washington DC

SAGE Publications Ltd
1 Oliver's Yard
55 City Road
London EC1Y 1SP

SAGE Publications Inc.
2455 Teller Road
Thousand Oaks, California 91320

SAGE Publications India Pvt Ltd
B 1/I 1 Mohan Cooperative Industrial Area
Mathura Road
New Delhi 110 044

SAGE Publications Asia-Pacific Pte Ltd
33 Pekin Street #02–01
Far East Square
Singapore 048763

Library of Congress Control Number: 2011929889

British Library Cataloguing in Publication data

A catalogue record for this book is available from the British Library

ISBN 978-0-85702-569-2
ISBN 978-0-85702-570-8 (pbk)

Typeset by C&M Digitals (P) Ltd, Chennai, India
Printed and bound by CPI Group (UK) Ltd, Croydon, CRO 4YY
Printed on paper from sustainable resources

CONTENTS

ABOUT THE AUTHORS

Peter Lunt is Professor of Media and Communication at the University of Leicester, UK. His research interests include audience research, popular television, the public understanding of media regulation and media and social theory and consumption research. He is the author of five books, including *Talk on Television* (with Sonia Livingstone, Routledge, 1994) and *Stanley Milgram* (Palgrave, 2010) and many academic papers. His research has received financial support from the Economic and Social Research Council UK, he has been a member of several European-funded networks and projects and has also conducted research for a number of public bodies including the Office of Fair Trading in the UK. He is currently working on a project on media, history and memory, focusing on the TV programme *Who Do You Think You Are?*, in collaboration with Claire Lynch at Brunel University. He is also writing about challenges to public service broadcasting and about the implications for media studies of the later works of Habermas. His future research plans include projects on the regulation of community radio and further work on the public understanding of media policy.

Sonia Livingstone is Professor of Social Psychology and Head of the Department of Media and Communications at the London School of Economics and Political Science. Her research examines children, families and the internet; media and digital literacies; the mediated public sphere; and audience reception for diverse television genres. She has been the author or editor of 14 books, including *Audiences and Publics* (edited, Intellect, 2005), *The Handbook of New Media* (edited, with Leah Lievrouw, Sage, 2006), *Harm and Offence in Media Content* (with Andrea Millwood Hargrave, Intellect, 2006), *Media Consumption and Public Engagement* (with Nick Couldry and Tim Markham, Palgrave, 2010), and *Children and the Internet* (2009, Polity Press). Sonia Livingstone serves at Evidence Champion for the UK's Council for Child Internet Safety, and has, at various times, also served on the Department of Education's Ministerial Taskforce for Home Access to Technology for Children, Ofcom's Media Literacy Research Forum, the Voice of the Listener and Viewer, and the Internet Watch Foundation. In addition she has been President of the International Communication Association (2007–8).

PREFACE

What do citizens need from the media and how can this be guaranteed? Who ensures that converging communications technologies serve the public interest? Do we even know what the public needs or wants? Can a single organisation balance industry and consumer demands in regulating media and communications? Can national governments still regulate in a global network society? Why does regulation increasingly rely on individuals acting responsibly? Who should participate in the process of regulation?

In response to globalisation, the increasing complexity of services and markets, and changes in welfare and governance, governments around the world are rethinking the nature, role and scope of regulation in a variety of markets. In this context, the UK's Communications Act 2003 established a new regulator for the media and communications sector, The Office of Communications (Ofcom), which, drawing on wider changes across Western democracies, also advanced New Labour's new regulatory regime. Ofcom took over the powers and responsibilities of regulators in the hitherto separate areas of telecommunications and broadcasting, and it has regulated the media and communications sector since 2003 through a mixture of measures to promote competition, plurality and diversity. Responsible for regulating television, radio, telecommunications and spectrum management (though not for all media, notably not music, film, the press or, curiously, that most convergent of all technologies, the internet), Ofcom has been closely observed by other countries also seeking a regulatory model to withstand the challenges of a globalising and converging media and communications landscape. Further, Ofcom exemplifies the regulatory innovations undertaken as part of the New Labour governments 1997–2010. For example, guided by principles of so-called 'better regulation', Ofcom has sought to reduce the regulatory burden on firms and to support self-regulation where possible. However, although Ofcom is a statutory agency with a wide range of legal duties, it has considerable discretion in how to meet those obligations, and its actions have resulted in public debate and occasional controversy.

Crucially, Ofcom is required to consult widely with its stakeholders, to conduct and publish market and consumer research and to measure the impact of regulation on markets and the plurality of both content and suppliers. Since many of these activities are conducted in and through public processes of deliberation, in this book we propose that Ofcom has acted, with greater or lesser success, as an institution in the public sphere. In today's complex societies, the potential of the public sphere – for impartial and inclusive processes of deliberation, the weighing of evidence and a recognition of diverse interests in debating policy and regulation – must increasingly be realised, if at all, through the institutional and civil society activities that bridge the oft-separated realms of policy making and the public. The 'public' of the public sphere should not, however, refer only to elites and experts speaking for people in their absence. We write as researchers of television audiences and mediated publics rather than as scholars steeped in the legacy of media policy research, and we have been struck by the relative absence of the voices and realities of audiences in policy analysis, including that conducted by the academy. Unsurprisingly, then, our main focus is on Ofcom's role in relation to the public interest – although of course we would acknowledge its significant activities in many other policy domains.

Intriguingly, Ofcom's primary duty was defined by the Act as the duty to further the interests of citizens and of consumers, a duty that has been regarded both optimistically and sceptically by observers of media regulation. Arguably, the public interest includes both the citizen and the consumer interest, although some would only align it with the former. Although Ofcom claims to represent the interests of citizens and consumers, to undertake consumer education and to engage with stakeholders (including audiences, through research and consultations with industry and the public), these regulatory roles require a difficult balance between economic regulation, consumer protection and furthering citizen interests. How, we asked, is this working, and with what consequences? In approaching these questions, our concern has been to explore how implicit and explicit conceptions of the audience shape policy developments in ways that may or may not serve the interests of citizens and consumers. Our interest in the lived realities of audiences has also attuned us to the discursive nature of policy making, leading us to look behind and beyond the actual decisions made so as to understand the processes through which decisions are reached, implemented (or not), and then re-made over time.

This book began life as an empirical project funded by the Economic and Social Research Council, which examined the design and activities of Ofcom and the Financial Services Authority, in particular the relations they established among regulators, firms, civil society, government and the public. In the project, entitled 'Public Understanding of Regimes of Risk Regulation', we asked, first, how the public is represented within the new culture of regulation and, second, how the public understands its changing role and responsibility within the communications and financial service sectors, with this potentially influencing individual and collective responses to risk. To some, this is a curious question – what does it matter how the public itself understands the regulatory institutions acting on its behalf? Is the public not simply uninterested in and ignorant of the activities of regulators? Does it not crossly endorse the tabloid view of regulation in terms of unwarranted interference and 'red tape' promulgated by the 'nanny state'? Our focus group interviews with diverse members of the public did indeed open with such accounts but, they then went deeper, revealing some subtle and complex views and thereby justifying our determination to include their voices here.

In the project, as well as in this book, we did not set out to answer the simple question, is Ofcom a good thing? And has it made matters better or worse? Is the Coalition government of 2010 right to reduce its funding and limit its policy functions? No simple answers are forthcoming. Rather, in our analysis we appropriate the neutral observer role claimed by social sciences – we note, chart, explore and seek explanations. On the one hand, we note the positive marks accorded to Ofcom by many, recently including those who – as the present Coalition government puts forward in its new Communications Act – realise that much of value might be lost. Ofcom has operated during an eventful period in which telecommunications have been opened up as a market, commercial broadcasting has survived, if not perhaps thrived, in an increasingly competitive market, the digital switchover in broadcasting is progressing rather better than expected, media literacy has been widely promoted in new and creative ways, community radio has flourished, and even public service broadcasting, although constantly threatened, remains strong. On the other hand, Ofcom's critics have never been shy and there has grown up, in contrast with the above judgements, a well-articulated critique of the past decade of UK media regulation that should also be heard. This highlights the continued threats – political and economic – to the support for and independence of the BBC and other public service broadcasters, the relatively unchecked rise to power of Rupert Murdoch's News Corporation, the apparent sidelining of citizen interests compared with both consumer and, more significantly, industry interests, and the gradual shift in regulatory power from Whitehall to Brussels as European policy making grows in importance, increasingly setting the agenda for national policy.

In the context of these fascinating and important debates, we set out to answer a more complex question. Ofcom, as we will demonstrate, has done much to provide the opportunities and the evidence base to enhance diverse forms of participation in public debate over media policy. As a competition regulator, it has extended the protection of consumers and the advancement of their interests across the range of its activities, complementing its facilitation of market and industry interests. To achieve these aims, Ofcom has operated as a publicly visible body, liaising with civil society and the public as well as with government and industry. In so far as this advances the avowed values of the public sphere – argument, accountability, inclusiveness, transparency, evidence-based deliberation and decision making – our judgement of Ofcom is broadly positive. But in asking whether, by acting as an institution in the public sphere, it has improved outcomes in particular areas of media policy making, our answer is more equivocal. We remain convinced that acting as an institution in the public sphere must improve policy making in the public interest, certainly by comparison with closed, opaque and top-down approaches. But the messy realities, conflicting interests at stake and the very indeterminacies introduced by public-facing, participatory or evidence-based regulation can nonetheless undermine public interest outcomes. We explore a number of case studies of regulatory practice – public service broadcasting, the protection of children, media literacy and community radio – which illustrate the new regulatory challenges in several ways. Each is shaped by specific contingencies, from legacy traditions of policy and regulation to the immediate glare of political attention or media publicity, from the invisible hand of market or state influence to the unexpectedly persuasive appeal of new arguments or compelling evidence turning a debate.

Eschewing an explicitly political or normative stance, our overall aim, therefore, is to integrate an analysis of Ofcom's processes of working as an institution in the public sphere with the particular relation between process and outcomes revealed through our case studies. Possibly, other case studies would lead to different conclusions, and we would welcome a larger field of scholarship conducting exactly such analyses. But time is short in the sense that Ofcom is already changing as we write, and following the design and implementation of a new Communications Act, it will surely change further. For now, therefore, we draw out the processes that have characterised media and communications regulation as regards the interest of citizens and consumers from 2003 to now, this representing a key decade in the history of the digital age. In so doing, we articulate a critical repertoire by which Ofcom's role, and that of any alternative approach to regulation (as may emerge in the UK or elsewhere, now or subsequently), may be evaluated, depending on the standpoint of future critics. And we hope that, taken together, these insights may positively inform the debates to come.

How has, and how can, media and communications regulation further the interests of citizens and consumers? Chapter 1 reviews the changing context of governance and regulation, particularly in an age of globalisation and digitalisation, drawing out the challenges that this raises for culture and citizenship. Chapter 2 situates current theories of regulation, which examine the various forms that regulatory agencies take, and the range of strategies that they adopt, in order to focus on our specific context of media and communication regulation. Together, these chapters locate media regulation within a framework which is both wide-ranging and highly specific. As Black (2005) observes, regulatory innovation across sectors has gathered apace in recent years, partly in response to the European Commission policy to encourage national regulatory agencies, partly as a response to the perceived problems of traditional forms of legal and regulatory intervention given notable technical and market innovation and, most generally, in response to the growing dispersal of power away from the nation state in a time of globalisation.

Chapters 3 and 4 focus the lens first on the discursive debates surrounding the framing of Ofcom's key purposes, namely on furthering the interests of citizens and consumers and, second, on the shaping of Ofcom as an institution that operates substantially in the public sphere. Hence we elaborate the context of its establishment, its statutory duties, regulatory structures and operating principles. As already noted, this means we examine how Ofcom balances its joint responsibilities to further both citizen and consumer interests, how it implements its statutory obligation to consult widely with stakeholders and to conduct and publish research so as to engage a wide range of participants in regulation and to foster public debate. Since it is beyond the scope of this book to offer a comprehensive view of all of Ofcom's structures and activities, we here review key areas of its core business, such as spectrum management and media plurality.

Four case studies follow, selected in order to reveal the processes of regulatory innovation, research, consultation and engagement noted above. Again, these may not seem 'typical' of Ofcom's main work strands, but they do, we suggest, reveal its workings in areas of regulation that matter to citizens and consumers (or, audiences). They also demonstrate ways in which Ofcom has operated principally (though not entirely) within the realm of public deliberation and debate. The first case study is, perhaps, the most obvious, that of public service broadcasting. As discussed in Chapter 5, Ofcom was required by the Communications Act 2003 to review public service television although it had only limited regulatory powers over the BBC, the cornerstone of the UK public service system. Given that public service broadcasting represents a hotly contested area of media policy, this case study demonstrates how Ofcom engages public debate so as to draw on and advance beyond the considerable legacy of policy deliberation. This case study also demonstrates the limits of regulation in an area that is strongly contested by powerful stakeholders, including the government, the media industry, civil society bodies and the public.

By contrast with the challenges of addressing this substantial legacy of policy work, Chapter 6 examines how Ofcom defined and scoped a new area of media policy – new at least to media regulators (though not educators) – that of media literacy, this being an intriguing requirement placed on Ofcom by the Communications Act. In this largely uncharted territory, Ofcom sought to develop policy to address a growing problem – the realisation that cross-border and convergent media technologies mean that regulatory control over media content is increasingly 'out of reach' of national regulation. Can enhancing media literacy among audiences, enabling them to exercise choice and adopt a critical stance on media content, meet this challenge, and if so, can the regulator promote this through effective stakeholder partnerships (rather than through traditional, top-down methods of control over media content and services)? Or is the promotion of media literacy less a policy designed to further the public interest than one motivated by those interests that are anxious to deregulate converging media platforms?

The protection of children has long been a specific and widely accepted role for media regulation, though our third case study – that of the regulation of junk food advertising in a context of fast-rising childhood obesity – proved no less controversial than the other two (see Chapter 7). We use this case to focus especially on Ofcom's research activities, research providing a key means by which the audience's interests and needs, especially in the lay voices of children and parents, can be recognised within the process of expert deliberation. The limitations of evidence-based policy provide a point of critical reflection on Ofcom's activities and the ambitions of the regulatory regime it represents. The outcome of this particular case also points up the persistently less than transparent relation between the regulator and the state.

Finally, we consider Ofcom's ground-breaking work on community radio in Chapter 8. Building on the work of one of its legacy regulators, The Radio Authority, Ofcom has succeeded in establishing a proper licensing system for community radio for the first time in the UK from 2004. This case study identifies the impact of Ofcom's commitments to enhancing plurality and diversity while also regulating competition (in this case between the emerging community sector and local radio). This case study also shows how Ofcom works closely with civil society bodies and promotes innovation in the media system by enabling the development of a licensed community radio sector in the UK, which had not previously emerged from either the public service or the independent sector despite considerable enthusiasm for the third tier of media. However, as we will see, this case study also reveals concerns over the way that regulation introduces controls that shape this emerging sector.

These case studies, we believe, demonstrate the complexity of the background and legacy that Ofcom inherited, the difficulties inherent in adopting a variety of regulatory strategies and powers, and the importance of partnership and engagement between regulators and stakeholders from government, commerce, civil society and the public. As a statutory agency working within a strong legal framework and policy context established by government, Ofcom has nonetheless had considerable discretion regarding how to meet its obligations from its inception in 2003 through to mid-2010. In the final chapter, we reflect on the changes brought in by the Conservative/Liberal Democrat Coalition government in May 2010, as part of a reformulation of the responsibility for public policy making, for the role of quasi-independent public bodies, and the broader relations between business, state and public, several areas of responsibility (including the review of public service broadcasting) and a considerable proportion of its staffing and budget were removed from Ofcom. At the time of writing, we can only begin to speculate here on how these changes may impact on the subtle and complex balance that Ofcom has sought to achieve when representing the interests of citizens and consumers.

ACKNOWLEDGEMENTS

This book draws on the research project directed by Peter Lunt and Sonia Livingstone, *Public Understanding of Regimes of Risk Regulation*, funded by the Economic and Social Research Council (ESRC) as part of the 'Social Contexts and Responses to Risk Network', directed by Peter Taylor-Gooby (RES-336-25-0001; see http://www.kent.ac.uk/scarr/). For the project website and publications, see www.lse.ac.uk/collections/PURRR/. We thank Peter Taylor-Gooby for his support throughout the project, Tanika Kelay, Laura Miller and Sarita Malik for their work on the project, and all those who kindly gave up their time to be interviewed.

We thank all the interviewees for the ESRC project. Please note that, throughout this volume, they are referred to in terms of their role at the time (notwithstanding that several have moved role or organisation since then). Interviews included (with roles in 2005 in brackets): Colette Bowe (Chairman, Consumer Panel), Neil Buckley (Policy Director, Consumer, Competition and Markets, Ofcom), Robin Foster (Partner, Strategy and Market Developments, Ofcom), Richard Hooper (Chair of the Content Board, Ofcom), Graham Howell (Secretary to the Corporation, Ofcom), Kip Meek (Senior Partner, Competition and Content, Director of Competition Policy, Competition and Content, Ofcom), Julie Myers (Policy Manager Consumer Panel, Ofcom), Helen Normoyle (Policy Executive, Director of Market Research, Ofcom), Matt Peacock (Director of Communications, Ofcom), Tony Stoller (Executive Committee, and External Relations Director, Ofcom), Rhodri Williams (Director, Nations-Wales, Ofcom), Claire Milne (Freelance Consumer Spokesperson, Antelope Consulting), Pat Holland, Jonathan Hardy and Gary Herman (Campaign for Press and Broadcasting Freedom), Jocelyn Hay (Chairman, Voice of the Listener and Viewer), Don Redding (Campaign Co-ordinator, Public Voice), Luke Gibbs and Russ Taylor (Founders, OfcomWatch blog), John Beyer (Director, MediaWatch-UK), Allan Williams, Senior Policy Advisor, Consumers' Association – *Which?*), Paul Skidmore (Senior Researcher, DEMOS think tank), Richard Collins (academic, Ex-Oftel Advisor), Stephen Whittle (Controller, BBC Editorial Policy, BBC) and Simon Pitts (Controller Regulatory Policy, ITV). As part of that same project, the authors conducted 16 focus groups with a cross-section of the UK public, totalling 116 people in all. The discussions ranged across risk and regulation issues broadly, though two sectors – communications and financial services – were explored in detail. We thank all participants for their lively conversations with us.

We note, by way of declaration of interests, that in relation to Chapter 6 ('Media Literacy'), Sonia Livingstone acted as a consultant to Ofcom in 2005, being commissioned to review the academic literature on adult media literacy (Livingstone et al., 2005). She is also a member of Ofcom's Media Literacy Research Forum and she and Andrea Millwood Hargrave responded independently to Ofcom's first media literacy consultation in 2004, advising on the definition of media literacy and its implementation and evaluation; she has also emphasised the importance of media literacy in formal responses to Ofcom's annual plans in 2006, 2007 and 2008. In relation to Chapter 7 ('Advertising Regulation and Childhood Obesity'), Sonia Livingstone acted as consultant to Ofcom in 2004 and 2005–06, having been commissioned by the Research Department to review the academic literature on the effects of food promotion (mainly advertising) on children's food choice and, ultimately, childhood obesity; this resulted in three reports, all publicly available (Livingstone, 2004, 2006; Livingstone and Helsper, 2004). From 2006–09, Sonia Livingstone served on the Board of Directors of the civil society group, Voice of the Listener and Viewer. Parts of Chapter 3 are developed from earlier texts published as Livingstone and Lunt (2007, 2011) and Livingstone, Lunt and Miller (2007a, 2007b). Earlier versions of parts of Chapter 4 were published in Lunt and Livingstone (2007). Earlier versions of parts of Chapter 6 have been published in Livingstone (2008a, 2009b, 2010). The focus group interviews are reported in detail in Lunt et al. (2008).

We warmly thank colleagues who have read earlier drafts of the chapters that follow: Robin Blake, Ian Blair, Bart Cammaerts, Nico Carpentier, Richard Collins, Divina Frau-Megs, Lawrie Hallett, Sylvia Harvey, Jeanette Hofmann, Dale Kunkel, Peter Lewis, Greg Lowe, Kathryn Montgomery, Jill Pitt, Nick Stevenson, Tony Stoller and two anonymous reviewers. We thank Ed Richards, Ofcom's CEO, and Colette Bowe, Ofcom's Chairman, for agreeing to be interviewed in February 2011 as we were writing the manuscript. We also thank Dawn Rushen and Yinhan Wang for tidying up our text. However, the opinions expressed in the book, and any mistakes, remain our own. Finally, we thank Mila Steele at Sage for believing in this project and for being, as always, a wonderful publisher to work with.

Peter Lunt and Sonia Livingstone
Leicester and London, 2011

1

MEDIA AND COMMUNICATIONS REGULATION AND THE PUBLIC INTEREST

Introduction

We are witnessing the increasing globalisation of the media and communications technologies which connect peoples across the world, crosscut the boundaries of nation states, enable a dynamic global marketplace and contribute to the emergence of a complex transnational culture. Indeed, fundamental changes in modernity itself have been stimulated by the rapid development of a global market in media and communications, extensive movements of peoples and the increasing viability of real-time connections between individuals, businesses, social institutions and states on an unparalleled scale. The importance of media, information and communications technologies to modernity has a long history; from print through telegraphy, radio, film, television and now digital and networked media, communication technologies have both shaped and been shaped by the diverse processes of social, economic and political life (Appadurai, 1996; Curran, 2002; Held and McGrew, 2003; Rantanen, 2005; Thompson, 1995). But today, globalisation, capitalism and the mediated network society (Castells, 2003) have all become inextricably linked: hence Tomlinson (1999: 1–2) defines globalisation as 'an empirical condition of the modern world, which I call *complex connectivity*. By this I mean that globalisation refers to the rapidly developing ... network of interconnections and interdependencies that characterises modern social life'.

Some commentators argue that modernity has not merely speeded up but also entered a distinctive new phase of late capitalism (Giddens, 1998), altered not least by the contemporaneous political transformations by which state socialist regimes and developing countries become absorbed into the dynamics of global capitalism. Global markets are qualitatively different from previous international flows of trade because they exploit the new level of coordination and integration of financial markets, real-time production processes, complex dynamics of distribution, and significant flows of people across national boundaries (Castells, 2003). Government control over markets, social life and culture is challenged by the perceived imperative to deregulate in order to open up markets and so maximise the benefits of globalisation. Global media markets in particular play a critical role in shaping these transformations by facilitating global connectivity and undermining state control while, at the same time, being themselves shaped by those same processes of globalisation.

From the middle of the twentieth century until the 1980s, governments were accustomed to media systems organised on a national scale, amenable to top-down regulatory control by the state and recognised for their central role in underpinning social cohesion and national identity. A broad consensus supported the institutional management of this strong regulatory approach, typically based on a mix, differently constituted in different countries, of economic policies focused on delivering accessible and diverse media content from a range of suppliers (more significant in the USA) and of state or public ownership of large portions of a national media system through public ownership of telecommunications and public broadcasters (more significant in Europe). In liberal democracies, regulatory legitimacy rested on the claim that these policies and institutions served the public interest. And this, in turn, was defined either descriptively – put simply, as what the public wants – or, alternatively, according to the important but more complex normative ideal of what would or should serve the public interest (Freedman, 2008). As will become evident as this book unfolds, the persistent tension between these contrasting images of the public interest – mapping on to the discursive figures of 'the consumer' and 'the citizen' respectively – has driven much regulatory and critical debate in the media and communications sector and also more widely (Clarke et al., 2007). Two key features of the emerging global media system have more recently put both of these approaches to regulation at risk: transformations in the production, distribution and marketing of digital media (Tambini et al., 2008); and the increasing power of global media corporations operating across national borders and pressing for open markets (McChesney, 1999). Not only is the development of multimedia and convergent devices and platforms revolutionising the character of media systems and markets and, therefore, the everyday experience of the public, but it also makes it increasingly difficult for governments to implement media and communications policies based on shared national values and aimed at delivering social and cultural policies. At the same time, the expectations of a well-functioning, secure and efficient communication system have grown hugely, as society places ever more reliance on media and communications for the conduct of its fundamental processes of commerce, political participation, education, community, health and more.

The UK's New Labour government of 1997–2010 responded to these challenges in the media and communications sector by creating a new regulatory regime instituted by the Communications Act 2003 and including the establishment of a newly converged regulatory agency for a converging technological environment: the Office of Communications (Ofcom). This has been controversial in its consequences for the media and communications sector in particular and in what it reveals of the workings of the New Labour approach more generally. Since Ofcom has acted on behalf of government while remaining relatively independent, it has suffered from the controversy that attaches itself to all 'quangos' ('quasi-autonomous non-governmental organisations'). Specifically, those from the neoliberal[1] perspective have feared that such bodies too easily become an insidious and unaccountable extension of the state; meanwhile, those taking a social democratic[2] approach to governance have hoped – albeit with critical doubts along the way – that such bodies can achieve beneficial outcomes precisely because of their political independence, their concentration of expertise and their flexibility in working with industry, civil society and the public. The present book tracks how actors from these two perspectives have viewed, and indeed become involved in, the day-to-day operation of Ofcom across a range of policy domains. But such activities, and the associated controversies, were all abruptly interrupted by the change of government in the UK in mid-2010, with a threat to the very existence of Ofcom being one of the incoming Coalition government's first acts, later modified but not entirely rescinded. The next steps in the history of media and communications regulation are, at the time of writing, still uncertain.

In this book, we position changes in media and communications regulation in the wider context of globalisation, market harmonisation (i.e. supposedly deregulation to reduce constraints on trade within states and across borders) and technological convergence (the much-hyped ability to deliver media content on a range of platforms and devices). Our focus is distinctive in that, rather than seeking to review any and all policy deliberations over the past decade or two, we ask more specifically about the particular implications of these developments for the public interest. From the early debates in Parliament during the passage of the Act in 2003, through to designing the institutional features of the new regulator, Ofcom and, then, the subsequent processes employed in reaching crucial policy decisions, the public interest has been framed in terms of the interests of citizens and those of consumers. Whether conceived of as mutually compatible or conflictual, these twin dimensions of the public interest provide a critical lens by which to explore the regulatory regime Ofcom had developed and how this compares with alternative approaches beyond the UK or within it (including Ofcom's legacy regulators). Thus rather than offering a more conventional analysis of how Ofcom has managed competition, issued licences, determined spectrum allocation, and so forth, we examine its consequences for a series of public interest objectives. In particular, we argue that the Communications Act 2003 and its primary offspring, Ofcom, have enabled new ways of governing, indeed a new model of governance emblematic of the ways in which liberal democracies are responding to the challenges of globalisation. In this new model, power is partly dispersed to new regulatory bodies which operate as public-facing institutions in the public sphere. As we shall see, such an argument requires, first, a theoretical and empirical argument about the role of institutions in the public sphere and, then, an analysis of whether and to what extent the operation of Ofcom as an institution in the public sphere has resulted in significant benefits for the public – i.e. the consumer and, especially, the citizen – interest. To be sure, many questions arise. Has this meant the (partial) withdrawal of the state from media regulation in order to embrace neoliberalism, allowing the market to dominate? Or has it facilitated a new form of state intervention, instituted through the many strictures of the Communications Act, to ensure that Ofcom regulates media so as to support social and cultural purposes? Before we can address such questions directly, we need to backtrack and argue the case more carefully for the ways in which globalisation is reshaping regulation, with complex consequences for society and the public sphere.

Regulation and the role of the state

From the beginnings of modern political theory there has been a debate about whether the state is best when this is small in scope, focused on creating the conditions in which people can live without constraint and allowing commerce to innovate and develop according to its own logic, or whether a strong state is necessary to counter the extreme effects of modernisation and capitalism so as to enable citizens themselves to further their interests and realise their potential. There are considerable intellectual, political and social challenges to be faced as the state seeks to balance the protection of public interests in the face of powerful global economic interests exerting long-term pressures towards deregulation. In Britain since 2010, the pendulum has swung back to emphasise the small state (or the 'big society' of Cameron's Coalition government), countering New Labour's reformist social democracy agenda of the 1990s as supported by a strong yet decentralised state. But in an international context, the politics of particular states takes them in divergent, indeed sometimes conflicting directions in this regard.

One vision of globalisation is that it creates the conditions under which transnational processes of governance, along with some rejuvenation of local and community-based organisations, can take over some of the functions previously managed by national governments (Held and McGrew, 2003).

Consequently, the power of national governments diminishes, being dispersed both upwards and downwards. As Jessop (2000: 75) puts it, in the trend towards the 'de-nationalisation of the state', there is a:

'hollowing out' of the national state apparatus with old and new state capacities being reorganised territorially and functionally on subnational, national, supra-national, and trans-local levels. State power moves upwards, downwards, and sideways as state managers on different territorial scales try to enhance their respective operational autonomies and strategic capacities.

However, although nation states have undoubtedly lost some autonomy and power in the face of global markets and culture, they remain important. Thus, however radically one conceives the challenge to the nation state, it is worth asking how the state adjusts to these changing conditions. One answer is that the state spawns new regulatory agencies that permit it to act in a more dispersed and flexible manner. Such regulatory reform enables the dispersal of power downwards, as functions of the state are performed through regulation rather than through legislation and the work of central government departments. This trades central control for the flexibility of quasi-governmental bodies working with industry, civil society and the public but accountable to Parliament, resulting in a form of governance and administration that involves strategic interventions at a variety of levels rather than prioritising executive, top-down control at the national government level.

Given such shifts, we use the term 'regulation' to refer to the relations between power and the ordering of social behaviour at all levels of society from the nation state up to the transnational organisation and down to the subnational organisation or community and, even, the individual. In late modernity, the hitherto predominant focus on the nation state is changing, and regulation takes on a new meaning and significance, part of a broader shift which allows for a more strategic, flexible relationship between the state and a variety of agencies, firms and publics. Jessop regards these changes in the role of the state as necessary if it is to stimulate a competitive, 'globalising, knowledge-driven economy'; hence the increased focus of states on the administration of everyday life and the conduct of business at the micro level as well as on the coordination of economic policy at the super-national level (Mulgan, 1997).

In addition to the 'de-nationalisation of the state', Jessop (2000) also identifies the 'de-statisation of the political system,' as reflected in a crucial 'shift from government to governance'. As Donges (2007: 326) observes, 'governance refers to the dynamic structure of rules between actors that are linked in different networks and permanently forced to negotiate, without a center that has the power to command and control'. The changes brought about by the knowledge-based economy are central here as the complex and dynamic nature of the economic system demands more flexible and responsive modes of coordination:

Accordingly there is a movement from the central role of the official state apparatus in securing state-sponsored economic and social projects and political hegemony towards an emphasis on partnerships between government, para-governmental, and non-governmental organisations in which the state apparatus is often only first among equals. (Jessop, 2000: 75)

In terms of regulation, again this implies a greater range of activities by regulatory agencies beyond their role as economic regulators. As we shall see, in the case of Ofcom this is evident in the efforts devoted to fostering partnerships and networks of connection among stakeholders in the media and communications sector, encompassing government, industry, civil society and the public, all in the interests of increasing flexibility and responsiveness, the development of expertise and the collection of knowledge about products, the market and audiences.

Finally, Jessop (2000) discusses the trend towards an 'internationalisation of policy regimes'. In the knowledge-based global economy there are increasing transactions and communications across national borders and the consequent need for coordination beyond the boundaries of the nation state. This trend intersects with the previous two because this coordination is not likely to be satisfied by traditional connections between national governments but rather demands interconnections among a diverse range of institutions and actors, at local, national and international levels. Jessop's three themes – the dispersal of power or denationalisation of the state, the shift from government to governance or the destatisation of the political system, and the internationalisation of policy regimes – together capture the changing obligations of governance and the state, resulting in the rationale for regulatory reform adopted by the New Labour government of 1997–2010 (and as discussed further in Chapter 2).

Regulation, civil society and the public sphere

A self-regulating media system must maintain its independence vis-à-vis its environments while linking political communication in the public sphere with both civil society and the political center; second, an inclusive civil society must empower citizens to participate in and respond to a public discourse that, in turn, must not degenerate into a colonizing mode of communication. (Habermas, 2006: 420)

What are the implications of such complex changes in the state for its relations with its public? Responding to widespread hopes and concerns over the potential for and the fragility of citizenship in complex, plural, frag-mented societies, Habermas's (1962/1989) theory of the public sphere critically examined the changing relations between commerce, state, civil society and the public. We turn to his work, and the theoretical develop-ments that followed, to provide the analytic criteria by which changing regimes of regulation (the institution of Ofcom, its relations with the state, stakeholders and the public) can be evaluated in terms of its advancement, or otherwise, of the interests of citizens and/or consumers. We also draw on Habermas's work to frame our focus not only on the practice of regulation, but also on the discourses surrounding regulation, for discourses and prac-tices cannot easily be disentangled. Moreover, while practices are situated, the discourses that surround and shape them draw flexibly on a more extensive landscape of ideas, including provision for the actions of citizens of the public sphere. Since the concept of the public sphere is an idealisa-tion of the contexts of social life in which citizens can, through the free exchange of ideas, form a collective representation of the public interest that may challenge and bring established power to account, a range of civil society organisations are also expected to support the public sphere. As Alexander and Jacobs argue, civil society works not only through its rela-tions with, or autonomy from, the state and economy, but also 'as a com-municative space for the imaginative construction and reconstruction of more diffuse, but equally important, collective identities and solidarities' (1998: 1). Hence discursive constructions of the citizen – and, in relation to media and communications, explicit or more often implicit construc-tions of the audience (Livingstone, 1998) – play a role in the design and practice of regulation.

In his early work on the public sphere, Habermas argued against the liberal welfare state in so far as this protects the economic and social well-being of the public while limiting citizen involvement to the actions of consumers in relation to welfare services and to the actions of voters in the political sphere. For Habermas, the decline of public engagement in modern society resulted from the tendency of public institutions to rationalise and manage – rather than stimulate and enable – public life. However, as a social democrat, Habermas is optimistic that it is possible, even in the large-scale, complex societies that we now live in, to create the conditions in which the public engage more thoroughly, and more consequentially, in social and political life. In his early work, he proposed that this could best be achieved by protecting the public from the influ-ence of both the state and the market by supporting an independent public sphere which sustains rational critical discussion that, in turn, gen-erates a freely developed consensus which any legitimate government would be bound to take account of. One key threat to this public sphere, Habermas further argued, comes from the media which have gradually become ever more professionalised and market-oriented, intervening in and compromising the public sphere by reshaping public discussion, especially in complex modern societies, according to their own commercial rather than public objectives.

Although Habermas's (1962/1989) theory of the public sphere was enthusiastically received by the academic community, it was also the object of considerable criticism and he was charged with, among other things, having adopted an idealised conception of public engagement and failing to come to terms with the realities of democracy in complex, plural societies. Instead of aiming to represent the public will through public discussion, alternative conceptions of deliberation favour the inclusion of diverse, even oppositional, interests in a republic of voices (Calhoun, 1993; Fraser, 1990), although just how these voices are to be articulated and brought to the attention of the political sphere remains unclear. One way forward, in a complex pluralistic society with multiple and dispersed interdependencies between institutions and publics, is for a range of institutions, including the media and regulatory agencies, to play a role in giving opportunities for expression and the interplay of different arguments and voices (Bohman, 1996; Dahlgren, 2009; Livingstone and Lunt, 1994). This includes, but goes beyond, the participation of individuals, as prioritised in the traditional theory of the public sphere, instead emphasising diverse forms and contexts of engagement over the capacity of a singular, independent public sphere to achieve a unique consensus. Although more easily applicable to today's social conditions, this approach also faces a significant problem, namely how public opinion can gain sufficient legitimacy to command the attention of established power. Collins and Sujon (2007) propose, following Hirschman's famous analysis of accountability in terms of the strategies available to the public of exit and voice, that in so far as they have any power, consumers hold broadcasters to account through their ability to exit, while citizens hold them to account, if at all, through voice. Further, as Gangadharan (2009: 337) observes of Ofcom's parallel in the USA, the Federal Communications Commission, 'participation may not be sufficient; a commitment to public-spirited decision making among agency officials is also needed alongside procedural safeguards for participation'.

In today's increasingly diverse and complex sphere(s) of engagement between public (citizens and consumers), civil society, state and, indeed, industry, we find Habermas's later emphasis on the role to be played by institutions in the public sphere particularly helpful. Applying this to the analysis of Ofcom's role as one among many dispersed agencies at arm's length from government, a critical analysis of its power and potential – for and against the public interest – is opened up. Thus we turn to an examination of Habermas's ideas, as developed in *Between Facts and Norms* (1996), in relation to the role of institutions in the public sphere. Habermas proposes that the network of state administrative institutions should each form its own public sphere, by contrast with his earlier formulation of a single national public sphere. Where the quality of democracy in Habermas's early work depended on a distinct public sphere able to generate consensus, in his later work it depends on effectively engaging publics as part of the operation of bureaucratic and administrative institutions (see also Bohman, 1996: 188). In other words, he now elaborates the normative expectation that the institutions of the state should make the processes within and between institutions more public and more deliberative. Habermas (1996) supports his argument about the normative role of institutions in the public sphere through recourse to the sociology of law. Specifically, he takes the law to be the paradigm case of a complex network of social institutions which has the potential for a radical reconstruction of society that combines effective enforcement with public engagement and reflexivity regarding the rationalising tendencies of institutions.

On this view, institutions should sustain diverse engagements in a networked society, promoting public deliberation with legal, administrative and regulatory agencies. The plurality of forms of association is critical to Habermas's arguments, and he draws on Cohen and Arato's extensive (1992) survey of civil society to support his case. He argues that civil society is organised in part through its connections with the other significant social systems but that it has two distinctive features; first, that it is strongly interconnected with the everyday lives of individuals, and second, that it articulates public opinion in a way that has a legitimate claim on government and administration.

> Civil society is composed of those more or less spontaneously emergent associations, organizations and movements that, attuned to how societal problems resonate in the private life spheres, distil and transmit such reactions in amplified form to the public sphere. (Habermas, 1996: 367)

Habermas imagines the process of engagement as a distillation of public opinion flowing from public discourse through processes deliberation in civil society to communication in the political sphere. He contrasts this with the managed expression of public opinion that emerges from the operation of opinion research commissioned by the administrative process. The value of the public sphere, then, lies less in its potential to produce a consensus (a potential about which many have long been sceptical) but in its heightened sensitivity to the problems experienced in people's everyday lives, in what he terms 'the lifeworld'. Additionally, Habermas draws attention to the specific potential of civil society in mediating the relation between public opinion and the social institutions of the state and commerce:

From the perspective of democratic theory, the public sphere must, in addition, amplify the pressure problems, that is, not only detect and identify problems but also convincingly and *influentially* thematize them, furnish them with possible solutions, and dramatize them in such a way that they are taken up and dealt with by parliamentary complexes. (Habermas, 1996: 359)

We suggest, therefore, that as part of the social democratic project of supporting public deliberation and engagement, regulatory agencies that engage multiple stakeholders have a potentially important role to play as institutions in the public sphere. Hence, in this book we examine Ofcom's work in the media and communications sector by drawing on Habermas's four criteria for judging whether the institutions of the liberal democratic state can exercise power effectively and with legitimacy so as to be collectively binding (Habermas, 1996: 384-6). While Habermas focuses on the relationship between the institutions of the state and the law, in what follows we apply these criteria to the workings of a statutory regulatory institution also charged with the legitimate and effective management of power, albeit at arm's length from the state. Habermas's criteria develop a normative vision, leading him to ask, as do we, whether the institution -

(i) recognises when it is dealing with issues of public concern, within a reflexive awareness of the problems of society as a whole, in such a way as to acknowledge and enable deliberation among the different and often unequally resourced viewpoints and interests at stake while effectively resolving the issue at hand;

(ii) recognises through its principles and practices that it represents one institution among many (state, corporate, public, civil society, etc.), each with its own logic and demands, while also dealing fairly with the public sphere (which operates within the 'lifeworld' rather than the 'system world', as Habermas terms it[3]), balancing these often conflicting requirements without sacrificing one to the other;

(iii) gives equal recognition to effectiveness (ensuring that markets are competitive and that consumers are protected) and legitimation (ensuring the engagement and assent of that public in whose interest regulation operates), for promoting one may or may not promote the other, and neglecting either risks a vicious circle of negativity and distrust;

(iv) respects rather than undermines the right to self-determination of citizens, judging the nature and consequences of its institutional processes and decisions reflexively as these unfold in practice (rather than presuming about them in the abstract).

These criteria – concerning the public interest, the balancing of constraints, the combination of effectiveness and legitimation, and reflexivity regarding consequences – combine to offer a normative account of regulation appropriate to the complex interdependencies of the knowledge society. For in the knowledge society, knowledge creation, use and distribution are vital to the economy, politics and culture, and yet they simultaneously exacerbate the limits on governmental power and public administrative institutions (Mansell, 2002). Although these criteria address the process of public deliberation in governance, clearly, their significance is more fundamental. For the implication must be that if, in addition to the effective management of markets and the conscientious administration of commerce, these criteria are followed – in other words, that regulators and other key social agencies act as institutions in the public sphere – the regulatory outcomes will indeed advance the public interest.

With this guiding idea in mind, we scrutinise Ofcom's actions and working methods, examining our selected case studies in terms of an assessment of both the processes and their ultimate benefits, or otherwise, in relation to the public interest. In short, we assess whether, as the Communications Act 2003 itself demanded of Ofcom, the regulator has furthered the interests of citizens and consumers. After all, from the outset, Ofcom was tasked with acting as a principled, converged, evidence-based regulator in an international context that increasingly favours self- and co-regulation rather than audit and supervision. The new regulator was accountable to Parliament, it followed operating principles emphasising high levels of public consultation, transparency and research, and it had an explicit remit to inform and educate the public to encourage them to be critical consumers of media services, while fostering an inclusive climate of public discussion and consultation to engage citizens (and their representatives) in media and communications policy making.

Market innovation versus social democratic values

It must be said that, in the media and communications sector, regulatory agencies, government departments, civil society bodies and public service broadcasters often claim to act in the interest of the audience, although they variously conjure the image of the citizen, the consumer, the public or the individual in so doing (Livingstone, 2005; Syvertsen, 2004). In this sense, it is commonly acknowledged that, although the pressing rationale for changing the regulatory regime in media and communications centres on market and technological innovations, the interests at stake are not only economic and technological, but also social, cultural and democratic. But although the arguments for regulation refer to the public interest or the public sphere, there are grounds for scepticism that such arguments are more than superficial. Some commentators have seen in Ofcom the triumph of neoliberal governance rather than any significant contribution to social and cultural policy. Others, no doubt because an important feature of the New Labour project was the attempt to find a 'third way' between state ownership and the *laissez-faire* economics of neoliberalism, have used criticism of Ofcom – a prominent child of New Labour – as a vehicle for expressing their wider scepticism about New Labour's version of social democracy (Giddens, 1998). But the history that led to the establishment of Ofcom is longer and more complex than such criticisms imply.

Nation states meet regulatory challenges from different starting points, with differing resources and particular political histories. In the UK, a well-developed media system – including a successful model of a public service broadcasting system, a flourishing industry, an international reputation for high-quality programmes and services and a track record of innovation – set the scene for a growing consensus through the 1980s and 1990s to release the potential of the market for media and communications while sustaining the important social and cultural value delivered by the media system. Such a decision relied on a longer history of investment in public policy to ensure that media and communications first and foremost serve the public interest by providing knowledge and information and recognising cultural diversity while strengthening cultural heritage, as well as connecting people in the public sphere and engaging them in the political sphere. From the 1950s to the 1970s, key social policy principles were 'hard wired' into the British Broadcasting Corporation (BBC), the public service commitments of independent broadcasters and the public ownership of telecommunications organisations committed to the principles of universal access and service. Indeed, an important legacy was the role that the media played in the post-war reconstruction of nation states and the emerging European project – reflecting the nation back on itself, in forming and maintaining a sense of unity and continuity in a fluid and uncertain world (Scannell, 1989; Uricchio, 2009).

Yet by the 1970s the need for technical innovation and establishing market conditions that would give commercial broadcasters and the telecommunications industry an equal opportunity for investment and innovation was being increasingly recognised. The BBC and universal telecommunications services, part of the pride of the post-war welfare contract, were increasingly claimed to have a distorting effect on the market for media and communications. At the same time, the rationale for thinking of media and communications primarily as a market was tempered by the realisation that this might put at risk the contribution that the media made to society, politics and culture, as had been guaranteed by public service broadcasting and universal access to publicly owned telecommunications services for nearly half a century. Would global media content dilute or replace locally and nationally produced programmes and so diminish the capacity of the media to define the national and the local? What of the key role played by public service broadcasting in national politics, enabling access to political argument and debate in a mediated public space at a distance from the centres of political power? And what of the role of the media in sustaining the cultural public sphere, supporting high culture in the face of difficult market conditions and providing a context for innovation in both popular and high culture. In so far as, during the twentieth century, politics, culture, community and identity had all become mediated to a significant degree, globalisation and privatisation threatened to disrupt a vital connection between media and society.

If the risks to social and cultural life from technological, institutional and societal change are high, so too are the risks of not responding to the imperatives of the global market and the competitive opportunities of the knowledge society. Indeed, at least in the UK, the fear of losing economic competitiveness in the digital era challenged complacent assumptions that all could be left alone, as was starkly put in the government's *Digital Britain: The Interim Report* (DCMS and BERR, 2009: 3):

> The Communications Sector is one of the three largest sectors in our economy alongside energy and financial services ... More importantly, the digital economy underpins our whole economy and builds our national competitiveness. Our readiness to adopt digital technology has driven productivity gains throughout our wider economy ... But our productivity still lags well behind the USA and we face new challenges from the innovative companies of the successful Asian economies.

Because of the necessity of developing a media and communications market as a point of entry into the developing global knowledge society, no government is able to ignore the need to review the regulation of media and communications. Knowledge is increasingly the most important resource in modern societies, paralleling the importance of labour power in industrial society. Extending far beyond the traditional provision of quality television programmes on a restricted number of channels, combined with universal access to telephony, the demands of the knowledge society require a very substantial investment in infrastructure and a media policy that is sensitive to market principles to ensure a dynamic approach to media content production for a global market. In the late 1990s, this was taken to require a radical overhaul of the regulatory regime, since European media markets were among the most highly regulated among Western industrial democracies. A critical question, therefore, was whether media and communications should continue to need special protections because of their important social, political and cultural roles, even though the historical justification for this on economic grounds was ever less compelling. If media and communications were to continue, even in part, to stand outside the market, then what proportion of not-for-profit media would be desirable and how could that be achieved while still encouraging and opening up the market? Such questions will raise difficult issues of governance if regulation is to meet the often contradictory needs of the market and society without favouring one and damaging the other.

Van Cuilenberg and McQuail (2008) suggest that we are entering a new age or 'third paradigm' of media policy due to the increasingly global spread of the media, the increasing power of global media corporations, the long-run trend towards deregulation, and the uncertainties over the potential effectiveness of regulation or government intervention. They propose that media policy must combine economic, social and cultural policies with a concern for the role of media in political culture. Yet regulation will have to strike a balance between political, economic and social concerns and pressures, being efficient in its coordination of the market while at the same time intervening – with legitimacy – in areas of political culture and social policy. It will also have to achieve all this without falling back on either the normative convictions of public service or public ownership or on the ideology of completely free markets since there is still no political consensus or public support for a completely deregulated media and communications industry. But what values can guide a regulator in this context?

While Habermas's criteria, elaborated above, concern the processes or operation of the regulator, accepting as he does the mutual dependency (rather than clear separation) between public and private spheres (and, thus, the interdependency of process and outcome), Van Cuilenberg and McQuail focus more on the values that should properly constitute its goals – freedom of communication, access and control/accountability. Freedom combines a reduction of the constraints on communication as much as possible (negative freedom) with a media policy that enhances positive freedoms such as public debate or creativity. Access concerns the accessibility of communication resources to individuals and groups. Accountability they link to control, for policy should address both who controls communication resources and also how that is justified or accounted for. All three are, in different ways, at risk in the new media environment – hence we are witnessing contemporary and upcoming struggles especially in relation to the balance between deregulation and the pluralism of media ownership, digital media and the internet over universal broadband and the digital divide, rights regarding personal information and surveillance, constraints on the right to communicate, and questions of accountability for online provision.

Similar arguments regarding the normative expectations of media regulation are suggested by Freedman (2008) in his comparison of the US and UK systems: in a post-war USA context, liberal pluralism is valued for holding in check the tendency towards a concentration of power among elites in a representative democracy, by its promotion of informed citizens, public access to media, the circulation of diverse and marginal voices, the communication of public opinion to the state, and the protection of individual freedoms from the state. The threat to such values – whether framed in social democratic terms (in Europe) or liberal pluralist ones (in the USA), come from the neoliberal commitment to 'free markets, individual rights, personal choice, small government and limited regulation' (Freedman, 2008: 36). But not all would judge that market failures will thereby cease. In particular, there is scant agreement on whether market failure should itself be defined in purely market terms or also include social and cultural values, and this leaves unchecked both the justification for state intervention and any arguments against it. This tension between regulating according to a market logic and regulating to promote the social democratic values of the public sphere is, in different ways, illustrated by each of our chosen case studies.

Introducing the case studies

In this book, we examine the emerging regime of regulation in the context of academic theories of globalisation and governance, while also emphasising the analysis of regulatory practice. In the three chapters that follow this, we look at the broader context of academic theories of regulation and then discuss the debates leading up to the establishment of Ofcom as a media and communications regulator, focusing on the arguments over whether regulation should serve the interests of consumers or citizens. We then trace this through to the nature of Ofcom as both a statutory agency and an institution in the public sphere, dissecting its internal and external relations, structures and functions. Our chosen case studies, in the following four chapters, explore how Ofcom has dealt with important areas of media policy, all of which are found on the agendas of many governments around the globe – the review of public service broadcasting (PSB), actions regarding the potential influence of advertising on obesity, work on promoting media literacy, and work on developing community radio.

Linking the first case study to the foregoing discussion, we note that Graham and Davies (1997) justify the continued public funding of public service broadcasting even from an economic policy perspective. They argue that it is possible to support public service broadcasting while enabling markets, and they doubt the claims that commercial broadcasting will deliver the social gains and public value provided by the mix of publicly funded and commercial public service broadcasters. They argue that the problems identified in emerging national markets of concentration of corporate ownership are also likely to arise in the global market (see also McChesney, 1999). Global markets and convergent technologies increase the potential for greater horizontal and vertical integration within those powerful media corporations with major stakes both within and across different sectors of the market. In turn, these corporations gain the power to influence governments to a degree that undermines the importance of ensuring a plurality of providers. This alone could justify governments continuing to regulate so as to protect the public interest at a national level. Graham and Davies' arguments are based on well-established ideas about the features of media and communications technologies and markets that lead to market failure. High production costs, along with the small purchase costs of media content, create a situation in which significant resources are required to produce television and radio programmes but each of these then sells for relatively small amounts of money, increasing the likelihood that only a few companies will have the resources to produce and distribute media content and will therefore dominate the market. In addition, there are reasons to think that as consumers audiences are unlikely to pay for public service content even if they agree as citizens that public service broadcasting is a good thing.

Inherent to this discussion is a distinction between the public's interest as consumers and their interest as citizens. The argument is that there are reasons to doubt that commercial broadcasters, oriented towards the public as consumers, will deliver the full range and depth of quality public service broadcasting we have come to expect in the UK and Europe more generally. On the other hand, public service broadcasters lack the direct accountability to audiences that consumer sovereignty brings to commercial enterprises. This points towards a future in which public service broadcasting must seek legitimation through increased public engagement and accountability, including a more explicit account of its public value. We examine Ofcom's position on these issues in Chapter 5 in relation to its reviews of public service broadcasting.

Public service media act, perhaps presumptuously, in the interests of citizens, creating trusted products and services. The broader move towards deregulation, the opening up of markets on a global scale and the reduced importance of public service media and national government policy point to a world in which individuals will increasingly have to take responsibility for their own use of technologies and consumption of media and communications content. In the emerging global, technologically diverse and fast-moving markets for media and communications, individuals will have greater choice and will need to rely much more on their own judgements of quality, truthfulness and enjoyment. This raises important questions of media literacy and, as we might expect of a broad-based regulator charged with furthering the interests of citizens and consumers, Ofcom has developed a media literacy policy, as we shall examine in Chapter 6.

Beyond this, Ofcom's role, as specified by the Communications Act 2003, also includes its intervention in broader public policy issues in which the media play an important role. The capacity of the regulator to act collaboratively with other branches of government, to manage a co-regulatory relationship with parts of the industry, to conduct research, and to formulate and influence policy is examined through the case study of Ofcom's intervention in the highly charged public debate about the role of advertising in increasing childhood obesity (see Chapter 7). Finally, Ofcom's intervention in the community radio sector, a case in which the media may (or may not) be regulated so as to support community engagement in mediated public life, is considered in Chapter 8. This brings to the fore the crucial question of how the media should be regulated if they are to support the capacity of citizens to make a difference to power through the expression of their views, voices and actions by being part of a republic of voices? Whereas the public service tradition spoke to power on behalf of the public, it is now increasingly asked if an alternative model – of a more diverse media, less centralised, more flexible – could afford greater potential for public deliberation and civic engagement, in other words for cultural as well as political citizenship (Stevenson, 2003)?

These selected case studies reflect part, not all, of Ofcom's scope, but they well exemplify the diversity of the regulator's activities as an institution in the public sphere, including its research, consultation, market analysis and policy review and enforcement, as well as its manifold practices of engaging with regional and global governance, national government departments, civil society bodies, industry bodies and the public. But before examining these, we consider in more depth the changing nature of regulation itself.

Notes

1 Neoliberalism is an approach to economic and social policy that emphasises the importance of market regulation. Pertinent to the present discussion, this positions audiences as consumers and seeks to turn knowledge about audiences into a tradable commodity (Freedman, 2008; Hamelink, 2002).

2 Social democratic approaches to regulation combine a focus on social justice that is typical of left-wing politics but reject the idea of a revolutionary change in capitalist economies in favour of a more gradual reform so as to incorporate social and cultural policies and thereby ameliorate the detrimental effects of the market on the public (Giddens, 1998).

3 By 'system world', Habermas refers to the dominant logic of strategic and instrumental rationality as it operates in institutions and other formalised structures, in contrast with the lifeworld, characterised by informal ways of life and modes of everyday communication, whether in the public sphere or the intimate realm of the family (Outhwaite, 1996).

2

REGULATION AND THE PUBLIC INTEREST

Administrative regulation – economic and social regulation by means of agencies operating outside the line of hierarchical control or oversight by central administration – is
rapidly becoming the new frontier of public policy and public administration throughout
the industrialized world. (Majone, 1998: 198)

From government to governance

Two questions are critical to regulation – in the media and communications
sector as elsewhere. First, should regulation address not only economic but
also social and cultural policy? Second, should regulation be centred on
top-down, state-led, command-and-control style regulation or should it be
more dispersed, encompassing both administrative regulation (as in the
above quotation) and even 'softer' or more discursive modes and techniques of power? Although we have posed this second question in terms of
modes of regulation, the underlying question goes broader: in what ways,
and with what consequences, is the nature of government itself changing,
with state power being supplemented or in some instances replaced by the
exercise of power by a range of agents – including both institutions and
individuals – resulting in the dispersal (or extension) of government
through diverse modes of governance (Foucault, 1991; Rose 1990, 1999).
Both of these questions are, at heart, political, raising in a modern form
some very old issues regarding the desirable form of government in a liberal
democracy (Held, 2006). Today, in the face of the combined challenges of
globalisation, political change and technological complexity, as discussed in
Chapter 1, the power of traditional, centralised, top-down government is
fundamentally challenged, resulting in a sense of crisis in the legitimacy of
institutions as they supposedly represent diverse and conflicting interests.
In consequence, new forms of governance – or the dispersal of power – are
emerging. At least two broad visions of the relationship between the state,
commerce, civil society and the public suggest how to govern in the

knowledge society – liberal pluralism (or, in its more recent and extreme forms, neoliberalism) and social democracy (or, as it is more often termed in the USA, civic republicanism).

Neoliberals argue for the deregulation of markets within and across states, the hollowing out of the state beyond government and an attempt to encourage local initiatives in social and cultural policy (termed by the 2010 Coalition government 'the big society'). A healthy democracy is one where government is small, transparent and accountable but powerful within its legitimate sphere of interest. But if the state grows, it becomes inefficient, counterproductive and open to influence by interest groups both in market intervention (leading to anti-competitive practices) and in social and cultural policy (leading to social dependency and an overextended welfare state). Consequently, where possible, the market should be left to regulate itself, leaving regulatory agencies as a measure of last resort should a market prove prone to failure for structural reasons. In economic terms, a 'perfect market' assumes high levels of competition, enabling consumers to make 'rational' choices among different providers of products and services on the basis of full information about price and quality in order to satisfy their needs optimally. The need for (state) regulation arises only when markets fall short of delivering either sufficient levels of competition to generate good products and services at fair prices or when the consumer is unable to act rationally so as to influence the market through their choices. It follows that economic regulation involves a careful scrutiny of markets, gathering information about whether confidence in the market is justified in terms of the level of competition, quality and access to goods, services and information. Thus even in the case of regulatory intervention to deal with market failure, regulators are understood to have specific market regulation and consumer protection remits. On this view, governing is a centralised activity of the small state, with the small state being regarded as cohesive, accountable and effective. Further, regulation should not exceed its legitimate sphere of interest, leaving business, civil society and individuals to manage their own affairs in so far as this is possible. For example, this view was commonly expressed by industry bodies during the passage of the Communications Act 2003 (and during Ofcom's consultations thereafter) – consider this complaint from America Online (AOL, 2002: 27): 'No justification is provided for why the UK Government's social policy objectives in the converged communications area should be financed by the UK communications industry – in contrast to the practice for all other aspects of social policy.'

The contrasting, social democratic view holds that democracy is best served if the boundaries of the political sphere are broad, supporting engagement by civil society bodies and the public in a participatory or deliberative democracy. As Raboy (2007: 344) said of media and communications regulation, this 'refers to all efforts to influence media ... [for] it is

REGULATION AND THE PUBLIC INTEREST

founded on the premise that as media are paramount social institutions, public intervention with respect to their orientation is both legitimate and necessary'. Although 'the idea that market forces can simply replace government regulation has proven to be naïve' (d'Haenens, 2007: 324), social democrats have increasingly, though not without contention, come to accept the liberal argument that markets must be deregulated (or in key respects re-regulated) so as to encourage competition and stimulate innovation while also protecting consumers, thereby differentiating themselves from the democratic socialist preference for state ownership and an extensive welfare state. However, social democratic governments aim to combine this with innovative ways in which the state can develop social and cultural policy by creating partnerships, encouraging deliberation and engagement through intergovernmental, regional or global cooperation (see Thompson, 2003). These aims focus on positive as well as negative freedoms, seeing the role of government as being not only to protect citizens and to release them from constraints, but also to enable them to lead good lives, and sustain the conditions for a vibrant civic culture, community and increased personal engagement and responsibility. The result is a government strategy involving the dispersal of state power (a larger state) to enable collaborative governance with a wide range of stakeholders.

Although very different in their politics, it is clear that both approaches are adapting to, and even in various ways advocating, the shift from government to governance. Our present analysis of media regulation, therefore, is positioned within a wider understanding of how the state is responding to changes in the relations of power and legitimacy in representative liberal democracies. Intriguingly, the shape and influence of the political projects of neoliberalism and social democracy (or civic republicanism) have not been long recognised. Writing in 1996, Barry et al. evoked a picture of instability in which the state (government, the law and public administration) seemed increasingly 'out of touch' and the certainties of the political terrain of the post-Second World War welfare contract were giving way to 'a proliferation of political doctrines and programmes that are unstable and difficult to classify in conventional terms' (Barry et al., 1996: 1).

Regulation is part of the machinery of government, a response to the broad economic, social and cultural changes that simultaneously challenge and undermine the power of the state. It is, moreover, the privilege of government to decide which approach to regulation to follow. Where neoliberalism accepts changing political and market conditions as an external reality and draws in the boundaries of the state – as has quickly come to characterise the Coalition government of 2010–date – the New Labour government of 1997–2010 worked with an alternative vision, adopting a policy of expanding the role of regulatory agencies in the hope that bodies such as Ofcom could remain independent of party politics.[1] New Labour thus sought a less hierarchical, more collaborative approach to government, operating through the activities of dispersed networks on different scales (Jessop, 2000). Newman (2005) suggests that compared to the traditional hierarchical relationships of government, which favour command-and-control regulation, this alternative model of governance operates strategically but flexibly by coordinating dispersed networks of actors, enabling them to collaborate in partnership so as to meet policy objectives by sharing the responsibility with other powers, including civil society and the public.

The theory of regulation

Why and how do governments regulate? Baldwin and Cave (1999) review a variety of economic reasons, including controlling monopolies, taxing windfall profits, overcoming asymmetries of power between producers and consumers and moderating anti-competitive behaviour by firms. In addition to these economic reasons, the possible social consequences of market activity may be ameliorated through regulation, such as protecting essential services, ensuring the fair distribution of public goods and protecting consumers. Beyond economic regulation and addressing the social effects of a market, regulation can also advance social and public purposes, and this is especially the case with a dispersed and collaborative or partnership approach to governance. At the same time, being an extension of the mechanism of public administration, regulators are conceived as bodies with a concentration of specific expertise to be used on behalf of and yet independent from government. The ideal, therefore, is of a rational bureaucracy working in the public interest at arm's length from government.

When it comes to regulatory practice, Du Gay (2000) distinguishes two conceptions of the relationship between public administration and government. One, derived from progressive US President Woodrow Wilson's early article 'The study of administration' (1887), proposes a clear division of labour between elected politicians who are responsible for setting policy goals and civil servants who are responsible for the administration and delivery of government policy. By contrast, in what Du Gay calls the 'Westminster model', public administrators participate in policy deliberations with government as well as being responsible for the operational delivery of policy. Although this model permits policy makers (ideally, politicians) to benefit from the expertise and understanding of issues of delivery held by civil servants, it blurs the distinction between administrators and elected politicians – and this was increased by the advent of special advisers, a characteristic of both the Thatcher and the Blair governments. New Labour's experiments in regulation further exacerbated this blurring by extending policy work beyond the Westminster village, encouraging high-level administrators to build collaborative relations with stakeholders, to undertake independent research and consultation, and so build an alternative site for deliberation and policy making. This included, as Newman (2005: 129) observed, 'deliberative forums; citizen panels; user empowerment; consumer consultation; user or citizen involvement in the governing boards of "public institutions"; participatory evaluation; and production of "games" designed to popularize public involvement in policy discussions.'

Should there be any doubt over the actions of regulators, public interest theory advocates a regulatory intervention by trusted and disinterested experts in order to balance competing interests. However, as Baldwin and Cave (1999) point out, there is always disagreement over what constitutes the public interest as well as practical doubts over whether or not regulators can meet the ideals of a rational, disinterested public administration given that all sides – government, industry, public interest bodies and the public – will relentlessly attempt to influence regulators. Scepticism about the Wilsonian ideal of separating policy making from administration has led rational choice theorists simply to make explicit the competing interests that shape regulation, the argument being that it is better to think of regulation as a means of reaching a compromise between competing interest groups rather than as the actions of a disinterested bureaucracy acting in the public interest (Baldwin and Cave, 1999). In particular, the Chicago School of Economics asserts that established, powerful interests such as governments or industries seek to influence regulation in order to stabilise otherwise volatile markets to the advantage of established and larger firms but at the cost of smaller and emerging businesses. On this view, the activities of engagement and discussion envisaged by public interest theories are regarded as largely rhetorical. Further, the pressure from competing interests results in what Baldwin and Cave describe as the natural life history of regulatory agencies, according to which they start out as disinterested bureaucracies acting in the public interest but are gradually taken over by powerful interests and consequently lose momentum and independence.

Regulatory agencies tread a difficult line between working on behalf of and being accountable to government departments and exercising critical, independent judgement (Millwood Hargrave and Shaw, 2009). Recent history in the UK illustrates the vulnerability of regulatory agencies to political interference, not just in relation to particular decisions or areas of regulation, but also in the more general sense that different governments will have radically different views about the proper powers, responsibilities and rules of engagement that regulators should be granted – consider, for example, the deregulatory wave of the 1980s prompted by the rise of monetarist economics and the political project of neoliberalism.[2] Indeed, the Thatcher governments viewed bureaucrats with antipathy, regarding their claims to be able to advise government on potential problems with their policies as an unwarranted intervention in the political process (Du Gay, 2000: 122). Strongly influenced by public choice theory, Margaret Thatcher was radically sceptical of the claims of bureaucracies to serve the public interest rationally and neutrally, whether these were professional bodies, the law or the civil service or, for that matter, public service media.

Thus Thatcher's government was determined to make sure that civil servants focused on operational issues in administration and that policy making was left, as far as possible, to elected politicians. The New Labour government, while also being concerned about delivery, adopted a position in which regulators were enhanced in their capacity, expertise and scope in order to take advantage of the power of regulatory institutions to develop policy and engage with stakeholders at arm's length from government. Thus in 1997 the New Labour government began a process of re-regulation in a number of sectors, including the financial services and media and communications, only to be followed by a swing back to deregulation under the Conservative/Liberal Coalition government (Tambini, 2010).

Strategies of regulation

Regulation traditionally centres on:

> (1) some sort of standard, goal, or set of values against which perceptions of what is happening within the environment to be controlled are compared through (2) some mechanism of monitoring or feedback which in turn triggers (3) some form of action which attempts to align the controlled variables, as they are perceived by the monitoring component with the goal component ... For classical regulation the goal component is represented typically by some legal rule or standard, the feedback component by monitoring by a regulatory agency, government department or self-regulatory organisation and the realignment component by the application of sanctions for breach of standards. (Scott, 2001: 3)

Thus the traditional regulatory strategy adopted by governments has long centred on command and control, regulating the conduct of firms by setting standards (e.g. quality of food production, levels of pollution in rivers, standard weights and measures) that were backed by legal enforcement for non-compliance (Baldwin et al., 1998). Despite the focus on centralised control the operation of this strategy may be flexible, involving both central and local agencies of government. In the UK, for example, trading standards officers working in local authorities support a centralised and more strategic Office of Fair Trading – this analyses broader market trends and works with global networks of enforcement regulators, thereby supporting the role of local agencies. What matters for the command-and-control strategy is the power to establish clear standards and sanctions that can be operated by experts (in measurement and law) working in the public interest so as to give consumers confidence in the market.

However, as Baldwin and Cave (1999) point out, one risk is that the close working relationship between regulators and industry, which is often invisible to consumers, permits regulator 'capture' by industry, with the result that the regulator loses its independence and power. A second problem is that command-and-control regulation can lead to the proliferation and increasing complexity of rules for operating in different markets, making it difficult for new firms to enter the market and so stifling instead of fostering competition and innovation. Third, although in some cases it may be straightforward to set standards, in others it is more difficult. In media and communications, for example, if a government wants to encourage diversity of content, how is an appropriate level of diversity to be judged? If government wants to support certain values through public service media, can these be left to a regulatory agency or how far should public consultation contribute to setting the goals? Finally, 'codes of practice and pledges are only as good as the monitoring system that ensures compliance' (Pitt, 2010: 13), yet an effective system of standards and enforcement might be restrictive, costly and unpopular.

These problems with command and control have led to the development of co- or self-regulation, in which firms set their own standards and police their own activities as reputable firms, often under the guidance of trade associations. In defining co-regulation, Held (2007: 357) emphasises the importance of the state in ensuring the legitimacy and effectiveness of regulatory bodies:

(1) The system is established to achieve public policy goals targeted at social processes. (2) There is a legal connection between the non-state regulatory system and the state regulation. (3) The state leaves discretionary power to a non-state regulatory system. (4) The state uses regulatory resources to influence the outcome of the regulatory process (to guarantee the fulfilment of the regulatory goals).

Since the second and fourth points afford pressure points for the state, if these are absent the system would instead constitute one of self-regulation, as preferred in the UK by comparison with Europe or the USA (Christou and Simpson, 2006; Tambini et al., 2008). In this approach to regulation, government departments or regulatory agencies do not disappear, but their role changes to one of holding firms or trade associations to account for their self-regulatory rules and procedures. When a trade association plays this role in collaboration with a regulatory agency or government department, this becomes 'co-regulation'. Governments can give self- and co-regulation 'teeth' by setting a high 'price' (in terms of adherence to the self-regulation requirements) for acquiring a licence or gaining the status of a regulated firm, and this the regulator can influence either directly, by setting conditions for firms, or indirectly, using co-regulation in collaboration with trade associations.

Self- and co-regulation often produce relatively high levels of compliance because firms or their representatives have been part of the process of regulation and thus party to the generation of well-formulated rules of business conduct. In addition, trade associations absorb some of the costs of regulation so that the cost to government is reduced compared to command and control. If a regulator has a policy-making remit, as has been the case for Ofcom, this gives regulated firms, industry representatives and, arguably, civil society groups and the public a potential role to play in the formulation of media and communications policy. Since the firms contribute to the regulatory process and so share in 'ownership' of the resulting policies, they are potentially more likely to take account of complaints from consumers and consumer representative bodies.

However, there are a number of disadvantages to self-regulation arising from the lack of transparency of rules and process, the expense of self-regulation, the lack of independence for compliance officers within the industry, the complexities of the relationship between sanctions by self-regulatory bodies and legal action and, in some cases, the public may not find it acceptable that a sector regulates itself and might then demand government agency regulation (Baldwin and Cave, 1999: 40–1). Such concerns are readily echoed by members of the public when asked to reflect on their experience of regulation in their everyday lives. Indeed, while legislation is understood, at least in its ideal incarnation, to result from publicly debated processes of decision making by elected politicians, backed by proportionate enforcement by legitimate and independent organisations acting in the public interest, regulatory bodies other than parliament are little understood – indeed they are often regarded with considerable scepticism. Seen as being run by non-elected bureaucrats and/or self-interested bodies, unaccountable and ineffective in terms of enforcement and redress, unknown by and often unresponsive to ordinary people, regulators of all kinds (self-regulatory, co-regulatory, national and European) have received little endorsement from our group discussions (Lunt et al., 2008).

Baldwin and Cave (1999) review alternative, high-level methods of regulation, such as incentive-based regulation where tax rebates or grants are used to shape firms' behaviour in directions desired by governments or the public and market-harnessed controls that use broadly-based competition rules and legal action to regulate the sector. The advantage of these methods of governing at a distance is they do not rely on a regulator's detailed involvement with the conduct of businesses but instead measure their impact on the market as a basis for regulation. The disadvantage is that the law can be a slow and blunt instrument while regulation may need to be flexible and fast-moving, especially in markets where innovation and development are the norm, as in media and communications. But its advantage lies in accountability and legitimacy, while not imposing an undue regulatory burden. Other methods of regulation based on outcomes include the strategy of 'naming and shaming' or disclosure regulation, in which firms are publicly exposed on the assumption that this will affect consumer confidence, though as with incentives, this is a blunt instrument and it hardly offers a comprehensive approach to regulation.

A key feature of Ofcom's approach to regulation has been flexibility in its array of strategies and practices, making it a hybrid regulatory institution as is appropriate to its wide remit. Not only was this characteristic of the move away from command and control towards a greater mix of regulatory strategies, including self and co-regulation, but also, more distinctively, it allowed Ofcom to operate across a wide range of areas of media and communications policy – through a dialogue and consultation with stakeholders, the conduct of research on markets, firms and public opinion and the advancement of policies that require some coordination with other agencies (as in the case of the promotion of media literacy or the reduction of childhood obesity or the development of public service broadcasting in a digital age). This takes us back to the question asked at the outset of this chapter, namely the issue of regulatory purpose. There is broad agreement that regulation has potential value as a flexible way of regulating markets, but there is less agreement about using regulatory agencies to influence social and cultural affairs. With the dispersal of power from the centralised state to a host of institutions with governance responsibilities at all levels from local to global, it is also 'increasingly difficult to uphold a clear distinction between *public* and *private* governance arrangements' (Zürn and Koenig-Archibugi, 2006: 251, emphasis in original). No surprise, then, that continuing controversies during the period of the New Labour government, widely expressed by the media using the pejorative tropes of 'red tape' and 'the nanny state', questioned the justification for the kind of regulatory regime instantiated by Ofcom. This in turn informed the actions of the 2010 Coalition government in retrenching regulation.

New labour, social democracy and regulation

A central feature of the Blair government's policies was an acknowledgement of the growing importance and impact of globalisation and the centrality of media and communications, both as the infrastructure for the knowledge economy and as a burgeoning global market in its own right. This acceptance of the increasing importance of global markets was a particular challenge to the social democrats, who had been strongly committed to the role of the nation state in public ownership and the welfare state. Driver and Martell (2002) suggest that there were three alternatives being considered across Europe by social democrats as responses to the challenges that globalisation posed for government intervention in economy and society. One was to accept that the power of governments was severely limited by economic globalisation and to focus on providing support and welfare to citizens in an increasingly uncertain world. The second was to develop new strategies through which the state could remain active in market intervention, and the third was to develop the links that globalisation opened up between governments, for example through European cooperation.

New Labour adopted neoliberal policies in macro-economic policy by focusing on competitiveness, low taxation, labour market flexibility and reducing regulation. However, this was combined with a number of policies that fell under the description of active state intervention to meet broad social policy aims. For example, elements of welfare state policy were reinforced with innovations such as the minimum wage, investing in education and training and infrastructure investment (so-called 'supply-side interventions'; Driver and Martell, 2002). Regulation was seen as one way of coordinating and bolstering such interventions. The third strategy of forming political alliances with European and global social democratic movements, being active in regional and international regulatory bodies and aiming to influence the world order was also adopted by New Labour (Held, 1995). Gordon Brown's interventions in the G20 summits towards the end of his term of office aimed at coordinating responses to the financial crisis of that time by governments around the world were an example of this focus on enhancing economic intervention through global cooperation. In addition, New Labour was committed to a variety of internationally coordinated policy developments, such as the Charter of Human Rights and the Social Chapter of the European Union (EU), as well as coordination on economic policy, such as cooperation on international regulation of markets. Nation regulatory agencies act as a mechanism for coordinating between nation states through the international networks of regulatory agencies and links to regional bodies. As we will see shortly, there were a number of initiatives to harmonise the European market for media and communications, balancing this with autonomy over important aspects of policy, which included encouraging nation states to establish regulatory agencies to fulfil social policy needs and trade agreements.

New Labour's economic policy was grounded in the idea that dramatic global changes rendered the Old Labour economic policies of public ownership, tax and spend, and the state management of demand no longer politically viable or relevant to global markets. As Driver and Martell (1998) put it, in response to radical change on a global scale New Labour aimed to hold on to the traditional aims of the Labour Party, particularly a commitment to social justice, but to achieve these through different means. Driver and Martell (1998) argue that New Labour's economic policy was conditioned by an acceptance that the combination of globalisation and post-industrial society meant that public ownership and planning were no longer viable. They also argue that the old debate between capitalism and communism had been resolved in favour of capitalism and that the question now was this – which form of capitalism would best serve broadly social democratic aims? New Labour policy makers considered the examples of three successful models of capitalism based on Germany, Japan and the USA. Although there was much debate and disagreement, Driver and Martell (1998) claim that New Labour settled on a number of principles in economic policy that combined ideas from these successful economies. First was the focus on inclusion to motivate a stakeholder society. This idea was derived from the analysis that both the German and Japanese economic successes were grounded in the broader social commitments that underpinned economic activity in those countries that also led to greater stability in industrial relations. However, in true 'third way' thinking, this commitment was combined with a US-style focus on flexibility in the labour market and welfare reform. Nevertheless, the stakeholder economy was to be encouraged, as Blair indicated in a 1996 speech:

The creation of an economy where we are inventing and producing goods and services of quality needs the engagement of the whole country ... We need to build a relationship of trust not just within the firm but within society ... It is a stakeholder economy in which opportunity is available to all, advancement is through merit and from which no group or class is set apart or excluded. (quoted in Driver and Martell, 1998: 51–2)

There was considerable discussion and controversy about what Blair meant by a 'stakeholder economy', but broadly speaking he intended that companies should see themselves as being in partnership with government, their employees and the wider community (Driver and Martell, 1998). Individuals were also to be encouraged to feel that they had a stake in their society. At a general level, this set a mission for government action focused on working collaboratively with firms to encourage corporate responsibility in return for economic stability and freedom in the market. This set the tone for Ofcom's approach to self- and co-regulation and an inclusive approach to consultation, and certainly its consultations have often been successful in terms of the number, range and quality of submissions. For individuals, stakeholder participation would be supported by a focus on education and training to enable them to survive in the new flexible labour market of a global economy that was supported by promoting enhanced consumer literacy. In relation to regulation, these policies led to a focus on consumer literacy and the widespread consultation of stakeholders, all of which are salient features of Ofcom's activities, as we will see in the course of this book.

Also important to New Labour policy was the concept of the 'hybrid state', which drew on elements of both neoliberal economic policy and social democratic intervention in the idea of combining effective economic management with social justice (Richards and Smith, 2004). Associated with the notion of the hybrid state was the idea, later much ridiculed precisely because it proved so hard to deliver, of 'joined-up government'. Joined-up government was intended as a solution to the longstanding problem faced by governments of different political persuasions, namely the difficulty of controlling and integrating policy across government departments, keeping public administrators on board and delivering policies beyond the central government departments of Whitehall (Driver and Martell, 1998; Du Gay, 2000). Joined-up government was intended, therefore, to strengthen both the centre and the periphery of government, and one means of achieving this was that the civil service should focus on evidence-based policy. Civil servants, in short, were to enable government by providing the evidence base for the development of government policy, to test ideas for delivery and to assess the effectiveness of policy. The evidence base is independent of government departments and so offers non-partisan direction for policy, potentially resolving internecine disputes between departments or between the centre and periphery while also, on occasion, challenging the direction of government policy. These ideas of hybridity of political purpose and convergence of policy across and beyond government are reflected in the dual purposes of Ofcom – to further citizens' and consumers' interests – and in the commitment to combine competition regulation with public purposes (Hesmondhalgh, 2005).

Certainly, many of the above ideas informed the design of Ofcom as a communications regulator – consider its substantial production and use of research to support evidence-based policy, its efforts to develop broad policies that joined up with New Labour's strategy of increasing competition alongside developing inclusive media policies, and its emphasis on a coherent approach to regulation. In addition, as a principled unitary regulator for an enlarging sector, Ofcom was also designed so as to integrate different parts of the media and communications industry under a coherent regulatory regime, while also connecting government to industry, civil society and the public.

It is noteworthy that Ofcom was not the first new style regulator introduced by the New Labour government. A similar approach was adopted in a very different market: financial services. The Financial Services Authority (FSA) was created in October 1997, with its powers redefined by the Financial Services and Markets Act 2000. Formed by conglomerating a number of sub-sector specific regulators in order to unify regulation across a broader area, the FSA developed a model that clearly influenced the design of Ofcom – notably, integrating market analysis, the regulation of firms and consumer protection. Consumer education (in Ofcom, this became media literacy) in financial services was one central policy, a deliberate counter-weight to the FSA's general preference for self-regulation. As with Ofcom, the FSA was designed to operate in an accountable and transparent way. Both bodies had consumer panels, although the FSA balanced this with two bodies that represented industry (large and small firms). This indicates that the New Labour government had a general commitment to principled, uni-tary regulation in markets that combined commitments to increased compe-tition with protecting the public interest. And the perceived success of the FSA encouraged the government to develop a similar regulator for the media and communications sector. To be sure, with the benefit of hindsight follow-ing the worldwide financial collapse of 2007–09, the FSA has been judged rather differently. As was also the case for Ofcom, the Coalition government promptly announced in 2010 that the FSA would be abolished (or, as things turned out, transformed by dividing its responsibilities – particularly those for firms and for consumers – among distinct agencies).

The European context

The final feature of New Labour policy underpinning the turn towards regulatory agencies (and so distinguishing New Labour policies from those of both Conservatives and democratic socialists) was a positive engagement with Europe (Holden, 2002). As we have seen, connecting national to regional governance was the third plank in building New Labour's response to the threat to government power resulting from globalisation. New Labour aimed to play a proactive role in regional if not global governance. As Europe sought to harmonise economic and social policy across member states, one key means was through the establishment of regulatory agencies in member states that would coordinate the governments who were oper-ating different national strategies.

This broad policy approach took a specific form in the media and com-munications sector, namely one with a focus on economic harmonisation at the European level combined with specific national policies for public serv-ice broadcasting (Sarikakis, 2007). This approach represented a hard-fought resolution of the fundamental tension between a cosmopolitan Europe committed to supporting economic cooperation and developing a shared European identity, on the one hand, and the strong desire to recognise and sustain social and cultural distinctiveness between and within nation states on the other (Collins, 1994). Indeed, the present contradictions in European policy should be understood as the outcome, satisfactory or otherwise, of some 30 years of conflict and compromise between the forces of harmonisation and subsidiarity.[3]

In response to the changes linked to globalisation and technical changes in media and communications, European member states began to reform their media systems by opening up markets and reducing public ownership. In telecommunications policy, for example, Fischer (2008) traces the far-reaching effects of European and international pressure to break up national monopolies, transforming both the market and its regulatory regime. In relation to broadcasting policy, the European Union (EU) thereby began a 20-year process (which is still not complete) in the early 1980s, ushered in by the European Commission's (CEC) Green Paper, *Television without Frontiers* (Commission of the European Communities, 1984), 'to navigate between the often competing demands of economics and culture' (Humphreys, 2008: 152).[4] For Michalis (2007) and Humphreys (2008), the resultant twists and turns of European audiovisual policy were exacerbated by the complex alignments of EU institutions, in which some parts of the Commission supported market liberalisation whereas the European Parliament and the Council of Europe supported the rights of member states to determine social and cultural aspects of media policy.

This led to a dual approach – legislative measures to open up competition within Europe alongside a series of communications and resolutions to safeguard such core public interest goals as cultural diversity, media pluralism and public service broadcasting. A crucial asymmetry arose, however, in that market liberalisation was backed by EU legislation through a series of EC Directives, while social and cultural policy objectives were implemented at a European level only through 'softer' policy processes focused on the coordination of activity, information sharing and best practice across member states (Feintuck and Varney, 2006; Humphreys, 2008). As a result economic policy in the sector has a firm legal foundation, with considerable clarity and coordination across the region, while the social and cultural aspects of media policy are dispersed to the member states (with some notable exceptions in the domains of consumer and child protection). Thus Humphreys (2008: 160) charts 'the Commission's increasing reliance, to be seen in other policy sectors as well, on "soft" policy instruments designed to achieve policy aims through the exchange of good practices and the exercise of peer pressure'. Interestingly, this neatly parallels Ofcom's handling of its dual role of representing the interests of both citizens and consumers, since as we show in this book Ofcom's policies to further the consumer interest are consistently clearer and more firmly grounded in rules and institutional structures than are policies regarding citizen interests – as examined in Chapter 3, these tend to fragment into a range of different policy initiatives that are only loosely supported by 'softer' regulatory practices.

So it was that, from the formulation of the *Television without Frontiers* Directive (Council of the European Communities, 1989) onwards, the EU provided the 'legal establishment of the single European market for television ... [but] did not provide a detailed, harmonized European regulatory regime for television content, which remained primarily a member state competence' (Humphreys, 2008: 155). This is not to say that the Directive was silent on cultural matters, and such provisions as were included remained controversial since the European Community Treaty in force at the time gave no competence to the EU in cultural matters.[5] This pattern of European regulation of markets, combined with subsidiarity over content issues, public service broadcasting provision and cultural diversity in the media, was consolidated in the Maastricht Treaty of 1992 (which gave the EU the competence to introduce measures under the title of 'Culture'; Feintuck and Varney, 2006). Further, evidence suggests the Directive has had some success in protecting indigenous production, diversity of production and common access to the broadcasting of key cultural and sporting events (Feintuck and Varney, 2006).

This approach was continued in the EU's Audiovisual Media Services Directive (AVMS Directive) of 2007, itself preceded by two extensive rounds of consultation between 2003 and 2005, again with similar coalitions of interest contradicting each other, although by this time the issues of digitisation and technological convergence were firmly on the agenda. On one side of the debate, commercial and new media interests sought to limit public service broadcasting to linear services, permitting new digital channels (the increased number of channels permitted by digital broadcasting was called the 'digital dividend') and the new media environment to be open to exploitation by commercial media. Against this, public service broadcasters, the European Parliament and some member states wanted public service broadcasters to share in the digital dividend and to develop, and even be innovators in, online services. The result, again, was a compromise in which those who wanted to put support for social and cultural aspects of media across Europe on a surer legal footing, as for economic policy, were disappointed; further, the difficulties of regulating the internet meant that content regulation for digital media was limited to controlling aspects of e-commerce, some protections for consumers and children, and adherence to the general legal requirements related to defamation (Humphreys, 2008). However, the AVMS Directive recognised important differences between the broadcast (or linear) and online (or non-linear) delivery of media content, introducing the principle that regulatory intervention would be greater for linear media. The result has been a graded system of regulation, with most intervention for linear media, less for non-linear media, and still less for telecommunications – a mixed model that works at national as well as regional levels and, further, one which meant that each member state had to have or establish a national regulatory agency in order to undertake its part of the task.

Thus national regulatory agencies are critical within the European approach for two reasons. First, they are responsible for implementing European and national legislation (following the direction of their governments). Second, they must play a key role in the coordination of such expanded regulatory instruments as self and co-regulation and in the coordination and implementation of 'softer' measures to promote social and cultural policy objectives through media and communications. Although the danger here is that the work of regulatory agencies in this regard could be dismissed as merely a 'talking shop', the changing nature of regulation itself increasingly means that institutional spaces for talk – in other words, for an evidence-based, consultative, multi-stakeholder engagement in the discursive framing and negotiation of policy – can be decisive in the process of policy making and its consequences.

The UK context

New regulatory authorities are being created, with new structures, degrees of independence and areas of competence: monitoring of public service missions, granting private licenses [with the] capacity to regulate and sanction. (Bustamante, 2008: 188)

New Labour came to power just as the European approach was consolidating around the Audiovisual Media Services Directive in 1997. Its thinking on regulatory reform, part of its broader commitment to constitutional reform, saw it adopt this emerging, broad definition of a converged regulator, with a range of powers, responsibilities and modes of regulation, in preparing for the Communications Act 2003. The result, as Doyle and Vick (2005: 75) put it, was 'a sweeping programme of regulatory change in the communications industries ... the most comprehensive legislation of its kind in British history'. Thereafter, Ofcom was closely observed across Europe precisely because it represented a prominent instance of the new regulatory authorities to be established in all member states. But while the dual European approach – of economic harmonisation, achieved top-down, plus a dispersed and softer approach to cultural and citizen issues – was, in key respects, replicated in Ofcom, in the UK context there was also a strong pressure towards a unified, consistent approach to regulation. Intended as a converged regulator for a converging media and communications sector, Ofcom was meant to solve the problem of regulatory confusion and consistency that was little fitted with the emerging digital landscape, one that could, also, learn from the differently-unified regulatory system in the USA (the FCC), the federalised system of Germany and elsewhere (Cowie and Marsden, 1998).

Writing more than two decades ago, Seymour-Ure (1987) scathingly described the confusion that was British media policy as 'now you see it, now you don't', reciting a litany of regulatory inconsistencies across the media and communications landscape which was itself ill-defined. The implication was that sector-wide consistency was desirable, as was echoed ten years later in Collins and Murroni's (1996) update on the continuing multiplication of regulators with different origins, operating under different auspices, and with diverse approaches and levels of regulatory effectiveness. The divergent and, arguably, disorganised nature of media and communications regulation reflected the lack of coherence in media policy by previous governments of both labour and conservative persuasions. This was evident, according to Collins and Murroni (1996), if one looked at the list of regulators in the media and communications sector – including the Broadcasting Standards Commission (BSC), the Advertising Standards Authority (ASA), the Broadcasting Complaints Commission (BCC), the Radio Authority, the Welsh Fourth Channel Authority, the Press Complaints Commission (PCC), the Independent Television Commission (ITC), the Independent Committee for the Supervision of Standards of Telephone Information Services (ICSTIS), the BBC governors, the Office of Telecommunications (Oftel) and the British Board of Film Classification (BBFC). As Baldwin and Cave suggest, media and communications regulation was calling out for reform:

There was a growing perception by policy-makers and legislators ... That certain industries and activities required a special and continuing form of control – that in relation to, say, discrimination or broadcasting, reliance could not be placed solely on sporadic forays by individuals in the ordinary courts. (Baldwin and Cave, 1999: 70)

The problem of regulatory effectiveness was only part of the story, for the view held was that there was a need to develop broad policies and strategies which were unlikely to emerge from court decisions. In addition, as Baldwin and Cave (1999) also point out, there was an advantage in having a mix of activities within an independent body combining adjudication, policy making and enforcement. The political orientation of government departments meant that they would not have the required independence to legitimate such a combination of functions. Also, as in the case of communications, markets and technologies were developing in complexity and sophistication to such a degree that there was a need to create agencies with the appropriate levels of professionalism and expertise to meet these challenges independent of government (see also Robinson, 2007, on wider changes in the British system of utility regulation).

Ofcom, established by the New Labour government through an Act of Parliament in 2003, represented a consolidation and extension of this process of re-regulation by forming a body that integrated the previously separate spheres of regulation (public sector broadcasting and commercial broadcasting, telecommunications and broadcasting, consumer and citizen interests). Majone (1998) illustrated the way that emerging European regulatory agencies functioned by comparing them with government departments. First, these bodies potentially provide the capacity and expertise to deal with complex technical and market issues facing both firms and consumers. Second, the political status of regulation afforded adjudication without legislation with the courts thereby providing the flexible regulation of firms. Third, these new forms of public administration afforded the opportunity for consultation and public engagement which was beyond the capacity and rules governing the actions of ministries and government departments. Fourth, while accountable to government, such agencies were sufficiently independent of party politics and could, therefore, potentially provide a source of continuity to markets and consumers in the face of changing governments. The relative independence of regulatory agencies also afforded a mechanism whereby flexible and pragmatic policies could be developed by governments in collaboration with regulatory agencies that worked with industry in the public interest (Majone, 1998: 199). Taken together, these features of regulatory bodies appealed to an incoming New Labour government that was looking to capitalise on the deregulatory tendencies of the previous neoliberal Conservative government while modernising governance and asserting revised social democratic objectives alongside the management of markets. Ofcom was an instantiation of these principles and as such represented an uneasy compromise between those who supported free markets and those who valued democratic control of economies through government intervention.

Regulation and the public interest

As we have seen, a new regulatory regime is now emerging in response to the challenges of global markets, the increasing complexity of media and communications technologies and the changing composition of audiences. This chapter has contextualised the rationale for this new regime, along with the design of the structures and functions of one particular regulator, Ofcom, to meet the economic and social policies of the New Labour government from 1997 and, yet more broadly, of the European policy context. To provide a critical analysis of these changes, we located debates concerning appropriate forms of regulation in relation to academic theories of regulation. One critical issue concerns the politics of regulatory decisions, since various structures, functions and purposes for regulatory agencies are favoured by governments of different political hues. A second theme, referred to above, which we have not yet developed, concerns the nature of the public interest. Although this is often put forward, in addition to or even in place of market competition, as the fundamental justification for regulation, it is surprisingly little examined critically. In this book, we take the public interest to underpin both citizen and consumer interest in the media and communications sector, and thus we shall conclude this chapter by examining what is meant by the public interest. We shall also end with a proposal for a normative account of the difference between citizen and consumers interest as the foundation for media and communications regulation.

Regulation represents an intervention in markets and in society, and it carries costs as well as potentially conferring benefits. Therefore it requires strong justification if it is to have legitimacy. The Communications Act 2003 placed the public interest at the core of Ofcom's activities, expressing this in terms of its primary duty to further the interests of citizens and consumers, a duty that was hotly contested as we shall see in the next chapter. Arguably, given the growing diversity in modes of regulation, it seems unlikely that a single definition of the public interest will suffice here. Contemporary regulatory agencies deploy hybrid methods encompassing command-and-control (rules, codes and compliance), informal regulatory mechanisms (e.g. the coordination and management of self and co-regulation), and a range of 'softer' interventions that aim to influence the actions of firms and publics, to create the conditions for stakeholder (including public) involvement, and to coordinate formal and informal regulatory initiatives of government at the national and European levels. Somewhat different conceptions of the public interest and, indeed, different publics, are mobilised in the justification of each of these. Unsurprisingly, then, the concept of 'the public interest' has proved difficult to define (Millwood Hargrave and Shaw, 2009). McQuail (1992) compares it to private interests, which centre on competition among individuals and/or groups in society for their own gain. Others define it as any justification for intervening in the market for social or cultural rather than economic reasons – notably, reasons such as media plurality, content diversity, public service values or the protection of audiences from harm and offence (Feintuck and Varney, 2006). Both are, essentially, negative approaches, defining the public interest against the apparently clearer and more straightforward conception of private interests (both market and individual).

More positively, considerable practical effort has been devoted to the development of public interest tests for media ownership and 'public value' tests for public service broadcasters (Just, 2009; Moe, 2010). Their purpose has been to measure the effects of intervention in the public interest in a manner that is comparable to more familiar efforts to measure the economic costs and benefits of regulation on the market. However, as regulation becomes 'softer' and more dispersed, operating through multi-stakeholder negotiation and cooperation, assessing its effects becomes ever more difficult, even contentious, and attention tends to focus on mechanisms more than on the evaluation of outcomes (Puppis, 2010). As we will see in Chapter 4, while reiterating that the citizen and consumer interests are its core focus, Ofcom emphasises its manner of working – through engagement, partnership and research – along with efforts to reduce the overall costs of regulation, as much or more than it does the particular benefits that accrue to the public interest.

Can we develop an account of the public interest beyond a discursive framing for particular regulatory processes or interventions? In Chapter 1, we discussed the normative expectations to be held of regulators as institutions in the public sphere (Habermas, 1996). In what follows, we consider a normative rationale for the public interest as a basis for regulation, drawing on Christians et al.'s (2009) analysis of theories of the media in democratic societies which, in turn, was inspired by Held's (2006) account of the main models of democracy. Our assumption is that, if different models of democracy can be analysed to specify different normative expectations for journalism, they may also be used to identify different conceptions of the public interest to be served by regulation.

Christians et al. (2009) focus on four traditions of democratic thought: two versions of liberalism (pluralism and administrative or elite democracy) and two republican (or social democratic) theories of democracy (civic republicanism and direct democracy). They compare these for their accounts of sovereignty (the legitimate expression of the public interest by the people), civil society, liberty (freedom), equality, public opinion, community and the expectations of journalism. Of these four models, two are particularly relevant to the work of a media and communications regulator such as Ofcom: liberal pluralism, we suggest, can underpin expectations regarding the furthering of the interests of consumers; and civic republicanism can be used to underpin expectations regarding the interests of citizens. The other two models of democracy considered by Christians et al. fit less well: certainly, there is little intention to follow the norms of direct democracy by Ofcom or any other regulator; it could be said that Ofcom's technical work on market analysis and spectrum allocation fits the norms of administrative, elite democracy, but this area of work is not our central focus. However the models of both civic republicanism and liberal pluralism could prove insightful in relation to Ofcom's work in the interests of citizens and consumers respectively.

Liberal pluralism conceives the legitimate expression of public interest in terms of sovereignty (or, as is sometimes said in relation to audiences, consumer sovereignty), the aggregated expression of the interests of individuals and groups across society (as in public opinion and market research measures). On this view, civil society is held to be a private space modelled on the marketplace, with freedom understood in terms of negative freedom – the removal of constraints on individuals' preferences and choices. By contrast, civic republicanism conceives the public interest as constituted through processes of recognition, public discussion and debate, which collectively and legitimately influence government and public administration. It also emphasises positive freedoms, for it works to create the conditions in which citizens can realise their potential through public engagement and self-actualisation. So, while liberal pluralism conceives equality in terms of equality of opportunity, for civic republicanism, equality is a matter of outcomes, and thus may require the (re)distribution of access to resources so that these outcomes, more than the conditions of entry, are made fairer.

Thus for civic republicanism, civil society is properly the place for articulating the public interest, through public discussion and debate in the public sphere. It draws upon the activity of communities, these providing the context for civil engagement (rather than representing mere functional groupings or sentimental attachments, as in liberalism). Further, civic republicanism conceives public opinion (regarding the public interest or anything else) as the collective outcome of a public sphere debate rather than, as in liberalism, as the aggregate of individual contributions. We could continue these contrasts, but suffice it to say that these two positions on democracy differ in their stances on the critical dimensions of political culture and society, including on the central opposition that runs through this book, that of citizen and consumer. On behalf of the consumer, for instance, the liberal pluralist is concerned to ask of the media, are they partisan or biased in relation to different interests? The civic republican, by contrast, is concerned to ask on behalf of the citizen, do the media facilitate deliberation and legitimately bring established power to account? Implicit in the foregoing is that liberal pluralism offers a rationale for furthering the consumer interest: it regards sovereignty in terms of the competition between private interests and thus holds out the normative expectation of regulation that it should adjudicate in conflicts in order to balance the interests of firms and consumers. The regulator, on this view, should act so as to reduce the constraints on individual choice and behaviour. Further, it should enable individuals to express their concerns or complaints, and ensure that these are addressed either proactively (by anticipating and removing problems or constraints) or by such means of redress as can compensate the individual for any cost or other loss. In parallel, we would argue that civic republicanism offers a rationale for advancing the citizen interest in relation to sovereignty. On this view, regulation should support an open and transparent process by which collective interests that are grounded in the lifeworld and that pertain in any way to the remit of the regulator (for

Ofcom, the power and potential of the media and communications sector) can be articulated. Further, this process should position civil society as a key mediator between government, public administration and the public, and it would legitimate interventions in the media and communications sector that contribute to the enrichment of cultural and social life and the potential for self-development of individuals, groups and communities.

For some commentators the definition of public interest is vague and, therefore, problematic, given that it is the core statutory duty of media regulators (e.g. Feintuck and Varney, 2006; McQuail, 1992). But arguably the problem is less that the term is vague than it is contested, since many parties would claim the right to define the public interest, including governments, public service broadcasters and civil society bodies. It seems plausible that the present mix of regulatory principles and practice represents a pragmatic compromise, though not a resolution, between the usually complementary but sometimes competing definitions of the public interest. In some respects, the public interest is ever more precisely defined – the efforts to develop a public interest test for media pluralism and public value tests for public service broadcasting are cases in point; here we can see an increasingly explicit, technical articulation of the public interest, although one that does not please every critic.

Ofcom's statutory duties require it to further the interests of both citizen and consumer. As we shall see in this book, this generally facilitates parallel work streams. For example, Ofcom is the body that consumers complain to about the quality of their broadband service, or about unexpected mobile phone costs, or market impediments to switching service providers. It is also the body that ensures compliance with the Broadcasting Code, adjudicating on and at times penalising those broadcasters who contravene the code by, for example, offending public tastes or breaking the rules on advertising to children. But sometimes these citizen and consumer interests conflict, and then one should ask, do its actions reflect the liberal pluralist idea that political subjects are individuals, that the public interest is the aggregate of individual consumer views, and that the role of regulation is to protect private interests, adjudicate in disputes, and relieve the consumer from market constraints and unfair treatment? Or, do its actions reflect the civic republican idea that sovereignty must be realised collectively, that the capacity of civil society requires support if it is to articulate the public interest and make it effective in relation to power, that the media may offer a public value that enables the realisation of human potential, and that opportunity is a matter not simply of equity but also of social justice? We will return to this question at several points throughout the book, ultimately concluding that, in cases where there is a conflict of interest, the citizen interest – and the civic republican vision that underpins it – tend to lose out to the consumer interest and, undoubtedly, the

market interest. This may be partly because Ofcom's self-avowed philosophy fits far more closely with that of liberal pluralism. It may also be
because of the particular interventions or actions of either industry or state,
as revealed in our case studies. But there are also some contrary cases
where citizens' interests have indeed advanced.

Notes

1 David Cameron's Coalition government took an alternative stance, reining in the
work of quangos and returning high level policy to government departments (cf.
the Public Bodies (Reform) Bill announced in the Queen's Speech of 25 May
2010).
2 Hood (1994, cited in Baldwin and Cave, 1999: 26) argues that this was an ideological move that could not be explained by pressure from interest groups, but
rather indicated that regulation colud have a political dimension.
3 Also complicating matters were the particular powers of the Commission,
including the powerful executive of appointed officials who could initiate
European policy, the European Parliament of elected members with limited
executive powers, and the Council of Ministers, which represented the member
states and ratified the proposals of the Commission (Collins, 1994).
4 *Television without Frontiers* built on Article 49 of the European Community
Treaty which defined television channels as providing services, meaning that they
should be available across borders within the European Union. Different countries within Europe had different media systems (Hallin and Mancini, 2004) and
operated with different standards and mechanisms of media content regulation
and consumer protection. As technology increasing allowed a cross-border traffic
in media services, several cases came before the European Court of Justice in
which member states were concerned about media services emanating from
other countries that did not conform to local standards and cultural values, pointing to the need to provide a legislative Directive to clarify the relative powers of
the EU and member states on these issues (Feintuck and Varney, 2006). While
powerful interests backed the idea that the emerging media environment represented a golden opportunity to develop a globally competitive industry if markets
could be liberalised (or 'deregulated'), an equally powerful coalition of interests
was convinced that media and communications played a vital cultural and social
role that was now threatened by market liberalisation (Humphreys, 2008).
5 Specifically, the *Television without Frontiers* Directive provided protection for
European production quotas in Article 4 (over 50% of the schedule should be
of European origin) and allocation of a proportion (10%) of production budgets
to European and independent producers in Article 5. Also, Article 3a provided
for public events that were considered of major importance to member states so
that these should be accessible by a significant proportion of the population; this
limited the introduction of paid-for television services for cultural events and
sports. Also, the EU provided waves of financial support for media production
aimed at preserving a diversity of cultural expression via the MEDIA programme (1991–2013; Feintuck and Varney, 2006).

3

OFCOM'S CORE PURPOSES: A DISCURSIVE STRUGGLE

Media regulation and the implied audience

While the 1990s saw growing acceptance of the need for regulatory change in relation to media and communications, there remained considerable disagreement over regulatory purpose, design and function. A key debate during the passage of the Communications Bill 2002 comprised an extraordinary struggle at the very inception of Ofcom regarding its primary duties. Centring on the fraught distinction between the so-called 'citizen' and 'consumer' interests, the debate had implications for the framing of the Act and, subsequently, the internal structures and external relations established for the regulator. It seems that asking the fundamental question – in whose interest would Ofcom act? – brought into the open a deep ambivalence among policy makers over the competing interests at stake in communications regulation. As this chapter will trace, the struggle over Ofcom's purposes was conducted discursively, but the conditions underpinning this struggle were shaped by the political changes, economic pressures and technological developments we have already elaborated in Chapters 1 and 2.

As we have reviewed so far, the television policy context in the 1980s and 1990s was shaped, on the one hand, by the relative scarcity of frequencies relative to potential broadcasters, so that 'those who were privileged enough to have a government license could be required to provide programming in the public interest' (Webster and Phalen, 1994: 20) and, on the other hand, by the reliance – to a greater or lesser degree in different countries – on advertiser support. For Van Cuilenburg and McQuail (2003: 195), by the end of the 1980s:

> Two main policy tendencies could be observed. One was simply to break monopolies and privatize as much as possible, under the banner of deregulation, along American lines, and harmonization of markets, European style. The second was to keep operating in the spirit of normative theory and try to develop new media potential by way of public investment and protectionism – in effect to apply the public service model to new territory.[1]

Conceptions of the audience were shaped commensurately – on the one hand, in terms of a citizenry or public (a diverse collectivity with established political, social and cultural rights; Livingstone, 2005; Murdock, 2005; Syvertsen, 2004) while, on the other hand, as consumers (i.e. individuals with preferences who are presented with choices) or even as a commodity (i.e. an aggregate to be sold to advertisers; cf. Smythe, 1984). Webster and Phalen argue that the persistent ambiguity evident in policy discourses over the naming of the audience is not accidental, for it has long allowed 'policymakers to avoid an explicit declaration of *their model of the audience*' (1994: 21, emphasis added). Hasebrink (2009: 147) goes further, arguing that 'the political and public discourse on the remit of public service media lacks systematic consideration of the users and audiences'. But the situation is changing, precisely because the conditions that permitted audiences to be tacitly spoken for, and taken for granted, have been undermined in an age of simultaneous technological and social divergence and convergence: as Webster and Phalen suggest, 'it seems likely that audience concepts that have been implied or fragmentary will have to emerge from beneath the surface and be considered in their own right' (1994: 21). Nearly two decades on, we would put this more strongly: today, the conceptions as regards audiences are far from implicit; indeed, they sit at the forefront of debates over competing visions of public rights and individual vulnerabilities, of agency and influence, of individualisation and collectivity (Livingstone and Lunt, 2011; Morley, 2006; Raboy et al., 2001). Or, as the debate over the Communications Act 2003 to be discussed in this chapter would have it, understanding the nature, concerns and rights of audiences lies at the heart of any analysis of the interests of citizen and consumer.

For the new regulator, these questions were hotly debated during the passage of the Act and subsequently, revealing how what might, at first sight, seem to be mere semantic struggles in fact pointed to a profound philosophical difference with very practical consequences. While not meaning to underplay the longer history of these debates (Collins and Murroni, 1996; Smith, 2006), in this chapter we shall focus on the series of steps from the 1998 Green Paper *Regulating Communications* (DTI/DCMS, 1998) to the Communications Act 2003, as specified in the setting and then the implementation of Ofcom's primary duty. As will be seen, its regulatory purposes were hotly contested on all sides. Even within government, ambivalence characterised the early shaping of the regulator, as represented in the different approaches of the two departments responsible for the Communications Act 2003 – the Department for Culture, Media and Sport (DMCS) and the (then) Department for Trade and Industry (DTI).

> Ofcom exists to further the interests of citizen-consumers through a regulatory regime which, where appropriate, encourages competition.

This mission statement hangs in Ofcom's entrance lobby, pinpointing Ofcom's conception of its regulatory purpose. It makes an interesting contrast with, say, the text on the wall of the BBC Media Centre, which states: 'Audiences are at the heart of everything we do'. Both statements prioritise ordinary people as prime beneficiaries, though whether this is as a Giddensian 'reflexive' or 'empowered' self or a Foucauldian 'governed self' is unclear. The BBC uses the 'old' language of audiences while Ofcom adopts the New Labour language of citizens and consumers (Clarke et al., 2007), a discursive shift which in its emphasis on values of transparency, consultation, accountability, and individual empowerment and choice was, as Fairclough (2002: 164) notes, enacted throughout the 'hardware' and 'software' of organisations. Consider how the Partner for Strategy and Market Developments (Robin Foster) explains the increased importance of regulation for the audience:

> [In a] very different and more converged world ... as regulators and policy makers we need to radically adapt the way we think about the communications sector ... We will have to learn to rely more on markets than ever before. And we need to rely more on individual consumers and on companies exercising responsibility in those markets, with increasing emphasis on self-regulation and co-regulation. (Foster, 2005: paras 2–3)

This can be read as both an opportunity and a threat to the 'individual consumers' in whose interest regulation is ultimately directed. The previously ambiguous language of 'audience' – albeit usefully embracing both the public/collective and viewer/individual – seems poorly suited to a converged media and communications landscape, and one that applies not at all to telecommunications or online media, while the language of 'users', increasingly prevalent in discussing mobile or internet services, fits poorly with broadcasting (Livingstone, 2005). A converged regulator needed a new language, and it so happened a new language – that of citizens and consumers or, especially, the citizen-consumer – was already well established as a core constituent of the New Labour lexicon (Clarke et al., 2007; see also Needham, 2003; Trentmann, 2006). But what does the 'citizen-consumer' mean in relation to media and communications regulation? And what did it mean to Ofcom?

Two distinct stages in the discursive process can be identified (as detailed in Livingstone et al., 2007a). The first stage, beginning with Tony Blair's

New Labour government in 1997 and culminating in the Communications Act 2003, was the struggle to resolve the plethora of everyday notions of the individual or audience or viewer or public into 'citizen' and 'consumer', two distinct terms that supposedly divided the semantic terrain neatly between them, closing down previous ambiguities and reframing the regulatory domain so that conflicting interests could be accommodated. The second stage, starting from when Ofcom began its work in late 2003, was the almost immediate unravelling of this two-term solution as ambiguities re-emerged and boundary disputes – provoked by civil society actors – problematised the proposed regulatory structures and direction, requiring remedial action on the part of the regulator.

Jointly produced by the DTI and the DCMS just one year into the New Labour government, the Green Paper, *Regulating Communications* (DTI/DCMS, 1998), favoured an evolutionary approach to the anticipated far-reaching technological changes, since 'mass markets for digital services do not yet exist … [and] how they develop depends on the behaviour of individuals and communities reacting to new technology and services' (Executive Summary). Stating that 'the public policy objectives which underpin regulation will remain largely the same', it prioritised serving the consumer interest; supporting universal access to services at affordable cost; securing effective competition; and promoting quality, plurality, diversity and choice. However, as diverse responses to the consultation on the Green Paper stressed, such a gradualist approach was considered insufficient and more radical measures were called for (Select Committee on Culture, Media and Sport, 2001).

The subsequent White Paper, *A New Future for Communications* (DTI/DCMS, 2000), consequently acknowledged that 'the communications revolution has arrived' and hence it sought to offer 'a new framework for communications regulation in the 21st century' (Foreword) in the form of an Office of Communications (Ofcom) tasked with:

- Protecting the interests of consumers in terms of choice, price, quality of service and value for money, in particular through promoting open and competitive markets;
- Maintaining high quality of content, a wide range of programming and plurality of public expression;
- Protecting the interests of citizens by maintaining accepted community standards in content, balancing freedom of speech against the need to protect against potentially offensive or harmful material, and ensuring appropriate protection of fairness and privacy. (DTI/DCMS, 2002: Executive Summary)

In short, consumers were to receive protection as in any other regulated market and publics merited particular positive freedoms ('regulation for'), while citizens – here making a first appearance in this process – were seen to merit negative freedoms ('regulation against'; Berlin, 1969; Corner, 2004). To achieve these objectives, the White Paper proposed two bodies: a Consumer

Panel, (semi-)independent of Ofcom, to further consumer interests where these were not met by the market and, within Ofcom, a Content Board, to ensure citizen interests in relation to broadcast content. As with each stage of the legislative process, a public consultation followed which, when it closed two months later, had generated over 250 responses. Many of these expressed support for the proposal, though some also expressed concerns (e.g. over 'regulatory creep') and some made new proposals (e.g. for a Citizens' Panel).

However, the Draft Communications Bill published in May 2002 marked a surprising linguistic shift, replacing both 'consumer' and 'citizen' with 'customer' (along with a sporadic use of other terms), perhaps suggesting lobbying pressure from the industry during the drafting process. Thus, it stated:

Part 1: Functions of Ofcom

3(1) (a) to further the interests of the persons who are customers for the services and facilities in relation to which Ofcom have functions ...

3(7) 'customers' means (a) a person to whom or for whose benefit that service or facility is provided or made available ...; (b) a person who is sought as a customer ...; (c) a person who wishes to be such a customer or who is likely to seek to become one. (Draft Communications Bill 2002)

Notwithstanding the attempt to clarify matters in paragraph 3(7), terminological confusion persisted over whether 'customer' (and 'consumer') was meant to include those without a contractual relation with a service provider, or even whether it referred to ordinary people at all as opposed to advertisers or businesses. Among the 300+ submissions to the public consultation, which concluded on 2 August 2002, Clause 3 ('General duties of Ofcom') attracted highly polarised responses. These included the Confederation of British Industry's (CBI) interchangeable use of 'customer' and 'consumer' in advocating an Economics Panel or Competition Board 'complementing the role of the Consumer Panel' and the Independent Television Commission's (ITC) assertion that 'audiences' could not be called 'customers' since, first, they received free-to-air public service networks and, second, 'they are members of the public as citizens'.[2]

A decisive intervention came through pre-legislative scrutiny of the Draft Bill by the Joint Select Committee for the House of Commons and House of Lords, an all-party committee chaired by Lord Puttnam, which reported at the end of July 2002 (Puttnam, 2002, 2006). Contributing to this was a coalition formed for the purpose among citizen, consumer and other civil society groups under the banner of The Public Voice. A cross-party alliance between opposition Conservatives and Liberal Democrats provided another notable source of input into the Committee's deliberations (Harvey, 2006). A pertinent effort here came in the form of a 'note on terminology' jointly issued by the DTI and DCMS (2002), which explained that, on the one

---

45

hand, '"customer" is used throughout the [Draft] Bill to refer to individuals or businesses who use or seek to use electronic communications networks and services or associated facilities, or whom providers seek as users of those things' and that, on the other hand, in the policy document accompanying the Draft Bill, the government had followed the approach of the White Paper rather than the Draft Bill. There, it stated, 'we have generally used the terms "consumer" or "citizen" rather than "customer" when talking about interest of members of the public', because:

> ... generally the term 'consumer' is used to indicate the purchaser or other user of a service, normally based on an economic relationship (either direct or indirect) between the individual and the service in question. Typically, though not exclusively, such interests arise in relation to networks and services rather than content. Meanwhile, the term 'citizen' relates to the individual as a member of society, and enjoying the rights and responsibilities such membership confers. In the electronic communications sector, these tend to arise mainly in the content area, where more cultural aspects, such as harm and offence, access to a wide variety of high quality programming, and the handling of political issues assume importance. (DTI/DCMS, 2002)

This clarified government thinking by mapping categories of the public on to areas for regulation and the institutional bodies to regulate them, thus revealing how discursive categories instantiate power relations among the state, industry and individuals:

	Consumer interest	Citizen interest
Approach:	Economic	Cultural
Object of regulation:	Networks and services	Content
Beneficiary:	Individuals	Community
Ofcom structure:	Consumer Panel	Content Board
Legacy regulator:	Oftel	ITC, BSC

Although supportive of the economic case for a communications regulator, the Joint Select Committee report (Puttnam, 2002) argued against an industry panel to balance the Consumer Panel 'because it was felt that consumers found it very difficult to get into the regulatory process, certainly far more difficult than the industry'. Consistent with public sphere values, the Consumer Panel was instead meant to rebalance the otherwise unbalanced representation of consumer versus industry interests. Further, the report criticised the omission of citizens' interests from the Draft Bill, asserting that 'this is more than a matter of semantics' (Puttnam, 2002: 11). Consequently, the report advocated two principal duties for Ofcom – to further the interests of citizens and to further the interests of consumers.

But, surprising to many, and contrary to the recommendation of the Joint Select Committee, in the Communications Bill of November 2002, Clause 3 ('General duties of Ofcom') specified only that Ofcom was 'to further the interests of consumers in relevant markets, where appropriate by promoting competition'. Although customers had become consumers again (specifically defined as including 'those who were not in receipt of services or unable to access them'; House of Commons, 2002: 13), any mention of the citizen had disappeared. As Jocelyn Hay (2002), then Chair of The Voice of the Listener and Viewer (VLV), commented:

> The continuing lack of recognition of 'citizens' and the public interest in broadcasting is, sadly, symbolic of a piece of legislation almost wholly concerned with the interests of commerce, for which members of the public are customers and consumers, not citizens ... The Bill simply re-iterates a, now largely discredited, faith that the 'market' and competition will provide choice and quality; it does NOT as experience shows.

A heated debate in the House of Lords followed in June 2003, with Lord Puttnam proposing an amendment to Clause 3 to reinstate citizen interest against the government (Hansard, 2003). The government response marshalled an array of arguments in its defence, notably claiming that citizen interest was already covered by consumer interest, that term 'citizen' could not appear in UK law for it referred only to immigration status, and that one might reasonably trust Ofcom to do the right thing. This last point was articulated by, among others, Lord Currie, incoming Chair of Ofcom, who urged that 'the dual concept of the citizen/consumer' would be recognised within Ofcom, whether or not the amendment was accepted. However, reiterating the oft-advocated position that the media represent a special case for regulation, Lord McNally argued that it was vital to specify the 'specific duties of Ofcom to protect the rights of the citizen ... the very reason we have a Communications Bill rather than leaving matters simply to competition and enterprise legislation is that communications is different'. Lord Peyton's attack on the government was more explicit in setting out the importance of explicit regulation in the interest of citizens:

> I believe the Government must be well aware that the forces of the market are such that 99 times out of 100 the real pressure of short-term demands, with the full support of the media moguls, would be more than sufficient to win the day. Supporters of the amendment fear that that position will be infinitely weakened by the pressures that the market and those who control the media – the moguls of television and other media – will be able to marshal against it. The consumer and the citizen are two sides of the same coin. All of us are both from time to time, but the consumer will almost always take a short-term point of view. In our time, we badly need reinforcement for the long-term view.

Lord Bragg offered an elegant summing up: 'I hope that your Lordships will fully support and champion that fine word and state of "citizen". It has a lengthy and distinguished pedigree'. However, Lord McIntosh, speaking for the government, rejected this:

It is not our intention – nor is it in the English language – to equate consumers with markets. The word that I have always used, in 50 years with the Labour Party, is that we have to be on the side of the 'punters'. I think everyone understands that ... 'Consumers' is not a doppelganger for the wicked and self-seeking market, which some people in the Chamber seem to fear.

Nonetheless, in a triumph for Lord Puttnam's Committee and the civil society coalition, The Public Voice and, arguably, for citizens at large, Blair's New Labour government lost the vote and the disputed amendment was passed with a sizable majority. The Communications Act received Royal Assent on 17 July 2003, and Clause 3 set out Ofcom's Statutory Duties as follows:

3(1) It shall be the principal duty of Ofcom, in carrying out their functions; (a) to further the interests of citizens in relation to communications matters; and (b) to further the interests of consumers in relevant markets, where appropriate by promoting competition.

Ofcom's remit – interpreting its primary duties

The Communications Act clearly distinguished citizen and consumer interests, putting the citizen interest first and specifying that the consumer interest alone is to be furthered by means of promoting markets. With the struggle apparently over, all that remained was for Ofcom to take up its duties following its official start in December 2003.[3] However, as Black (2002) observes, the letter of the law is meaningful only through its interpretation, and interpretation is a collective and pragmatic act. Just a few days after the Lords' debate, David Currie (2003), Ofcom's first Chair, commented with some frustration:

You may well have noticed that the careful balance established in the Communications Bill between the duties to citizens and those to consumers has been upset by a recent House of Lords amendment, pressed by Lord Puttnam, that requires Ofcom to give paramountcy to the citizen in all matters concerning broadcasting and spectrum. That represents a considerable departure from what has been the case for the two existing broadcasting regulators (the ITC and Radio Authority), who currently work to a balance of these interests. This late change ... seems to us to be unfortunate.

Stephen Carter, Ofcom's Chief Executive Officer (CEO), was equally concerned. Having earlier asserted that 'we are all of us both citizens and consumers ... it will be against that combined citizen-consumer interest that we will benchmark all our key decisions' (Carter, 2003a), he characterised the attempt to distinguish citizens and consumers in biased terms as a struggle between:

> ... those who hoped or feared that Ofcom would approach its tasks wholly through an economic prism and would sweep away anything subjective that could not be encompassed by a market analysis; and those who hoped or feared that Ofcom would give primacy to the cultural and political themes and would intervene subjectively and distortingly into market choices. (Carter, 2004)

From the start, Ofcom's interpretation of its general duties followed Lord Currie's hyphenated term, 'citizen-consumer', which, though this formulation appears nowhere in the Act (Harvey, 2006), was held to 'reflect a truth that is at once simple and more complex than the crude characterizations of each side of the debate', namely, that broadcasting depends on the market and that telecommunications must accommodate civic needs (Carter, 2004). Carter's proffered resolution was that 'the promotion of civic values must infuse all our actions; economics should be the basic tool which underpins all our actions'. In short, civic values may inspire goals, but economic realities will dictate outcomes. Speaking to an industry audience, Currie (2005) was more blunt: 'Let's be clear. Our objective is to create an environment which will help markets to grow, not to stifle innovation'.

So, as expressed in its mission statement, Ofcom was (re)interpreted as primarily an economic or market-focused regulator, first, by conjoining citizen and consumer as the citizen-consumer and, second, by foregrounding competition as the primary instrument to further the interests of both. Don Redding, Campaign Coordinator of the civil society body, The Public Voice, protested to Ofcom about the hyphenated formulation, arguing that in the mission statement:

> ... the two twin but separate and distinct principal duties become aligned and subordinated into the consumer, essentially but principally because you say, well, the vehicle is competition. Well the Act doesn't say that. The Act says, normally you'd expect the vehicle to be competition when you're dealing with consumer issues but no such link is made with citizens' issues ... Last year in their annual plan consultation there were eight, nine, ten out of whatever it was sixty, sixty-five responses that raised that issue about the mission statements and said please change it. It had no impact ... and there it is now, they've stopped apparently using 'citizen-consumer', hyphenated, to show that they don't con-flate the two anymore. But they still say, 'both where appropriate through competition'. (Interview with the authors; see also Redding, 2005)[4]

His argument was carefully framed, referring to the wording of the Act (since 'Ofcom is a creature of statute'[5]) to demand that this self-avowedly consultative regulator take note of the public response. After all, scope for

OFCOM'S CORE PURPOSES

misinterpretation was rife: in an interview with us,[6] Ofcom's then Content Board Chair, Richard Hooper, made exactly the mistake Redding was concerned about, in regarding competition as a means of furthering citizen interests:

Our major clause says we are in the business of furthering the interests of citizens and of consumers, where appropriate by competition. That's what our job is, our job is to basically instil competition into the markets and to make sure the consumers and citizens are satisfied.[7]

Do words dictate actions? Arguably not, but they may legitimate priorities and ease omissions. Notably, the hyphenated formulation has only recently and rather quietly disappeared from Ofcom's walls, reports and website – which is itself extraordinary, as no publicly available minutes of the Board record a decision to change Ofcom's mission. Nonetheless, Ofcom continues to refer inconsistently and apparently haphazardly to the interests of consumers, citizen-consumers or 'citizens and consumers', though rarely to those of citizens. More significantly, perhaps, from 2003 onwards Ofcom established institutional structures and roles relating to consumer policy: it publicly reported its progress in meeting consumer concerns;[8] it adopted the 'consumer interest toolkit' developed by the Consumer Panel to ensure that consumer interests were taken into account at all stages in policy development; and it established a range of public-facing initiatives to offer advice to consumers directly. The conception of a demanding consumer was, it seemed, readily congruent with Ofcom's conception of what market-focused regulation was: as its first chair, David Currie said, 'consumers are demanding access to any service, any time and anywhere', for 'the digital era is shifting the balance of control towards consumers'.

Strikingly, little equivalent activity or accountability was forthcoming regarding actions to further citizen interests. Repeated requests from academics and civil society groups to define and report on Ofcom's efforts to further the citizen interest received a scant response, even when expressed as part of formal public consultation processes. For example, although Ofcom announced 'Identifying and defining citizens' interests in relation to communications matters' as a new work area for 2005/06 (Ofcom, 2005a: 39), noting its determination to 'identify and articulate more clearly how the interests of citizens should be incorporated in Ofcom's decision-making process in a transparent and systematic way', nothing materialised. In the Draft Annual Plan for 2006–07 the term 'citizen' barely appeared and was consistently replaced by 'consumer', as was pointed out by civil society actions in response to the consultation. Perhaps this reflected Ofcom's view, *contra* that of its critics, that 'consumer and citizen interests are closely related and that for many people, the distinction is not very important' (Ofcom, 2006a: 8).

In its report, *Taking Account of Consumer and Citizen Interest: Progress and Evaluation – 12 Months On*, Ofcom (2007a) elided the twin duties into one by stating that 'Ofcom has a principal duty to further the interests of both citizens and consumers'. This evaluation report detailed numerous consumer-related activities organised around 'a framework, which Ofcom can use to prioritize and plan its consumer policy programme of work and response appropriately to consumer interest related demands'. As it explained, outcomes were to be disseminated publicly 'to ensure we articulate and communicate our decisions in a way that allows consumers to understand our decisions and explains what the outcomes are for citizens and consumers'. As in this last sentence, although 'citizens' does appear on rare occasions in this supposed progress report, it seems that no particular significance was attached to such mentions.

Whether elided or kept distinct, the terms 'citizen' and 'consumer' remain unstable, resting on vague terms (needs, values, choices), mapping uneasily on to Ofcom's structures and available policy tools, and interpreted variously by different stakeholders less for reasons of semantics than because of their conflicting interests. Though the terms easily 'pass as ordinary' precisely because of their everyday familiarity (Born, 2004), they remain awkward and, as we document elsewhere (Livingstone et al., 2007b), key Ofcom figures sought various ways of avoiding them. To quote Matt Peacock, Ofcom's then Director of Communications, 'citizens/consumers, people basically, as I prefer to call them'. But Ofcom was constrained by its statutory obligations. While a civil society campaigner was free to comment 'I think it's horrible, the "citizen-consumer" opposition',[9] Kip Meek, Ofcom's then Senior Partner (Competition and Content), more cautiously observed of the Communications Act that:

> It was hard fought over because as with many of these things, it became a metaphor for [...] whether, you know for the sort of it was a the sort of 'soul of Ofcom' was being fought over and the, you know, if you include the word 'citizen', QED Ofcom will not just be an economic regulator, it will look more broadly than that and that is what it was about.[10]

This question of Ofcom's 'soul' takes us back to the special status of the media's role in the public sphere, in relation to democracy rather than markets. The critical concern was that citizen interests would be subsumed by consumer interests, an outcome that can be read as being in step with New Labour thinking more widely, as:

> ... replicating patterns of choice and power found in the private economy. The consumer is primarily self-regarding, forms preferences without reference to others, and acts through a series of instrumental, temporary bilateral relationships. Accountability is secured by competition and complaint, and power exercised through aggregate signalling. (Needham, 2003: 5)

Critiquing market rhetoric and insisting on the inclusion of citizen interests does not, however, make it easy to specify just what this means, even for civil society critics and academics. Allan Williams, then Senior Policy Advisor to the Consumers' Association, explains:

The risk is if you have just the language of citizens then you end up with, with a load of nebulous and quite high level public interest-type objectives rather than actually looking at are people getting the best deal in this market.[11]

Jocelyn Hay, Chair of The Voice of the Listener and Viewer (VLV), concurred that:

It is much easier to regulate consumer issues which are basically economic issues and redress and fair representation and so on than citizenship issues which involve social, cultural, democratic issues which are far more difficult to quantify and measure.[12]

Colette Bowe, then Consumer Panel Chair (and Ofcom's Chair from 2009), added:

The citizen issues are much harder because you have to find some other deliverers who you can forge an effective alliance with to deliver. Doesn't mean you're not still responsible for doing something, but it's a harder and more complex, more diffuse.[13]

The BBC's then Controller of Editorial Policy was the most forthcoming, readily using a language of positive public values (value, culture, education, nation) that was little employed by Ofcom's senior managers:

My concern would be ... that citizen is indeed understood in the broader sense of issues around public value, and that is not just about information, it's also about culture, it's about encouraging the British story, so to speak, being reflected within British production. And also it's around educative programming as well.[14]

However, if the citizen interest, by contrast with the consumer interest, is difficult to define clearly and unambiguously, if it requires the construction of diffuse alliances with other stakeholders and is not readily amenable to quantifiable research, this makes it hard to allocate resources to furthering the citizen interest, notwithstanding its inclusion in the regulator's general duties. As Ofcom's Director of External Relations asked, 'if you engage with consumers, do you engage separately with citizens?' He continued, yet more sceptically, 'do we get better advice from self-appointed, probably issue-driven, non-representative groups?'[15] His question implies that even if civil society groups had adequate resources to challenge Ofcom, the regulator would question whether they reasonably represented either the citizen or the consumer or if they were partisan. His scepticism is presented with a degree of equivocation (via the modal qualifier 'probably', together with the pauses and hedges apparent in his utterance), for Ofcom is driven by the imperative to be efficient, clear in its purposes, transparent in its workings, perceived as legitimate by all stakeholders.

Arguably this was a point at which academic stakeholders could and should have advocated a decisive account of the citizen interest (in terms of the democratic public sphere and the requirements of mediated civic participation), thereby redressing the semantic confusion and, in consequence, providing a clear rationale for policy action. But they did not. Civil society voices, it seems, have been somewhat content and have focused more on consumer rather than citizen interests. In the early days, Allan Williams suggested that Oftel, Ofcom's legacy telecommunications regulator, 'didn't understand what consumers actually wanted, what the actual problems in the market were and they didn't understand that you couldn't just make competition work through increasing choice at the supply side'.[16] Claire Milne, a freelance consumer spokesperson, agreed: 'another difference between Ofcom and Oftel, of course, is that Ofcom is explicitly tasked with putting consumer interest first which Oftel never was'.[17] Moreover, since furthering the consumer interest appeared to be sufficiently advanced by Ofcom's activities, once Ofcom's Consumer Panel was established the Consumers' Association decided that consumer interests in communications had been suitably addressed, and so reduced their activities in this domain.

Moreover, unlike in some other domains of regulation, the audience itself rarely expresses views on media regulation in public forums, although as surveys repeatedly show, values of objectivity, impartiality, diversity and quality receive consistent and strong support. But the main route to communication offered to the audience by regulators is through the mechanism of complaint which, while periodically used to real effect by audiences, positions the audience as consumer rather than citizen, able only to represent a particular harm done to them as individuals rather than to express any larger concerns or to participate in the debates held on their behalf regarding the public interest.

Speaking up for the citizen or public interest, however, Ed Richards (2003), then Senior Partner for Strategy and Market Developments at Ofcom and its CEO from 2006, argued from the start that 'at the very heart of Ofcom is the duality of the citizen and the consumer'. Indeed, far from interpreting the key terms of the Act as identical (the citizen-consumer, two sides of the same coin), these are now opposed (citizen versus consumer). Richards' 2004 speech on broadcasting contrasted the 'consumer' and 'citizen' as follows. First, he argued, the consumer rationale is focused on wants and individual choice. In times of scarcity, market intervention is required to maximise the range and balance of content, but this requirement 'will gradually reduce over time' as we enter the digital age of abundance. In the future, therefore, broadcasting will become more like the publishing, film and music industries, and regulation can recede.

The citizen rationale, by contrast, Richards argued to be focused on the benefits broadcasting offers in the long term to society, bringing 'broader social benefits' to democracy, culture, identity, learning, participation, engagement in a manner that goes 'beyond our interests as private consumers'. Since the market can and does deliver just some of this, there is a continued justification for market intervention. That this assertion of a binary discourse, mapped below, bears striking similarities to the DTI/DCMS terminological note to the Joint Select Committee is perhaps not accidental, since in 2002 Richards was Senior Policy Advisor for Communications in the Cabinet Office.

Consumer rationale	Citizen rationale
Wants	Needs
Individual level	Social level
Private benefits	Public/social benefits
Language of choice	Language of rights (inclusion)
Short-term focus	Long-term focus
Regulate against detriment	Regulate for public interest
Plan to roll back regulation	Continued regulation to correct market failure

This elegant solution, however, met with some difficulties when it was translated into regulatory practice. One such, expressed by Ofcom's then Partner for Strategy and Market Developments, Robin Foster, developed the accepted view that television raises particular citizen interests by implying, more controversially, that as the media and communications environment diversifies, the citizen interest in communication matters will decline:

The point about television as a medium is that it is ... special because it has the potential, whatever is on it, to have a powerful impact on our lives and the way we think about ... the society we live in. Therefore it becomes important to pay a particular interest to the nature of the content and the providers of that content ... Now, I don't think you can say that about many products, I don't even think you can say that about a lot of media.[18]

Another intriguing realignment emerged when Ofcom's Consumer Panel (2005a)[19] expanded its 'consumer' remit by 'building citizen considerations into our work'. As its then Chairman, Colette Bowe, explained, it was also the Consumer Panel's role to address:

... important questions ... which are about access – or the lack of it – to communications that arise because of where people live, or because of who they are. We call these 'issues about people as citizens'.[20]

Though not incompatible with Richards' scheme above, this vision decouples the citizen interest from both broadcasting and the Content Board, instead aligning it with telecommunications and the Consumer Panel, contrary to the Act's mapping of purposes on to structures (although, to be sure, the rationale for universal service in telecommunications policy has always rested on a conception of the citizen – or public – rather than the consumer or market interest; Simpson, 2004). Unrepentant, the Consumer Panel has since advocated affordable universal broadband provision on citizen as well as consumer grounds, as is evident from its annual reports and as subsequently taken up by *Digital Britain* (BIS and DCMS, 2009). As Bowe goes on to explain:

> We realised very quickly ... that what we were talking about was not consumers. We were talking about citizens. We were talking about people who were perfectly capable in principle of going to the shop and buying the thing as a consumer, but actually might they be isolated from our society in a way that made it difficult to know that that was what they should be doing?

Far from seeing the consumer interest as subsuming the citizen interest, Bowe thus argues that consumer interests, in reality, are citizen interests. For example:

> You can start off thinking that an issue like digital switchover is about consumer issues. I – I, we regard consumer issues as being about price, choice, access. So you might say, well, you know digital switchover is about consumers. Actually where the problems come, and why they are important, is in the area of citizens when it's about ... where you live and who you are.

So while the consumer interest is reduced to a practical list (price, choice, access), the citizen interest is elevated to a fundamental concern, one that may go beyond concrete evidence and measurable targets, according to Colette Bowe:

> I've had many groups of people come to talk to me about citizen issues. And it's actually through talking to those concerned groups that I've realised that actually most of what we do is about citizen issues, and that part of our really important role in life is to not be afraid to stand up and say 'I can't give you hard and fast evidence about this but I'm prepared to assert that it is important that people stay connected to communications because otherwise our society will lose some of its cohesion.'

This attempt to stretch the consumer interest to encompass citizen concerns derives directly from two of Ofcom's core working principles. The first, as Colette Bowe indicates above, stems from Ofcom's commitment to be open to diverse stakeholder views. If civil society groups choose to represent their concerns to the Consumer Panel, the Panel listens and, in this case, expands its remit to accommodate the normative within a largely economic model of regulation. The second, as Helen Normoyle, Ofcom's then Director of Market Research, explained, derives from its commitment to empirical evidence:

... the primary interest for most commercial organisations would be the consumer-type person, they tend to be less interested in the citizen-type issues. Whereas as a regulator, the consumer and the citizen aspect ... [are] of equal and critical importance to us.[21]

For a market researcher, in other words, consumers and citizens become population types that any sampling strategy must include if it is to claim representativeness. The expectation that Ofcom should 'protect these citizens and ... make sure that they don't get left behind because the market by itself will not take care' (ibid.) becomes a matter of good science, following on from the empirical demonstration that vulnerable groups exist, as conscientiously documented in many of Ofcom's research reports.

Although this is explicitly to recognise the limits of a market approach, more subtly the use of statistics also reifies the priority accorded the consumer over the citizen, since the latter, on this logic, represents just a small fraction of the population. Hence, it is a negative definition of the citizen interest that results, citizens being the vulnerable minority excluded by the market and only revealed through research and not, as in the more usual sense of the term, all members of the public, with the right to represent themselves in matters that concern them. This somewhat counterintuitive definition is recognised by the Consumer Panel's then Policy Manager Julie Myers, albeit in a return to the language of consumers:

You have consumer groups who may well represent sort of low income consumers, consumers with disabilities, but you know, who's there actually talking for people who aren't in any of those particular groups? The generality of consumers.[22]

Actions to further citizens' and consumers' interests

There are two ways of developing this unfolding analysis of what Ofcom has done for 'the generality' of consumers and citizens. The first is to examine their actions in relation to specific policy domains (as we do in our case studies in Chapters 5–8). This is to judge Ofcom by its actions, not its words, for it remains possible that the citizen interest has nonetheless been furthered in practice. As Ofcom's then Secretary Graham Howell put it, 'Maybe we do deal with the citizen. Maybe in what we do and how we regulate we are doing all we can to help the citizens. It's just we don't quite word it like that'.[23]

The second is to take forward the narrative developed thus far in this chapter regarding the contested notion of the citizen interest. This we undertake below in concluding the chapter, taking as our focus Ofcom's belated (2008a) discussion paper, *Citizens, Communications and Convergence*, put out for consultation in July 2008, five years after the Communications Act was passed:

> The purpose of this paper is to discuss and clarify Ofcom's role in furthering the interests of citizens. It sets out our thinking on this issue and we hope that it stimulates debate.

Noting that 'the fact that we have not published an equivalent statement on citizens has led some stakeholders to suggest that Ofcom lacks commitment in discharging its responsibilities in this area' (Ofcom, 2008a: 4), the paper documented how Ofcom has, in practice, furthered citizen interest in some key ways: public service broadcasting has been at the top of the agenda for the past five years; the question of a universal service for broadband is rising up the agenda; community radio has been strengthened by Ofcom's efforts; and its digital dividend review, digital inclusion and media literacy strategies, among others, have all advanced citizen interest. But as Chair of the Content Board, Philip Graf (2008) told the civil society group, VLV, that these and other activities result in 'a bit of a laundry list'. What is still lacking is a coherent and principled framework for scoping, underpinning and furthering the citizen interest in communications matters.

The view that Ofcom possesses the necessary vision for such a framework was undermined by its curious observation that 'we tend to think of a market as a vibrant, enticing place where consumers interact, but there is not an equivalent metaphor for the way that citizens interact in civil society' (Ofcom, 2008a: 8). The 'we' of this claim is surely unfamiliar to those suffering from the credit crunch, fuel poverty or even mobile phone scams. The excitement of the market is surely also foreign to those who fear the might of Rupert Murdoch, the end of regional television news or the future for indigenous children's drama. Furthermore, academics, civil society and new social movements can indeed think of some engaging, even vibrant, metaphors – notably that of the public sphere, whether envisioned as the Athenian forum, eighteenth-century coffee houses or today's blogosphere.

Ofcom's hope that it might stimulate some debate, however genuinely meant, was frustrated. There were only 25 responses, few compared with many Ofcom consultations, of which eight were from individuals (one or two of which were self-described campaigners), four from industry, four from groups advocating local or community television, two (or three – classifying such organisations is not always straightforward) from civil society groups specialising in media matters, two from academics (including the second author of this book, though additionally some of the civil society responses were written by academics), and one each from Ofcom's Consumer Panel, the British Humanist Association, the Communication Workers' Union, a councillor and Friends of the Lake District (concerned with the environmental impact of ill-regulated cables and overhead wires).

Beyond the perhaps surprising paucity of academic input, given the number of scholars concerned with media, democracy, citizenship and the public sphere, it is also noteworthy that several responses – particularly those from industry and from individuals – offer little or no comment on the 'citizen interest' at all. Instead, they have treated the consultation as an occasion to advance their own agendas of complaints from silent calls and telephone number systems to the quality of broadcast transmission. Some of these were creative in their determination to make their point. For example, the Broadband Stakeholder Group (BSG) advocated citizen over consumer interests because the latter generate bureaucratic regulations on industry (designed to protect individuals) whereas the public interest in the long term, they imply, is best served by encouraging (i.e. deregulating for) investment and innovation. In a similar vein, British Telecommunications plc (BT) advocated that the citizen interest should be served by establishing a universal service obligation for broadband: few would demur, but it seemed that self-interest more that the public interest dictated the plea, placed in both bold and italics, that in future 'BT and its customers are not constrained in improving its services by more regulation'.

Most unusually, months after the consultation closed, nothing had resulted, despite queries from several of those who had responded and Ofcom's website promises that for all consultations:

The team in charge of the consultation will review all the responses we have received. They will then prepare a summary for our Board or another group responsible for making the relevant decision. We usually aim to produce this summary within 2 weeks of the consultation closing. (Ofcom, n.d.-a)

Should it be concluded, then, that Ofcom had little interest in this consultation, having instead become the 'cheerleader' for 'the dominant market rhetoric of competition' (Harvey, 2006), with the citizen as the loser (Redding, 2005)? Ofcom insiders had always disavowed such a conclusion, saying in 2005 that 'I think the good thing is that on the whole I don't think there are citizen groups out there who think that the citizen has been neglected' (Richard Hooper, Content Board Chair), and that:

I think it's one of those things that the board is very alive to, the citizen-consumer, and what comes up quite often during board discussions is, 'are we really gripping the citizen end of this because we get so much of it's a consumer focus' ... I'm not conscious of us being put under pressure by citizens' groups to suddenly bring citizenship up the agenda. I think it's more a feeling that maybe we haven't quite brought it out.[24]

Finally, nearly two years after the consultation, in April 2010 Ofcom published *Citizens, Communications and Convergence: A Summary of Stakeholder Responses, and Our Next Steps* (Ofcom, 2010a). After summarising the consultation document and the responses received, Ofcom observed in April 2010 that:

We recognise the depth of concern among those who responded on this aspect of Ofcom's work and agree that we need to more clearly identify the citizen issues which are relevant to our policy appraisal. To ensure a consistent approach, policy managers will be provided with a toolkit, requiring them to identify relevant citizen issues and explain how they have been taken into account in the policy appraisal process. Where the interests of citizens and consumers are in conflict, managers will be required to justify how they have sought to achieve a balance. (Ofcom, 2010a: 8)

This is a key statement, acknowledging that Ofcom has not managed the public-facing aspects of the citizen interest well while also giving nothing away in terms of actual consequences for citizens. However, in parallel with the consumer interest toolkit developed by the Consumer Panel, Ofcom hereby proposes a citizen toolkit. Exactly what this will contain, and when/how it will be implemented, remain to be seen.

Citizen interests in a wider perspective

As we have seen, both the formulation of Ofcom's primary duties and its accountability regarding furthering the interests of citizens and consumers have been unsatisfactory processes. But it is always easier to criticise than to contribute in a creative and effective manner. What, one wonders, would academic critics and civil society groups wish to see in the proposed citizens' toolkit? Or what alternative approach to furthering the citizens' interest would they advocate, should they be seriously listened to (Schlesinger, 2009; see also Boaz et al., 2009)? And how would they even define citizen interest? Although academic and civil society actors are often vocal in relation to specific issues (public service broadcasting, children's television, advertising, broadband policy, and so forth), the general principles – the key statement of citizen interests that guides and frames these more particular contributions – tend to remain implicit.

One obvious suggestion, given Ofcom's constitution as a public consultative body – even, as we have argued, an institution in the public sphere – is that it should host a wide-ranging debate among media scholars, political scientists, journalists, civil society groups, alternative media providers, activists, human rights specialists and the wider public to scope what might be envisioned and what could be done. A wider debate would force a recognition that citizens are genuinely diverse, even agonistic in their goals (Mouffe, 1992), a point masked by the bland use of 'we' and the presumption of consensus (as in, 'As citizens, we participate in society'; Ofcom, 2008a: 6). Our analysis in this chapter indicates that Ofcom is insufficiently equipped to address such a charge, having framed citizens confusingly either as 'us' or as 'other' (i.e. 'the vulnerable') but precisely not as plural, diverse, alternative, radical or justifiably disaffected.

It may be argued, however, that a greater engagement with the diversity of contested views regarding the citizen interest would, in turn, support Ofcom's efforts to maintain a plural media system and to evaluate the diversity of content, reflecting the range of choices, opinions and tastes that is (or could be made) available. For critics, the risk of a creative and cultural mainstreaming of media representations along with the marginalisation of diverse voices, especially on mass media platforms, is of growing concern. In addressing the United Nations (UN) General Assembly on the question of content diversity, Mansell (2007) argued that 'even where it works, however, the liberal mainstream news media are severely limited. They are self-contained, self-referential, and often elitist, rarely crossing difficult boundaries.' If, as is sometimes implied, it is expected that individual citizens – as active searchers of online content, for example – will overcome such mainstreaming tendencies on the part of industry, then serious questions remain to be asked of the public's critical media literacy.

Further, a wider debate would surely push Ofcom's philosophy beyond its general focus on consumers and technologies (as in *Citizens, Communications and Convergence*) rather than citizens or their civic or political needs and rights. So instead of starting with the technology and speculating about its potential value for citizens (a technologically determinist approach that is more concerned with means than ends), the starting point could be a wider analysis of citizens' communication needs and rights before scoping the communication environment that could better serve these interests; only then should particular technologies be weighed in terms of the means of achieving this. For example, Ofcom's (2009a: 1) research report on citizen's digital participation usefully recognised that, 'people do not necessarily identify their actions as citizen participation, but when we asked them about specific activities, it became apparent that most of them are, in fact, participating as citizens'. But it presented findings that pointing to technological barriers and enablers to participation for the internet alone, leaving unexplored the contribution of television or other media to citizen engagement, and refraining from evaluating participation against the normative expectations held of a democracy; most obviously, Ofcom offers no account of regulatory issues relating to media and communications technologies that insufficiently support such participation.

How should the purpose, the eventual benefit, of furthering the citizen interest be understood? Raboy et al. (2001) offer a rethinking of the citizen interest in terms of 'social demand' (cf. Hardy, 2008, on the parallel notion of 'public demand'), so as to bring democratic and cultural 'needs' within the language of economics favoured by regulation (since demand 'is more easily measurable when it comes time to evaluate policy's effectiveness in meeting desired goals', Hardy, 2008: 106). Thus, Raboy et al. (2003: 324) call for 'the legitimation of types of cultural policy which incorporate a fuller conceptualization of the public interest and its ties to the exercise of citizenship', the emphasis on citizenship being thereby 'recentered as the main mediating category between the state and the self' (Hardy, 2008: 107). Whether this will win over the economists seems unlikely, though some have advocated such a path (Garnham, 1999). Whether either citizen or consumer will survive into the new Communications Act (first announced in 2011 to come into law in 2015) remains equally unknown. But certainly, it would seem necessary that civil society groups will, once more, need to organise if their voices are to be heard in a forum otherwise substantially populated by those apparently satisfied with the status quo.

This could – indeed should – mean taking seriously the notion of communication (or information) rights or entitlements in scoping the citizen interest, where 'communication rights are based on a vision of the free flow of information and ideas which is interactive, egalitarian and non-discriminatory and driven by human needs, rather than commercial or political interests' (Hamelink, 2003; see also Garnham, 1999). In other words, social demand is merely to be met through the tools offered by the media but, in a heavily mediated society, communication rights are vital for and endemic to cultural expression, civic engagement, democratic participation, valued identities, mutual understanding and more. Referring to all media, not just the internet, Tambini (2006: 121) asserts that 'electronic communications are becoming ever-more central to exercising citizenship rights, just as a basic level of education and welfare have been'. Only thus can citizens connect horizontally (peer to peer) and vertically (to institutions, sites of established power), on an increasingly global scale. Ensuring diverse and effective routes to public connection is vital if the democratic deficit, political disengagement and rising distrust are not to increase (Couldry et al., 2010). How far can the media play a role here, and are they being enabled or impeded by regulation? What are the successes and where the difficulties? And what kinds of alliances are required to take forward such an agenda?

These are, it must be said, ambitious questions. But then Ofcom has presented itself as an ambitious regulator, one that often refers internally and externally to its 'philosophy'. As the Senior Partner for Competition and Content says of the contrast between consumer and citizen interests: 'It's a question of … can Ofcom straddle these things? I think it can straddle these things, it's just that the philosophical route is rather different I think in competition and markets versus content and standards.'[25] Nonetheless, Ofcom's attention to the citizen interest contrasts strikingly with the efforts invested in the consumer interest. Furthering the consumer interest has always seemed a sensible goal to Ofcom, and the Consumer Panel has pushed Ofcom forward at times when market pressures threatened to undermine it. Moreover, Ofcom's actions in relation to consumers have been relatively little contested, for in the regulation of any largely or wholly private sector domain, from energy to health to financial services, and notwithstanding the populist rhetoric of the market liberals, it is accepted that regulation has a role to play in ensuring fair pricing, consumer rights and redress, and even social welfare considerations of inclusion and protection for the vulnerable – all directed towards the better regulation of the market. The difficulty is that Ofcom gives the impression of being more comfortable dealing with consumer than with citizenship issues and that in this, as we have indicated, the regulator has not been helped by the tendency of academic work to offer critical rather than constructive commentary and contribution.

Notes

1   Hardy (2008: 77) saw a parallel tension evident in the New Labour approach more generally, arguing that, in the late 1990s, 'The principal role for governance and regulation was redefined as facilitating the conditions in which markets could operate dynamically, efficiently and effectively, namely through competition. However, Labour's neoliberal embrace of the market was tempered by a critique of the inability of the market, under certain conditions, to adequately ensure public policy objectives.'

2   Originally online at www.communicationsbill.gov.uk/pdf/response_OFCOM. pdf (and accessed during 2006), regrettably these responses no longer appear to be publicly accessible.

3   Although as a shadow organisation, Ofcom began its work earlier in 2003.

4   Author interview with Don Redding, Campaign Coordinator, The Public Voice, 09/05/05. Cf. The Public Voice's response to Ofcom's consultation on its draft annual plan for 2004/05.

5   Author interview with Robin Foster, Partner, Strategy and Market Developments, Ofcom, 09/06/05.

6   Author interview with Richard Hooper, Chair of the Content Board, Ofcom, 20/06/05.

7   Author interview with Robin Foster, Partner, Strategy and Market Developments, Ofcom, 09/06/05.

8   Ofcom publishes annual reports on its website, also consulting publicly before finalising each year's annual plan.

9   Author interview with Gary Herman, academic member of the Campaign for Press and Broadcasting Freedom (CPBF), 21/07/05.

10 Author interview with Kip Meek, Senior Partner, Competition and Content, Director of Competition Policy, Competition and Content, Ofcom, 20/07/05.

11 Author interview with Alan Williams, Senior Policy Advisor, Consumers' Association (*Which?*), 04/03/05.

12 Author interview with Jocelyn Hay, Chairman, Voice of the Listener and Viewer (VLV), 19/04/05.

13 Author interview with Colette Bowe, Chairman, Ofcom Consumer Panel, 28/09/05.

14 Author interview with Stephen Whittle, Controller, BBC Editorial Policy, 08/07/05.

15 Author interview with Tony Stoller, Executive Committee, and External Relations Director, 10/08/05.

16 Author interview with Allan Williams, Senior Policy Advisor, Consumers' Association (*Which?*), 04/03/05.

17 Author interview with Claire Milne, freelance consumer spokesperson, 20/04/04. This is perhaps an overly tough judgement. In its first submission to the Culture Media and Sports Select Committee Inquiry into audio-visual communications and the regulation of broadcasting (*Beyond The Telephone, The Television and The PC – II*, January 1998, para 30), Oftel proposed three high-level goals for the communications sector: 'Deliver the Best Deal for the Consumer in terms of Quality, Choice and Value for Money', 'Secure Maximum Economic Benefit for the UK' and 'Enhance Social Cohesion and Promote Welfare'. See http://www.ofcom.org.uk/static/archive/oftel/publications/1995_98/broadcasting/betel198.htm.

18 Author interview with Robin Foster, Partner, Strategy and Market Developments, Ofcom, 09/06/05.

19 Note that the Consumer Panel was renamed the Communications Consumer Panel in 2008. The Conservative/Liberal Democrat Coalition government decided in 2010 to abolish the panel.

20 Author interview with Colette Bowe, Chairman, Ofcom Consumer Panel, 28/09/05.

21 Author interview with Helen Normoyle, Policy Executive, Director of Market Research, 27/06/05.

22 Author interview with Julie Myers, Policy Manager, Consumer Panel, Ofcom, 28/06/05.

23 Author interview with Graham Howell, Secretary, Ofcom, 09/06/05.

24 Author interview with Graham Howell, Secretary to the Corporation, Ofcom, 09/06/05.

25 Author interview with Kip Meek, Senior Partner, Competition and Content, Director of Competition Policy, Competition and Content, Ofcom, 20/07/05.

4

OFCOM AS A REGULATORY AGENCY

Ofcom's remit and rationale

No matter which type and form of national regulatory authority a country adopts, the prime regulatory objective should be the establishment of trustworthy, sustainable and legitimate structure and functions for the authority in order to serve specific policy goals, including the public interest one, efficiently. (Spyrelli, 2003: 3)

Ofcom was established as a regulatory agency to facilitate the UK government in addressing the emerging opportunities and dangers of an increasingly complex, convergent global media and communications landscape. In addition to the technological and market challenges outlined in Chapters 1 and 2, the implications of these changes for citizens and consumers were becoming ever more pressing. For example, television and radio programmes previously provided only on terrestrial analogue channels were becoming increasingly available on multiple digital and online platforms, requiring a shift in regulatory strategy to address the decoupling of content and platform and, further, the diversification of both contents and platforms. Relatedly, access to broadband was beginning to transform people's mode of accessing both familiar and new media services, challenging, for instance, the nature of public service broadcasting (itself being redefined as public service media). Audiences were increasingly exposed to both the opportunities and dangers of an ever more complex mix of media services, raising new questions of consumer protection and media literacy that required an agency with the scope and expertise to span the media sector.

To meet these challenges, Ofcom was designed – as specified in the Communications Act 2003 – with the capacity to analyse markets and consumer behaviour, to take account of stakeholder interests, including those of citizens, and to advise and regulate in a flexible style that would reflect contemporary expectations regarding public engagement and governance. The regulator was given a wide and, some would say, contradictory remit, as illustrated in the controversies over its formation discussed in Chapter 3. In this chapter, we consider Ofcom as an organisation – its philosophy, legal duties, institutional structures, key activities and relations with stakeholders. As befits a principled regulator committed to transparency and accountability, these are outlined in its Annual Plans and on its website, www.ofcom.org.uk. We outline the statutory obligations, operating principles and structures of this innovative regulatory agency. We give examples of areas of operation and note ways in which Ofcom was designed to operate as an institution in the public sphere. The chapter provides an introduction to what was intended to be a new approach to regulation to deal with convergence in a principled, transparent and accountable way, while engaging stakeholders in the regulatory process and representing the interests of citizens and consumers.

As we noted in Chapter 2, Ofcom was not the first of this new style of regulatory regime introduced by the New Labour government. It was preceded by the Financial Service Authority (FSA), which was also a converged regulator, formed by amalgamating several previously separate regulatory bodies. Similarly, too, the FSA combined expertise in market risk analysis with a statutory consumer panel and a remit to enhance consumer literacy (although this was termed consumer education by the FSA). Ofcom therefore takes forward a larger political project centred on powerful regulatory agencies working at arm's length from government, following principles of better regulation and combining a wide range of key aims, including consumer protection, securing citizen interests, promoting competition and innovation in the market, and maintaining infrastructure while seeking to minimise a direct regulatory intervention.

Ofcom is a statutory regulatory agency established by an Act of Parliament with a series of requirements, including its principal duty as set out in the Communications Act 2003:

> 3(1) (a) to further the interests of citizens in relation to communications matters; and (b) to further the interests of consumers in relevant markets, where appropriate by promoting competition.

Section 3(2) of the Act requires Ofcom to ensure that the wireless spectrum is used optimally, that a wide range of such services is available throughout the UK, that a range of broadcast services is available throughout the UK delivered by plural providers, that the public is protected from offensive and harmful broadcasting content and from unfair treatment by programmers or unwarranted invasions of privacy. Ofcom classifies its legal duties under the Act within three broad areas: telecommunications, broadcasting, and consumer protection. In relation to telecommunications, Ofcom has sought to ensure that the radio spectrum is used optimally and to enhance the communications infrastructure with a particular emphasis on the development of high-speed broadband. In relation to broadcasting, Ofcom's focus has been on monitoring media ownership with the aim of ensuring a plurality of providers and a diversity of broadcast programme content. In relation to consumer protection, Ofcom's actions have aimed at protecting audiences from material that might cause harm and offence and at ensuring that people are treated fairly when represented in programmes and that their privacy is protected. As outlined in Ofcom's Draft Annual Plan 2010–11, these areas of regulation are pursued through five main objectives: supporting and protecting consumers; securing citizen interests as guided by Parliament; promoting competition and innovation in media and communications; maintaining and strengthening the communications infrastructure and reducing the regulatory burden.

In this way, work that had previously been divided among five legacy regulators (Independent Television Commission, Broadcasting Standards Commission, Radio Authority, Radio Communications Agency and Oftel – The Office of Telecommunications) was integrated within the remit of a single converged regulator, encompassing both telecommunications and broadcasting in order to face the current and coming challenges of a converging media and communications sector. Then still conceived in terms of 'the information society', later reframed in terms of 'the digital economy', this converged sector required regulation, as broadly agreed on all sides, to deal with issues that were of concern to both consumers (as individuals and as a market) and citizens (again, as individuals and collectively as a democracy). However, important areas of regulation were not included in Ofcom's remit, limiting the neat management of this complex and burgeoning sector by bringing everything under the umbrella of a single regulator. A range of other regulators continued, including ICSTIS (now PhonepayPlus, the regulator for premium rate phone-paid services in the UK), the Advertising Standards Authority and the BBC Governors (later the BBC Trust). As we will see in our case studies, it was crucial that Ofcom established working relationships with these bodies, including developing memoranda of understanding (e.g. with the BBC) and co-regulatory arrangements (with ICSTIS and the Advertising Standards Authority). Yet other areas remained wholly outside of Ofcom's purview – the press, subject to self-regulation by the Press Complaints Commission and, more problematically, given the convergence of digital platforms, the internet.[1]

Thus the rationale of a sector-wide media and communications regulator, which integrated the market and provided a unitary and principled approach across convergent media, was only partially realised by the formation of Ofcom. Notwithstanding fears that a converged regulator, sometimes dubbed a 'super-regulator', would become too powerful,[2] this rationale centred on the prospect that firms would become subject to consistent and principled regulation. Although with the exception of the Radio Authority, the legacy regulators were statutory bodies, they had been established on different terms and had developed different regulatory approaches, so that an increasingly convergent market was witnessing the imposition on firms of different regulatory regimes even for the same media content and services. In short, the prospect that Ofcom would provide a unitary approach was important, as was the idea that this would rest on clearly articulated principles and sound evidence-based practice.

From guiding principles to working practices

Ofcom interpreted the principles according to which it would operate broadly as follows. It would strive to deliver public policy objectives only when the market did not deliver these adequately. When it judged this to be the case, it would then seek to find appropriate strategies, such as supervision, incentives or other forms of regulatory control. If it did intervene, it would aim to do so in a timely and effective way, always aiming to use the least intrusive regulatory strategy or instrument at its disposal (Ofcom, n.d.–b). In all of this, it would follow good practice in regulation defined as acting on the basis of evidence, in a proportionate and consistent manner, and making both its deliberations and the impacts of its interventions transparent and accountable to a wide range of stakeholders. To enhance transparency and accountability, Ofcom would, in accordance with the Communications Act 2003, consult frequently and widely, and complement this by publishing an annual report and an annual plan which would lay out its policy objectives and priorities for the coming year. In addition, it adopted a philosophy of enhancing the broader evidence base in media and communications and its own capacity as a regulatory agency by conducting research into markets, technologies and audiences.

These commitments had some notable consequences: Ofcom gave priority to market solutions where possible; it used the lightest touch regulation that would be effective; it acted as a principled, evidence-based regulator; it sought to be transparent in its policies and practices, and to be accountable to Parliament, government, firms and the public. It worked in partnership with commerce but also provided an opportunity for civil society bodies and the public to express their views on policy matters. Representation of the consumer interest in particular was supported by the work of the complaints team and the Consumer Panel and by consumer research. In short, Ofcom advanced a new regime of regulation through its design (as an integrated statutory regulatory agency), through its practice (acting in a consistent and principled way), through its relations with stakeholders, and through the very breadth of its scope. From the beginning, Ofcom (n.d.-c) regarded itself as offering a new approach by bringing together the best of corporate and administrative thinking:

There have been mergers and de-mergers of communications regulators before, and there have been a number of converged regulators created over recent years. However, Ofcom represents a departure from much of the UK public sector norm; a merged regulator in the form of a statutory corporation, independent of Government, covering the whole sector of electronic communications, and organised around a model which owes at least as much to private sector as to public sector precedents.

This significant claim positions Ofcom as a body between government and commerce; on the one hand, an extension of government, a quasi-governmental regulatory agency; on the other hand, a body that works with and on behalf of a spectrum of stakeholders from industry, civil society and the public. This commitment is reflected in Ofcom's structure, which borrows features from corporate management – notably, in being governed by a board and executive committee chaired by the Ofcom chair and Chief Executive Officer (CEO) respectively and in publishing an annual plan and annual reports. However, while the overall framework borrows from corporate governance, some of the boards within Ofcom reflect the bureaucratic structure of public administration. For example, the Policy Executive operates as a forum for the discussion of Ofcom's regulatory agenda (developing Ofcom's 'philosophy'), the Content Board focuses on quality and standards issues in the style of a more traditional media regulator, and the Operations Board deals with consumers, fielding complaints, giving advice, and managing the department that grants licences.[3]

Central to advancing Ofcom's aims is the effort to take account of the recommendations of the Better Regulation Task Force, which the New Labour government established when it came to power in 1997, 'to advise the Government on action to ensure that regulation and its enforcement are proportionate, accountable, consistent, transparent and targeted'.[4] The Task Force, replaced by the Better Regulation Commission in 2006 while retaining the same basic principles, focused on 'efficiency' – the incremental reduction of the regulatory burden – on the grounds that regulation reduces competition and tends to have more detrimental effects than market failures. Harvey (forthcoming) consequently describes Ofcom as a reluctant regulator since it aims to intervene using command-and-control strategies only as a last resort, and to lower its costs and activities incrementally to reduce the overall burden of regulation. For example, in its Annual Plan 2010–11, Ofcom reports having cut its operating budget by 3.9 per cent in real terms in the previous year.

However, as we have indicated, Ofcom is an active regulatory agency both in the exercise of its duties, in conducting research and consultation and, as a body subject to a complex range of duties, in using its discretion to determine appropriate and varied regulatory strategies. What Ofcom seeks is a balance that favours deregulation or self-regulation, where possible combined with the use of indicators of the effectiveness of regulation to help decide when greater intervention would be desirable. Thus it adopts a process of impact assessment of its own regulatory activities not only after, but also in advance of policy formation, as part of the decision-making process. In this way, Ofcom seeks to anticipate the potential impact of regulation, including any unintended consequences. In addition, it aims to regulate in a manner proportionate to the potential detriment that might result to consumers from the activities of media institutions. But how does this play out in practice? Such a question is best addressed through a consideration of particular areas of policy. In this book, we ask whether and how Ofcom may have furthered the interests of citizens and consumers in relation to public service media (Chapter 5), media literacy (Chapter 6), regulating food advertising to children (Chapter 7) and community radio (Chapter 8). To be sure, these case studies are only representative of part of Ofcom's core business in pursuit of its overall objectives of supporting and protecting consumers, securing the citizen interest, promoting competition and innovation, maintaining and strengthening the communications infrastructure and reducing regulation. However, our chosen cases clearly illustrate the public-facing nature of Ofcom's work – incorporating consultation, deliberation, evidence and public debate – and they also show how this work shaped the process and consequences of particular policy areas, specifically those focused on citizen interests, the 'softer' and arguably more easily neglected areas of its work. In recognition of important areas of regulation not otherwise covered in this book, we examine below Ofcom's activities in relation to telecommunications, spectrum management and media plurality, all of which are areas of its core business which aim to further the interests of citizens and consumers and also all areas of work that have rightly absorbed much of Ofcom's energies.

Core business: telecommunications, spectrum management and media plurality

Ofcom's Annual Plans and Annual Reports give a clear overview of its core business and strategic priorities. From early on, Ofcom organised its core activities into a number of strands: Strategy and Market Developments; Competition and Markets; Content and Standards, External Relations and Support Services. This work was generally headed by a senior partner who supported these activities and each area of work encompassed a range of activities. In Strategy and Market Developments, Ofcom conducted research and analysis to understand markets in media and communications. For example, in 2004, the Strategy and Market Developments group had several key responsibilities: working on Ofcom's strategic planning, including leading strategic reviews in telecommunications, spectrum issues and broadcasting; coordinating market, audience and consumer research; developing Ofcom's technology strategy; conducting specialist economic analysis as required; advising the Secretary of State on public interest issues in mergers and acquisitions; and reporting publicly on key features of the media and communications markets. The group was also responsible for driving forward government commitment to the digital switchover by creating certainty over the timing for this, using spectrum pricing to provide incentives for the switchover, raising public awareness for it through a national advertising campaign, coordinating the switchover effectively, and providing financial support to consumers to enable it (Ofcom, 2004a).

In its early years (2003–04), the Strategy and Market Developments division conducted several extensive strategic reviews of telecommunications, spectrum issues and public service broadcasting (which we examine in detail in Chapter 5). The strategic review of telecommunications set out to answer key questions regarding this essential infrastructure of the network society, focusing on the characteristics of the telecommunications market in so far as these do (or could) provide for the interests of citizens and consumers. The aim was to recommend which areas of telecommunications would be best served by competition, to identify the incentives for investing in next generation telecommunication networks that would be critical to the delivery of broadband and convergent media, and to determine the optimum level of (de)regulation in the telecommunications market (Ofcom, 2004a). Ofcom was also concerned to examine whether the private monopoly of British Telecommunications plc (BT) should be broken into operationally separate companies and how this would affect the development of broadband and local loop unbundling so as to enable access to the market for a greater range of service providers. Finally, Ofcom's review looked at how mobile phone networks do and should protect consumer interests, including reviewing contracts to protect consumers from mis-selling. This strategic review and the regulatory interventions that resulted demonstrate the depth and range of Ofcom's expertise in relation to the telecommunications infrastructure and services, building on the work of the legacy regulator, Oftel (Ofcom, 2004a).

A separate group at Ofcom has been responsible for Competition and Markets, aiming to give greater choice and stimulate innovation in the media and communications market. This division attempts to enable increased choice and innovation by promoting greater competition across the sector, by using its resources to investigate complaints and disputes concerning competition. In addition, it was responsible for issuing broadcasting licences and planning the use of wireless frequencies, and for conducting regulatory impact assessments. The management of the radio spectrum, also the responsibility of the Competition and Markets group, is a key plank of Ofcom's activities, a task which illustrates the question of whether a crucial and scarce resource should be positioned as a valuable public good or opened up as a profitable market. It also illustrates the highly technical nature of some of Ofcom's core business, in key ways justifying the establishment of an independent regulator that concentrates expertise while in other ways revealing the difficulty of acting in an inclusive and consultative way over such a complex an issue. Currently, the radio spectrum is used for a vast range of different communications[5] and about 70 per cent of the available spectrum is marketised (Ofcom, n.d.-d). But Cave's (2005) audit of UK spectrum holdings conducted for the Treasury suggests that while technical changes allow for the release of a more usable spectrum, this is unlikely to meet the growing need for spectrum in the medium term.[6]

In addition to the task of supporting the market and investor confidence, in developed countries spectrum use is regulated for three reasons. First, regulation ensures the efficient use of services and stops interference or jamming from competing users of the same spectrum. Second, since some users of the spectrum are commercial operations and the use of the spectrum is a valuable resource, the government can charge for its use through licence agreements. Third, regulation allows the government to reserve parts of the spectrum for important public services, including broadcasting and communications for essential services and the military. The availability of the spectrum forms part of our case studies on public service broadcasting (see Chapter 5) and the licensing of community radio (see Chapter 8).[7] The regulation of the spectrum is, in short, a fundamental aspect of media and communications regulation with significant implications for other areas of media and communications policy.

Ofcom has developed a spectrum strategy to guide its work, conducting auctions for spectrum and seeking flexible regulation as regard access to and use of the radio spectrum. Recognising that a mix of regulatory approaches is required to realise the potential of the spectrum, in some areas Ofcom has retained control over spectrum allocation, determining either use or the technologies to be deployed. In other areas a market for spectrum was established through licensing, allowing firms to decide on whether or not to bid for the spectrum and its efficient or desirable use. In addition, some services, particularly those using low power radio transmissions, were judged to be best left unregulated so as to enable the development of uses and services, most notably wireless computer networks (Ofcom, n.d.-d).

Ofcom conducts periodic reviews of spectrum use to identify where congestion and available space exist. This highly technical task has, for instance, led to the realisation that no additional spectrum was required for low

OFCOM AS A REGULATORY AGENCY

power applications such as Wi-Fi and that the availability of unlicensed spectrum for low power use need not inhibit bids for licensed spectrum for innovative or specialised services such as multiple use mobile phone services. In general Ofcom has been against using spectrum allocation as a policy tool in order to protect the £40 billion per year that licensing generates for the UK economy, arguing that granting free spectrum to public projects or services risks reducing the value of the market for spectrum as a whole. However, on the enforcement side, Ofcom is sanguine about the possibility of commercial players hoarding spectrum and speculative trading in the spectrum as these are, within reason, normal features of markets. Thus Ofcom commits itself to only act when there is evidence that such behaviour is anti-competitive, this leading to an approach in which regulation is 'lighter' in the commercial and the unregulated sector than in the public sector, where allocation and use is more controlled by the regulator. This pattern is repeated in the case of community radio, which we examine later in Chapter 8.

This case illustrates Ofcom's general commitment to transparent, principled regulation, since its principles for spectrum allocation are available on its website. However, its juxtaposition of an assumed idealised perfect market with specific problematic examples of regulatory intervention clearly indicates Ofcom's preference for market solutions. If a market is working well, then the justification for regulators to step back and establish general rules and guidelines for self-regulation and licensing will surely be judged a reasonable one. However, Ofcom's rhetoric misses out two important exceptions: when markets are less than perfect and cases where making the spectrum available for social purposes is justified. The focus of Ofcom's recent work on spectrum is laid out in the 2010 Annual Report (Ofcom, 2010d); here the key issue identified is that of the strategic release of spectrum gained through the digital switchover (the digital dividend). Government will make the final decision, but Ofcom anticipates being asked to implement a liberal regime to release spectrum to the market to complement the review of spectrum by the public bodies discussed above.

A further plank within Ofcom's activities has been to ensure a plurality of owners for media and communications enterprises so that an open and competitive market flourishes, while also furthering public interest through content that satisfies diverse needs and tastes. As media ownership is increasingly privatised, many are concerned about the concentration of power that owners potentially wield over a sector that is so vital to the social and cultural life of liberal democracies. As Barnett (2010: 1) caustically observes, 'concentration of media ownership within too few hands contradicts the basic tenets of democracy, threatening diversity of expression and risking autocratic control of communicative spaces ... [yet] recent policy initiatives have moved inexorably in the opposite direction, towards relaxation of restrictions and hence greater consolidation'. However it is Parliament and not the regulator that establishes the rules for media ownership, and as Ofcom (n.d.-e) notes:

> Parliament has put in place media ownership rules for television, radio and newspapers. In the interests of democracy, their aim is to help protect plurality of viewpoints and give citizens access to a variety of sources of news, information and opinion.

Ofcom's duty in relation to media ownership is to put its considerable resources and expertise at the service of the government in reviewing the operation of media ownership rules and analysing the impact of mergers or acquisitions as regards both market and the public interest. The Secretary of State for Culture, Media and Sport may ask Ofcom to report on the operation of media ownership rules at any time, and the Secretary of State for Business, Innovation and Skills may ask it to investigate mergers or acquisitions that might adversely affect the public interest. Additionally, Ofcom can be called on by the Secretary of State (DCMS) to conduct public interest tests regarding any proposal for cross-media ownership or mergers between existing newspapers or broadcasters (Puttnam, 2006: 126), this complementing the market testing that the Competition Commission can call for.[8]

For the most part, Ofcom has supported the maintenance of existing restrictions on media ownership in the interests of sustaining a plurality of media sources and content.[9] However, when it was tasked by the *Digital Britain* report (BIS and DCMS, 2009) to examine how the operation of media ownership rules affected the sustainability of local media, it supported the relaxation of ownership rules in order to make it possible for a single company to control a newspaper and also hold licences for television and radio stations in the same local area, although it also pointed out that enabling the financial viability of such a company might place too much control under the same ownership, thereby risking plurality (Ofcom, n.d.-e). As Ofcom argued, the Coalition government's plans for an extension of both BBC and commercial local stations potentially compensated for this concentration of ownership by delivering alternative sources of local media. At the time of writing, the prospects for local media remain uncertain, notwithstanding strong advocacy on the part of the Secretary of State.

Equally uncertain at present is the wider situation regarding media ownership. In late 2010/early 2011, there was a lively public debate surrounding Vince Cable's request, as Secretary of State for Business, Innovation and Skills, that Ofcom investigate the proposed acquisition of BSkyB by News Corporation, a debate that became yet more lively when Cable was caught out by expressing his hostility to the Murdoch proposal. The responsibility was then passed to Jeremy Hunt, Secretary of State for Culture, Olympics,

Media and Sport. Unexpectedly, Hunt sidestepped Ofcom's considered advice to refer the proposed takeover to the Competition Commission, instead seeking undertakings from Rupert Murdoch that the public interest would not be damaged should the deal go through. This process, in turn, became mired in claims that News Corporation was not a 'fit and proper' owner of a broadcasting licence, as required by the 1990 Broadcasting Act (and as judged by Ofcom), following the phone hacking scandal of News International's newspapers in 2011.

The Secretary of State did, however, follow the approach adopted by Ofcom (2010e) in its audience research on media plurality in the core assumption, arguably contestable but in practice little contested, that media plurality matters for news alone. Since, as Ofcom's research showed, the proposed takeover would indeed reduce the plurality for news, Hunt's resolution was to permit the takeover (with no referral to the Competition Commission) provided Sky News was omitted from the deal (becoming, thereby, an independent operation divorced from News Corporation). Ofcom's research assumptions played a key role in shaping the policy decision – it assumed, notably, that a threat to media plurality could be adequately assessed by a projected reduction in the number of news sources accessed by the population, that media plurality itself only mattered for news (and, by implication, not indigenous production, documentary and current affairs sources, or other types of significant cultural production), and that media plurality could be assessed in terms of media ownership rather than content diversity (something that would be more complex to measure even if, for many, content diversity was equally important). Whether the outcome, should it come about, namely a considerable concentration of ownership in News Corporation – plus a new independent player (of uncertain financial and institutional viability) in the form of Sky News – ultimately damages either the news environment or the wider public interest remains to be seen.

Freedman (2008) compares the US system in which government tends to stay at arm's length, leaving the Federal Communications Commission to regulate except when there is widespread public concern, with the UK context in which the New Labour government and, at least in the above case, the new Coalition government became closely involved in media ownership policy. Freedman interprets New Labour's hands-on approach within its political strategy in gaining support from Rupert Murdoch's News Corporation during the 1997 General Election campaign. On the one hand, since the tabloid press had vilified previous Labour election campaigns, this could be seen as an attempt to ensure that New Labour could explain its policies to the electorate. Freedman (2008), however, gives a more conspiratorial critique, suggesting that New Labour's deregulatory approach to media ownership was a *quid pro quo* for political support from multinational media players. Illustrative of New Labour's 'third way', Collins and Murroni

(1996) working with the think tank IPPR (Institute for Public Policy Research) instead argue that media ownership rules should focus on guarding against the concentration of power rather than seeking to prevent cross-media ownership (e.g. owning a newspaper and a television channel) *per se*, especially as convergence becomes the rule rather than the exception. In this undoubtedly political debate over the nature and direction of regulation, Ofcom has generally supported existing media ownership rules, including those that serve the public interest. Nonetheless, the risk is a serious one in that, as Freedman (2008) warns, market considerations may undermine social and cultural priorities.

In addition to Ofcom's work in furthering the interests of consumers through a strategic review and the work of the groups on Strategy and Market Developments and Competition and Markets, the Communications Act 2003 established a statutory body to represent specifically the interests of consumers to Ofcom. The Consumer Panel, renamed the Communications Consumer Panel in 2008, was established by the Act as independent of Ofcom, with an appropriate budget, the power to set its own agenda, and the requirement to make its views public. Generally dubbed Ofcom's 'critical friend' – at arm's length from, but resourced and administered from within Ofcom – the Panel may be seen to embed the concerns of a statutory civil society body within the regulator.[10] Its broad purpose is to gain an understanding of consumer interests through consultation, apply the expertise of Panel members, including through research, and generally make sure that this collected wisdom was sufficiently taken into account in Ofcom's decision making, thereby furthering the consumer interest. In addition, the Panel was able to advise other bodies, including the government and European institutions, as it saw fit on matters related to consumers of media and communications, and to make the results of its research and deliberations public. The thinking behind the Communications Consumer Panel, modelled on the Financial Services Consumer Panel, was stated in the Communications Bill thus:

> The Consumer Panel should be the conscience, not the creature, of OFCOM. It will have a vital role in providing OFCOM, and other relevant bodies, with advice on the interests of consumers ... it will be expected to provide a counterweight to advice and lobbying from the corporate sector. (House of Commons, 2002: 19)

The areas of consumer interest covered by the Panel were specified in section 16(3) of the Communications Act.[11] Consumer interests were clearly delineated from those of citizen interests in both the Communications Act and the resulting structure of Ofcom (with these interests mapped on to the Consumer Panel and Content Board respectively), although not without some contestation, as discussed in Chapter 3. Indeed, the Act specified explicitly that the Consumer Panel should not advise on 'any matter that concerns the contents of anything which is or may be broadcast or otherwise transmitted by means of electronic communications networks' (section 16(5)). In addition, individual consumer complaints were not to be addressed by the Communications Consumer Panel but by Ofcom itself. In *Putting the Consumer First*, the Communications Consumer Panel (2010) noted its successes in advising Ofcom and gaining tangible benefits for consumers regarding mobile coverage, complaint-handling, easing the process of switching supplier, stimulating digital participation, and ensuring equality in the provision of universal broadband.

However, one of the significant changes instituted by the incoming Coalition government was to axe the Communications Consumer Panel (along with other consumer protection organisations such as Consumer Focus and the Office of Fair Trading), handing the task of representing consumers to Citizens' Advice as part of a general programme of reducing the number, size and scope of non-government agencies, including regulators (as announced on 14/10/10).[12] Although, at the time of writing, the Panel continues to exist (being mandated by an Act that is not yet superseded), this threatens to remove an important source for the independent scrutiny of Ofcom's work, weakening the direct role of consumer representation in regulatory policy and practice. As the Communications Consumer Panel itself commented, perhaps hinting at some scepticism regarding the capacity of Citizens' Advice to be as effective:

We want to see that the interests of consumers in the communications sector continue to be protected and promoted effectively. To this end we will seek to ensure that the benefits of the Panel model are enshrined in the new system, including the ability to advise on Ofcom proposals early in the decision-making process before they are made public and to use its communications sector expertise to counterbalance industry lobbying.[13]

Ofcom's response was that, having learned from the work of the Communications Consumer Panel, it had learned as an institution to embed the interests of consumers more thoroughly within its activities.[14] In Ofcom's 2010 Annual Report, the Chairman reflected on its continuing commitment to 'be a powerful agent for consumer and citizen interests' (Ofcom, 2010d: 6). Many of the activities outlined above – to make strategic interventions in market developments and to enable the development of competitive markets – are aimed at benefiting consumers, acting on their behalf to deliver a market that they can have confidence in which in turn will benefit the market as the choices of increasingly knowledgeable consumers have an effect on the price and quality of service. Ofcom responds to consumer complaints, monitors markets in media and communications, and adopts a strategic view of market and technological developments to this end. As the 2010 Annual Report states, there are positive developments in the continuing process of digital switchover, in Ofcom's interventions in problematic markets such as mobile phone contracts, and in the increasing availability of digital television with ever more choice for the consumer. And as elsewhere, Ofcom's role here includes advising the public, making information about services publicly available (e.g. independent evaluation of the speed of Broadband Services), and dealing with consumer complaints. However, while in a general sense these activities benefit people as consumers, our principal interest in this book includes the ways in which Ofcom addresses citizen issues more directly, it being significantly an institution in the public sphere.

Ofcom as an institution in the public sphere

How does Ofcom proceed with its work in the various domains that fall within its remit? In Chapter 1, we introduced the notion of Ofcom as an institution in the public sphere, in which it would play an important role in public debate and deliberation, enhancing the capacity of a broad range of stakeholders to contribute to regulation and make its judgements and research publicly visible and accountable. We drew on ideas from public sphere theory to propose criteria to judge Ofcom's work as an institution in the public sphere. Notably, would it generate a public sphere of discussion and debate around its work, providing multiple points of engagement for a range of stakeholders, including civil society bodies and the public, and not just disseminate its work but also publicly reflect on the purposes and impact of regulation? As Spyrelli (2003: 35) observes:

> Public hearings, public notices, consultative documents followed by consulta-
> tion periods, meetings with industry and consumer groups, sharing of informa-
> tion among other authorities are the basic tools for informing the public of
> matters that have to be taken care of and at the same time fulfil the requirement
> of transparency, and empower the integrity and ultimately the legitimacy of the
> regulator.

Ofcom is required by the Communications Act 2003 to consult widely as a means of engaging its many stakeholders in the development of media and communications regulation. As observed in Chapter 2, this reflects the New Labour government's focus on public engagement, deliberation and accountability in the 'stakeholder society'. Ofcom's guidelines for its consultation process emphasise that the aim is to enable the widest possible range of stakeholder voices (companies, industry representatives, consumer groups, civil society bodies and individuals; Ofcom, 2007a) to respond to the options under consideration and have a say in how the regulatory process may affect them before any decisions are made.[15] The guidelines also require any consultation to be conducted in an open and transparent manner but with efficiency in terms of cost and time (Ofcom usually sets a deadline for responses of one month from the date of publication of the consultation document).

Of course formal consultation has its limitations, as Ofcom is well aware. Not all stakeholders are equal in the expertise and resources required to frame their responses to what can be very long and technical consultation documents. In particular, individuals and community groups may be less able to provide detailed or professional responses compared with well-resourced firms with a strong interest in the issue at hand. Ofcom claims to overcome such structural asymmetries by issuing press releases to announce its consultations, holding public meetings and briefings, and developing a dialogue with particular stakeholders. This includes a dialogue with a range of civil society groups claiming to represent the citizen and/or consumer interest – such as Consumer Focus, Which?, The Voice of the Listener and Viewer, the Community Media Association, the Telephone Helplines Association, the Royal National Institute of Blind People, Age Concern, Help the Aged, the National Consumer Federation, TAG (the Telecommunications Action Group), the Trading Standards Institute and Citizens Advice. While many of these regularly respond to Ofcom consultations – which is a considerable effort given the scarcity of time and money that is available to many of these and similar organisations – Ofcom also organises its address to them through the Consumer Forum for Communications, in which civil society organisations periodically meet Ofcom representatives.[16] Whether such consultation processes redirects policy, however, remains a moot point.

Particularly interesting in this regard is Ofcom's very substantial investment in original research. Ofcom has a rolling programme of research into the media and communications market, public service broadcasting, the experience of consumers and many more issues. Its annual Communications Market reports are widely valued and its many specialist reports have provided a substantial part of the evidence base across a number of fields – the case of media literacy, examined in Chapter 6, is one such field in which the evidence base has been transformed by Ofcom's research contribution. In addition to research reports, Ofcom also regularly publishes research data on specific topics such as digital television, the telecommunications sector (quarterly) and broadband speed. As might by now be expected, it is also noteworthy that much of this research is publicly reported, with the data often being made available for further analysis and public scrutiny.

However, in addition to its commitment to evidence-based policy making, Ofcom also regards the conduct of public opinion research, both qualitative and quantitative, as a valuable means of reaching the wider public (as required by the Communications Act 2003). In other words, research is also framed as part of Ofcom's role as an institution in the public sphere, a means especially for including those who, for whatever reason, do not find themselves sufficiently represented among those parties who put themselves forward in consultation processes. Thus research significantly complements the consultation process, enabling Ofcom to understand how, for example, policy decisions may impact on disadvantaged or marginalised groups. This sustained effort by Ofcom reflects its commitment, therefore, to evidence-based policy and to the inclusion of diverse stakeholder experiences, as well as providing a means by which the regulator sustains its independent analysis in key areas of policy. This last aspect is, however, a double-edged sword, for the difficulty faced by those who might wish to contest Ofcom's research or its interpretation, or to counterpose their own research, and who find their own resources challenged in the effort to keep up with and gain attention for alternative evidence (Freedman, 2008). As a Senior Policy Advisor at the Consumers' Association (Which?) put it, 'it's a capacity issue, you know, that there are lots of issues that we can deal with as a consumer organization and we try and prioritise'.[17] The Chair of The Voice of the Listener and Viewer was more blunt: 'We don't have the resources to do the research that is necessary in order to make it objective.'[18] A member of the Campaign for Press and Broadcasting Freedom[19] added that a debate held in terms of research evidence was one that had already narrowed the range of possible contributions:

> an underlying concern is that the sort of survey and research data which seeks to identify consumer attitudes is not the same as a mechanism to empower discussions around citizenship which would involve identifying and making political decisions about regulation and regulatory governance.[20]

One may wonder how much research or public consultation would be enough? The campaign coordinator of Public Voice told us that:

> We suggested that they [should] have a research project to identify, define and build consensus around what were citizens' issues in communications across the whole view of the sectors [... but] they came back and said, 'we don't want to, we've got so many people we have to consult with already, we've got so much apparatus in terms of the Content Board, the panels on disabled and elderly people, the nations and regions representation etc. and the Consumer Panel that we feel we're well enough in touch.[21]

The Director of Media Watch UK read this as complacency on the regulator's part, arguing instead for the importance of '... views that are expressed to Ofcom, not just in focus groups, not just in consultations, but from the general public, which they should canvas ... But they don't do that, because it creates too much work for them.'[22] A picture emerges from these critics of a debate that is subtly framed by the regulator to further its own interests, despite its explicit claims to openness.

The regulator offers two responses. First, that it conducts far more consultation than ever before, its doors being generally open. Unfortunately, it suggests, the public does not always respond: the policy manager of the Consumer panel explains: 'It's very hard to get consumer people to come to an event'.[23] Second, and more contentiously, the regulator is itself critical of those voices striving to be heard. She continues, the regulator always has to be asking itself, 'Alright, so we've got some consumer groups at an event, but how far do they actually represent the interests of the generality of consumers, and how much do they actually just represent, you know, particular groups of consumers?' Ofcom's Director of External Relations is yet more sceptical, asking rhetorically, 'Do we get better advice from self-appointed, um, probably issue-driven, non-representative groups?'[24] In short, Ofcom's stress on market research is, in part, due to its statistical claims to the representativeness of the entire population, not just its more vocal or partisan elements.

The question of representativeness is clearly fraught. For an institution in the public sphere, the key questions are which voices should be included and how should they be weighed? For a civil society body in the public sphere, the questions are equally critical: how can it participate on equal terms with other competing voices; how can it sustain the capacity to develop an influential and sufficiently expert or technical critique without relying on the provision of resources (finance, connections, expertise) that may compromise its perceived, and actual, independence? For Habermas (1996), the key role of the civil society bodies lies less in awareness-raising, nor in the provision of public information to consumers, nor even in the conduct of independent research, but rather in the galvanising of public opinion so as to bring consumers' views to the attention of policy makers, firms and regulators. Undoubtedly, Ofcom quickly became a significant focus for consumer representation and deliberation among stakeholders. Yet paradoxically, the more open the regulator, the greater the problems of capacity for consumer representatives: many civil society workers are unpaid, or working with very limited budgets, and the regulator holds so many meetings and consultations that it easily exhausts the capacity of civil society organisations, particularly by comparison with the far larger resources of the industry to represent the market perspective in the same fora. Hence the civil society bodies are stretched, face tough decisions about their priorities, and worry about their funding base, while the regulator is frustrated by the difficulty in obtaining sufficient representation from a diversity of stakeholders, and disappointed that so few participate.

The content board and (communications) consumer panel

Although the Communications Act 2003 sought to map regulatory purposes (the interests of citizens, the interests of consumers) on to institutional structures – specifically the Content Board and Consumer Panel respectively, however, what was also foreshadowed in the previous chapter is the way in which the regulatory design may unravel as the regulatory practice unfolds. The Content Board, a committee of Ofcom's Board, was given the primary responsibility for setting and enforcing broadcasting policy standards. In addition, it was to provide advice to Ofcom's Board on issues related to broadcasting when requested. It was also tasked, in more general terms, with developing an understanding of and championing the voices and interests of audiences in their guise as listeners, viewers and citizens. The deliberate focus on citizen issues was reinforced by a remit to tackle public interests that were not handled by competition and market forces. Content Board members included officers from Ofcom, lay representatives from the four nations (England, Scotland, Wales and Northern Ireland), and other members who represented the public or had been invited on account of their experience in broadcasting. The deputy chair of the Ofcom Board chairs the Content Board and it reports annually as part of Ofcom's annual report.

In pursuing citizen interest in broadcasting, the Content Board works in three broad areas, which it defines as 'tiers': tier one is concerned with protecting audiences from harm and offence; tier two with accuracy and impartiality; and tier three with making sure that citizens are treated fairly by the media and that their privacy is protected. All broadcasters are to be monitored under these three tiers by the Content Board, with the exception that the BBC Governors (later the BBC Trust) deals with complaints about accuracy and impartiality on its services. The Content Board also has specific responsibilities for setting quotas for independent television, regional and original UK production and for regulating the commercial public service broadcasters (ITV, Channel 4, Channel 5). These quotas are intended to sustain independent production, regional programming and original UK/EU production, representing an important means for ensuring a plurality of producers and diversity of content. All of these issues are vital to Ofcom's strategic work on reviewing public service television, examined in Chapter 5. In addition, the Content Board was tasked with taking forward Ofcom's strategy in media literacy, which we examine in detail in Chapter 6, and aspects of radio regulation, as examined in Chapter 8.

In addition to these areas of strategic review and regulation, the Content Board is responsible for drafting Ofcom's Broadcasting Code in accordance with the Communications Act 2003, the Broadcasting Act 1996, the European Commission's *Audiovisual Media Service Directive* 2010, and the European Convention on Human Rights (particularly Article 10 which deals with the right to freedom of expression). Clearly, the legislative background to the Broadcasting Code is complex and the code therefore needs periodic updating as legislation is introduced. Ofcom implemented the most recent changes to the Code in 2010. The Code generally applies to all broadcasters who are licensed by Ofcom, with the BBC retaining control over some areas as a self-regulatory body. When applied to 'general services' delivered by broadcasting it is able to go beyond broadcast content and include interactive features of broadcasting such as telephone phone-ins. In the case of breaches of the code, Ofcom's first recourse is to publish the findings of its investigation, and for more serious breaches of the code Ofcom has been empowered to impose statutory sanctions, including fines. Here we can see the advantage of a convergent regulator as it can unify the code for broadcast content that was previously conducted separately for public service and commercial, independent television and for radio.

The Content Board also manages co-regulatory arrangements between Ofcom and the Advertising Standards Authority (ASA) and ICSTIS (the industry body that regulates premium rate telephone services in the UK) – we examine the co-regulation in advertising as part of our case study on the regulation of junk food advertising to children in Chapter 7. Finally, the Content Board is responsible for dealing with complaints made to Ofcom about broadcasting, these being first fielded by the Ofcom Contact Centre, which, if need be, will pass on particular issues to the Content and Standards Group working under the direction of the Content Board.

Defining citizen and consumer interests in practice

How clearly did the institutional design of Ofcom resolve the relation and balance between citizen and consumer interests? In any given year, the (Communications) Consumer Panel establishes its policy priorities, and in 2010 these included matters of digital participation and inclusion, mobile phone coverage, consumer protection and empowerment, consumer engagement with the internet, and evaluations of universal service provision. This is a wide range of topics relevant to the consumer interest and not, furthermore, always clearly distinguishable from citizen issues. In a series of interviews that we conducted in 2005, the Senior Partner for Competition and Content discussed the contrast between consumer and citizen interests thus:

> It's a question of ... can Ofcom straddle these things? I think it can straddle these things, it's just that the philosophical route is rather different I think in competition and markets versus content and standards. So, that doesn't mean it's irreconcilable, indeed if they were done by completely separate organisations ... you'd still hope for ... some sort of consistency, and there are some benefits from doing it all in one organisation. But nevertheless there's different types of thinking associated with both approaches.[25]

However one academic commentator spoke for many critics in suggesting that 'there's an asymmetry ... in that the Consumer Panel represents the consumer interests on every topic except content, which by and large, we would see as more of a citizen interest than a consumer interest ... The Content Board inside Ofcom represents the citizen on all issues to do with content – broadcast content, but no other issue.'[26] Ofcom's then Secretary to the Corporation defended their approach as follows:

> On the telecoms side really we are trying to help competition, we're trying to give the consumer open competition and in simple terms, trying to make sure BT doesn't maintain its monopoly and therefore, in some way, disadvantage consumers. In a sense that's what we do in telecoms. But on the broadcasting side, it's much more citizen-based, isn't it, because we're not really stopping competition, we're being more restrictive on, 'well this is what you can and can't see on your television' ... it's very interesting how ... the two things split.[27]

Yet things are not so simple, as when the then Policy Manager for the Consumer Panel argued that there were 'consumer issues around broadcasting ... like digital switchover'[28] and when the then Policy Director for Consumer, Competition and Markets explained that there were also citizen issues in relation to telecommunications:

> There are complexities to just perhaps having a simple distinction – where the market works, that's about consumer issues, and where the market doesn't work, that's citizenship issues. Because you know sometimes it's about how the market works but it could work better, or how the market works but we need to support confidence in the market by taking particular forms of action. And there you'll sometimes, you're coming from it from a very consumerist policy but it's underpinned by what I would, you might call, citizenship-type concerns.[29]

For those outside the regulator, the pertinence of both citizen and consumer issues to both broadcasting and telecommunications is unsurprising, as noted by the BBC's then Controller of Editorial Policy:

You can characterise the interests involved in two ways. That there is a citizen interest in broadcasting because we have always traditionally taken the view that broadcasting is a matter of public space and of public value ... Equally, there's a consumer interest too, in terms of how it's paid for and in terms of what services are delivered to you, and whether or not the price you are having to pay is a reasonable or fair one. And that was a concept [that] ... Ofcom translates into the telecom sector, because again, in the telecom sector, the original requirements laid on BT were that it should provide a universal service, that the possibilities of universal access to telephony was a part of their responsibility. So even again in the telecom sector there's a tradition of, you know, you don't just provide to the people who it's easiest to get to.[30]

However, for Ofcom, there is a tension between the strategy of fudging the boundaries between citizen and consumer and that of protecting the binary mapping of consumer and citizen on to the Consumer Panel (and other Ofcom units) and Content Board respectively. Ofcom's then Partner for Strategy and Market Developments described the relation between Ofcom's duties and its organisational structures as 'a delicate balancing act', noting of the citizen interest that:

It was ... largely talked about in terms of the media, the broadcasting side of Ofcom's activities, but in fact when you, the more you think about it, the more some aspects ... of the issues which actually the Consumer Panel, so-called, is very interested in, are in many ways what I would describe as citizenship issues. They're about universal availability of telecom services around the country, they're about affordable access to, telephony services ... for the less well off. They're about protecting the more vulnerable groups to make sure they have access to, uh, to communications. And all of those actually feel more like citizen rather than consumer issues.[31]

The Chairs of both the Content Board and the Communications Consumer Panel were more forthcoming in challenging the neat binary mapping of Ofcom's general duties on to its organisational structure. As the Chair of the Content Board said, 'it's just that I think the way that the Communications Act set us up ... they set up this rather strange structure that there was a Content Board inside covering certain issues and a Consumer Panel outside covering certain issues but not content'.[32] The Chair of the Consumer Panel concurred, having no problem in expanding the definition of the citizen interest:

If we were all to accept that ... there's consumer detriment that flows from confusion over mobile phone tariffs, then we'd say, OK, let's do something about it. There are all sorts of ways you can tackle that, there are websites that give comparisons, you know, there's a raft of things you can do. There's a kind of standard ... consumer policy response, all of which is within the ... capability, of a regulator. If, however, you say, well, actually, there's another set of issues over here, which, let's generalise it and say there's an issue for many people in our society about how they choose, this technology,

... televisions, phones, whatever, and how they use them. That then becomes an issue that extends beyond just this regulator, it becomes an issue about public policy quite broadly defined. Doesn't let the regulator off the hook, but it means they have to find ways in which to collaborate with other deliverers of public policy outcomes in order to secure an outcome.[33]

Her argument was that, first, the regulator has a standard, well-recognised repertoire of interventions to address consumer detriment; second, communications technologies also occasion public policy challenges (i.e. the citizen interest) which the regulator must address; but fortunately, third, it is safe for the regulator to acknowledge this because, together with the public policy focus comes a wider range of stakeholders who must collectively meet the challenge. It is this third area of her account that provides the key to understanding how citizen interest is framed by the regulator – as 'another set of issues over here' – thereby implying they are external to the work of the regulator and, instead, a matter of public policy. But, rather than simply state that this has nothing to do with Ofcom, she advocates a new kind of citizen-facing agenda, one requiring a dialogue with other stakeholders (and, as we have seen, one that befits the new regulatory regime). Ofcom is, in short, already furthering the citizen interests in some ways, and is also already in dialogue with those who should further them in other ways. As its then Secretary observed:

We're not a private sector outfit ... because we're in the public sector, we have to be much more transparent, much more open ... there's a sense of trying to be as open as we can about everything.[34]

The Director of Nations for Wales added:

We have to be able to demonstrate that we ... are doing what Parliament told us to do. That we are actually safeguarding the interest of citizens and consumers in the field of communications.[35]

This need for transparency was one driver of change, as the Policy Manager for the Consumer Panel explained:

The tone has changed, there has been very much more emphasis on consumer issues ... the point of what Ofcom are doing is about, you know, consumer objectives and citizen objectives. Whereas before they were left implicit, um, and you know the tone has changed significantly ... it's a cultural change for the organisation ... it's not going to happen over night.[36]

Significantly, if somewhat contentiously, the Chair of the Consumer Panel suggested that the citizenship agenda should be built into the very structure of Ofcom, and that Parliament would hold Ofcom to account for delivering on its twin duties:

OFCOM AS A REGULATORY AGENCY

The scrutineer is the public, I mean literally the scrutineer has to be Parliament, I think. Parliament acting on behalf of the public, has to be. Parliament needs, I think, to be able to say this is what we want this regulation to deliver, this is why we legislate it. And, you know, interestingly in Ofcom's case, the word 'citizen' is used in the legislation as well as 'consumer', and I think it's for Parliament to hold Ofcom to account for how it's interpreting that remit.[37]

Public views of regulation

There are other ways of representing the opinion of ordinary people that differ both from the minority participation of strongly-motivated individuals contributing to public consultation processes and the bland collation of views that typically result (in practice, if not necessarily) from much social and market research. Academic qualitative research, by contrast, adheres to methodological principles that respect the context, complexity, diversity and reflexivity of the public (Denzin and Lincoln, 1994).

Discerning people's views about regulation is no easy matter – while people are used to complaining about silly or irritating regulations, commonly captured by the derogatory mention of 'health and safety', they are less used to being listened to regarding the fundamental dilemmas of regulation: state or individual, regulation for or regulation against, favouring the interests of the competent or the vulnerable, top-down or participatory. Yet in our focus group interviews, we held some lively, hotly contested and strongly deliberative discussions with people of all ages and social backgrounds (Lunt et al., 2008). The discussions freely mixed bits of knowledge, anecdotes, popular media stories and personal experiences, generally reaffirming a common-sense view in which rules and regulations appeared to be misguided or intrusive, but then questioning these interpretations as the contingencies and complexities of applying abstract regulatory principles to particular circumstances were mulled over. Time and again, the view was expressed that the real problems of society (e.g. crime, immigration, corruption) weren't being tackled while faceless bureaucrats developed elaborate systems of rules to constrain or intrude on the freedoms of the majority and while people themselves had little or no influence on how regulation was formed or shaped, as fairly passive recipients. Also problematic was that people tended to confuse different forms of regulation - for example, regulation was viewed as quasi-governmental rather than independent; legal and regulatory systems were often described as the same thing; concerns over the political relation between Britain and Europe framed ideas of regulation, with EU policy frequently mentioned in relation to the recurring idea of 'unnecessary regulation'. The result was a powerful sense of 'us' and 'them', and yet when these normative understandings were challenged in the groups, people were ready to step back, question, and rethink.

It would be easy to disregard people's views as incoherent or ill-informed, but this would be to ignore both the often heartfelt pain or anger that punctuated the focus group discussions and people's genuine willingness to engage with abstract issues that mattered to them and others. Thus we read the focus group discussions as showing that people were interested in issues of risk and regulation that were important in social and political terms as well as acknowledging their personal significance in their everyday lives. Some have strong, principled ideas of how regulation that were impacts on their lives, grounded in daily experiences, their experiences of regulation at work, social norms and attitudes to society generally and media representations of risk and regulation. Indeed, despite the dissent due to people's different positions in life and their different experiences, the shared agenda of concerns about risk, and doubts about regulation, was striking.

We discerned widespread public support for regulation to address an array of risks and, at the same time, considerable criticism of recent trends in regulatory practice. People argued that there was both too much regulation in some areas while others were neglected, and they expressed frustration that regulation was insufficiently grounded in common sense and social tradition but rather emerged from 'them' – faceless bureaucrats driven by commercial or political agendas. The sense that regulation had taken a 'wrong direction' was associated with a sense of uncertainty and powerlessness, revealing a disconnect between how the public felt they were represented or communicated with and the regulators' claim to have become more open and 'public-facing'. Nonetheless, there were some interesting paradoxes in how the public understood regulation and risk, paradoxes that also had echoes in expert analysis. For instance, people endorsed a strong ethos of personal responsibility but also wanted protections and backups in place. They wanted more choice but recognised that they might struggle to understand complex information regarding the decisions they faced. They worried about the vulnerable and, at times, recognised their need for protection from themselves, yet they attacked regulation for its intrusion in their lives. They saw themselves as outside the regulatory decision-making process yet knowingly passed up opportunities to become engaged, especially in forms of collective action; they were also reluctant to complain when they lost out.

Possibly because of the institutional contexts with which they were familiar, people were more comfortable with the positioning of the public as consumer, though they had many more criticisms of how consumer needs and protections were met than there was a recognition of their role as citizens in relation to regulation. Nor had they much expectation of or interest in being consulted, with this in turn depressing levels of trust and efficacy while raising doubts about institutional legitimacy (Couldry et al., 2008). The evident risk of consumer detriment in domains such as financial services, welfare or heath was less salient in relation to media and communication matters, though people had strong views on a range of issues from harm and offence in media content or the protection of children from commercial media to fair dealing in mobile phone contracts or personal privacy for those in the public eye.

There is, then, a task facing today's regulators in managing public expectations, not least because people are familiar with and tend to prefer traditional regulation based on supervision, enforcement, and consumer protection. People are worried about taking on the burden of risk management themselves as a cost of increased consumer choice, especially in relation to complex decisions, vulnerable groups, or in those cases when things go wrong. Wider problems of trust in institutions and disaffection with routes to participation also colour their perceptions of regulation. Attempts by regulators to work 'with' the public may be (mis)understood as attempts to work 'on' the public – via increased personal risk, surveillance, managed choice, or the provision of over-complex information. Attempts by regulators merely to summarise what people do say miss the significance of what people do not say: crucial silences in the focus group discussions included a consideration of the work of regulators in monitoring market trends, product innovations and emerging risks in the market, or in managing relations between regulators and firms other than through traditional notions of regulation as supervision and enforcement, or in ensuring processes of effective consumer representation and consultation. In so far as people are unaware of these processes, it is important to inform them before canvassing their views, this pointing to careful processes of deliberative polling rather than market surveys.

Conclusion

In the first four chapters of this book, we have examined the broader context within which regulatory reform has been adopted as a governmental strategy aimed at combining economic and social policy in response to the pressures and opportunities of globalisation. In Chapter 2 we examined academic theories of governance and regulation in order to understand the options available in regulatory design, and in Chapter 3 we brought out the political dimension of regulation in an account of one key public and parliamentary debate leading up to the Communications Act 2003. In this chapter, we have focused on the structures, policies and practices of Ofcom as a new-style regulatory agency aiming to provide a principled, unitary approach for a significant portion of the convergent market for media and communications acting in the public interest. We have also identified a number of issues in principle with this approach to governance and regulation, including the balance of consumer and citizen interests, the relationship between government and regulator, the balance between the public sector and the market, and issues related to Ofcom's use of consultation and research.

This review of Ofcom's statutory obligations, structures and operational principles demonstrates that, as often stated, it is a creature of statute with a broad range of responsibilities. The result is a demanding remit for a regulatory agency requiring it to act across previously separated areas of the marketplace, to be flexible in regulatory strategy, to demonstrate a consistent reduction in the regulatory burden, to submit its work to review for effectiveness, to make regulatory policy transparent and accountable, to conduct research and make the results of much of this public. As a regulatory agency, therefore, Ofcom has had to balance traditional rulebook or command-and-control regulation (e.g. in competition policy and content regulation through the Broadcasting Code) with innovations in regulatory interventions (e.g. self and co-regulation) and a set of 'softer' modes of engagement with stakeholders through research and consultation, providing the evidence base for government decisions, raising public awareness and understanding of media policy as an institution in the public sphere and, at the same time, seeking to minimise regulatory intervention.

The way that the Communications Act was drafted outlined a wide range of specific duties but left the detail of their implementation to Ofcom. The emphasis on impact assessments has ensured that market impacts – often drawing on the data and analyses of market activity provided by media and communications firms and institutions – have been significant in the regulator's activities. Ensuring that policy and practice reflects Ofcom's statutory duties has offered a defence against 'regulatory creep'. Further, the continued unfolding of societal, technological and market developments has meant that Ofcom needed a range of consultative, collaborative and deliberative strategies in order to undertake the wide range of duties required of it. Being relatively independent from the state, commerce and civil society, this approach – acting as an institution in the public sphere – depoliticises the regulatory process in some respects. By being highly visible and by making its processes transparent, accessible and reflexive – following the principles of 'better regulation' – media and communications regulation has become more salient on the public agenda. At the same time, these changes render regulatory power both diffuse and more complex, complicating its claims for effectiveness, accountability and transparency.

Ofcom's guiding principles have been to encourage competition in the market while protecting the pluralism of media ownership and production and diversity in media content, an approach that has raised critical concerns. Could Ofcom also have implemented an assessment of the impact of its work on social life and the cultural sphere, as well as the market? Why were the potential effects of regulatory policy and practice on the social and cultural aspects of media and communications not given equal weight as a test against which all departments and activities in Ofcom should be judged? Could there have been a citizens' toolkit, to assess the furtherance of the citizen interest to match the consumer toolkit introduced – to broadly positive effect – by the Consumer Panel?[38] Are there alternative, and better ways of engaging with the public who are, ultimately, the beneficiaries of regulation? These and other questions will doubtless be debated for years to come as Britain's media and communications landscape continues to evolve.

Notes

1 As regards the internet, the UK's then Secretary of State for Culture, Media and Sport, Tessa Jowell, announced in 2002, 'we do not intend to regulate the internet' (see House of Commons, 2002, *Hansard*). Yet arguably, such an ambition was already recognised as implausible (notably following the publication of Lessig's *Code and Other Laws of Cyberspace* in 1999 – see Tambini et al., 2008; Livingstone, 2011). Moreover, it was already under threat from the revisions to the Television without Frontiers Directive (see http://www.ofcom.org.uk/research/tv/twf/twfreport/).

2 The regulators themselves recognise that power brings resources and vice versa. Richard Hooper, Chair of Ofcom's Content Board (interview, 20/06/05), pointed out that, especially by comparison with the legacy regulators, Ofcom has very considerable power which, he is convinced, is used to improve the quality of regulation. Talking of Ofcom's size and scope, he said, 'I think people say that's both a strength and a weakness, I think when the arguments were going on in the late 90s, people said no politician would ever give Ofcom the amount of power it's got but they were wrong, they did ... I think one of the striking differences for me between Ofcom and the predecessors is that this is really seriously evidence based. I mean people are staggered by the amount of research we do and the amount of evidence we bring to the market.'

3 Below the level of the boards, Ofcom consists of a number of committees that represent either specific public interests or the application of specific expertise to the Ofcom Board and Executive: the Consumer Panel (later renamed the Communications Consumer Panel); national advisory committees for England, Northern Ireland, Scotland and Wales; a spectrum advisory board; and a committee advising on how communications issues affect older people and people with disabilities. Regrettably, we cannot cover the work of all these bodies in the present volume, important though they are.

4 The documents of the Better Regulation Task Force appear to be no longer publicly accessible, though this quotation has been reproduced at http://en.wikipedia.org/wiki/Better_Regulation_Commission#cite_note-0

5 This includes, at very low frequencies, communications with submarines and below ground. The lowest part of the spectrum of radio frequencies used for broadcasting is between 30–300 kHz, which is used for AM (medium wave) radio as well as navigation communications and time signals. The wavebands between 3 and 30 MHz are used for shortwave radio, citizens band and amateur radio, radio-based radar, and mobile telephones. Between 30 and 300 MHz, the

FM wavebands are located for radio and television as well as aircraft communications. Notably, between 300 and 3,000 MHz the applications include television, mobile phones, wireless LAN, Bluetooth and GPS, although some wireless LAN services operate between 3 and 30 GHz. There are higher frequencies, but these are used for specialist services, not for the technologies covered by Ofcom (see Cave, 2005).

6 Cave therefore recommends a dual strategy of a periodic review of spectrum usage and increasing pressure on public sector spectrum management so as to release spectrum for commercial use.

7 The case of community radio illustrates the importance of the introduction of digital media, which allows a compression of broadcast signals and therefore increases the number of stations that can use a given band of the radio spectrum. In the past, community media have been elbowed out of the spectrum by public service and commercial media, and the additional channels that are possible due to digitisation open up the possibility of granting licences to such stations.

8 In these actions, decisions on mergers and acquisitions are taken by the relevant Secretary of State supported by Ofcom's analysis and evidence on the potential impact on competition and the public interest. In the case of mergers between two newspapers, the public interest was defined in the Communications Act 2003 as the requirement for an accurate presentation of news, a free expression of opinion, and a sufficient plurality of views across the market as a whole. In the case of broadcasting or cross-media merger proposals Ofcom would, if requested by the Secretary of State, examine whether the merger would affect the plurality of ownership in the system as a whole to the detriment of either particular audiences or areas of the UK, whether it would diminish the quality of media content and the diversity of tastes and interests to which it appealed, and whether the people or enterprises who would increase their ownership of media had a genuine commitment to standards of accuracy of reporting, impartiality, not giving harm and offence, and acting to protect fairness and privacy in the media (Puttnam, 2006: 127).

9 For example, restrictions on the cross-media ownership of independent broadcasters and newspapers at the national level have been continued.

10 Section 16(10) of the Communications Act 2003 laid out the grounds on which the relationship between the Communications Consumer Panel and Ofcom should be established, requiring Ofcom to provide facilities and funds for the Panel to do its work, to publish the advice given and research conducted by the panel, and to ensure that the panel was involved in an advisory capacity at all stages of the regulatory process. This relationship would be subject to a memorandum of understanding which reaffirmed the independence of the Panel and its importance as a means of consulting consumers and conducting independent research which complemented that done by Ofcom, adding to the evidence base for regulatory policy and practice. The relationship is intended to be professional and business-like, with the Panel playing the role of a trusted critic of Ofcom.

11 Section 16 of the Communications Act, entitled 'Consumer Consultation', identified the Consumer Panel as a means for Ofcom to deliver its broader commitments to consultation by establishing a relatively independent body that would exist to advise Ofcom on the experience of consumers across the range of services for which Ofcom was responsible. Interestingly, the Panel was required to give advice on behalf of both individual consumers (which the Act calls 'domestic consumers') and small business consumers. The overall scope of the Panel was

summarised by Darlington (2008) as including: the provision of electronic com-munication networks; the provision of services and facilities; the supply of appa-ratus; the supply of directories; the financial and other terms on which such services, facilities, apparatus and directories were supplied; the standards of serv-ice, quality and safety of such services, facilities, apparatus and directories; the handling of complaints by companies providing such services, facilities, appara-tus and directories; the resolution of disputes between consumers and compa-nies providing such services, facilities, apparatus and directories; the provision of remedies and redress in respect of matters that were the subject of such com-plaints or disputes; the information about service standards and the rights of consumers made available by companies providing such services, facilities, appa-ratus and directories; any other matter appearing to the Panel to be necessary for securing effective protection for consumers.

12 This was welcomed by Citizens Advice in a press release of 14/10/10 (http://www.citizensadvice.org.uk/index/pressoffice/press_index/press_2010141), although in the following months they said little in public beyond a response to Ofcom's proposals on mobile charging for 0800 numbers (http://www.citizensadvice.org.uk/press_20101217).

13 'Panel responds to quangos announcement', Communications Consumer Panel news update, 14/10/10.

14 Author interview with Colette Bowe, Chairman of Ofcom (22/2/11). In a follow-up email, Max Beverton, also present at the interview, stated that the seven members of the Consumer Policy Team in 2005 had risen to 15 by 2009 and 22 in the newly-formed Consumer Group by 2011. The partner for the Consumer Group sits on both the Executive Committee and the Policy Executive, ensuring the direct representation of consumer issues at the highest level in Ofcom. He added that the consumer toolkit has played an important role in ensuring that Ofcom's projects examine the consumer interest in a sys-tematic way. Its approach has become embedded into Ofcom's processes and culture, helping to define the consumer interest in scoping work, collecting and assessing evidence and proposals, and guiding how Ofcom communicates the consumer interest internally and externally. The Communications Consumer Panel has conducted several audits of Ofcom's work in respect of the toolkit, with an annual publication, *Consumer Experience*, assessing the impact of Ofcom's work on consumers. It would be interesting to speculate about the possible contents of publications entitled *Citizen Experience*, or *Putting the Citizen First*.

15 See Ofcom's Consultation Guidelines on its website (n.d.-a)..These are its gen-eral principles of consultation, but Ofcom emphasises that the range of issues that it deals with includes issues of general public concern (e.g. the future of public service broadcasting) and issues that are highly technical and of direct interest to only a small, specialist audience (e.g. technical aspects of spectrum allocation), so it varies its approach to consultation, always making transparent the approach it adopts in each case.

16 We thank Robert Clark of The Voice of the Listener and Viewer for drawing this to our attention and kindly sharing his meeting notes with us.

17 Interview with Allan Williams, Senior Policy Advisor, Consumers' Association (Which?), then at the Ofcom Consumer Panel, 04/03/05.

18 Interview with Jocelyn Hay, Chairman, The Voice of the Listener and Viewer, 19/04/05.

19 The Campaign for Press and Broadcasting Freedom is a not-for-profit group which campaigns for a diverse democratic and accountable media.

20 Interview with Jonathan Hardy, The Campaign for Press and Broadcasting Freedom, 21/07/05.

21 Interview with Don Redding, Public Voice, 09/05/05.

22 Interview with John Beyer, Media Watch UK, 12/07/05. Media Watch UK is a not-for-profit group that campaigns for family values in the media.

23 Interview with Julie Myers, Policy Manager, Ofcom Consumer Panel, 28/06/05.

24 Interview with Tony Stoller, Director of External Relations, Ofcom, 10/08/05.

25 Author interview with Kip Meek, Senior Partner, Competition and Content, Director of Competition Policy, Competition and Content, Ofcom, 20/07/05.

26 Author interview with Richard Collins, Academic, Ex-Oftel Advisor, 19/04/05.

27 Author interview with Graham Howell, Secretary to the Corporation, Ofcom, 09/06/05.

28 Author interview with Julie Myers, Policy Manager Consumer Panel, Ofcom, 28/06/05.

29 Author interview with Neil Buckley, Policy Director, Consumer, Competition and Markets (consumer policy, media literacy), 10/06/05.

30 Author interview with Stephen Whittle, Controller, BBC Editorial Policy, 1807/05.

31 Author interview with Robin Foster, Partner, Strategy and Market Developments, Ofcom, 09/06/05.

32 Author interview with Richard Hooper, Chair of the Content Board, Ofcom, 20/06/05.

33 Author interview with Colette Bowe, Chairman, Ofcom Consumer Panel, 28/09/05.

34 Author interview with Graham Howell, Secretary to the Corporation, Ofcom, 09/06/05.

35 Author interview with Rhodri Williams, Director, Nations (Wales), Ofcom, 11/08/05.

36 Author interview with Julie Myers, Policy Manager Consumer Panel, Ofcom, 28/06/05.

37 Author interview with Colette Bowe, Chairman, Ofcom Consumer Panel, 28/09/05.

38 Mick McAteer, Senior Policy Advisor to Which?, expresses scepticism: 'It's very easy to have consumer representation by creating panels. And you know that's very different to actually representing the consumer interest, the whole way through what we would call the regulatory supply chain. You know just as firms have a supply chain so does regulatory policy where the policy's actually made way upstream before it even gets to the stage of consultation or discussion you know.' Note that our interview with McAteer concerned both Ofcom and the Financial Services Authority – here he is speaking about the latter's Consumer Panel.

5

OFCOM'S REVIEW OF PUBLIC SERVICE TELEVISION

Introduction

Public service broadcasting plays an important role in a democracy; certainly it has long done so in the UK. It provides independent news and current affairs, including critical reflection on government, together with high-quality programming that is accessible to all and that meets the needs and interests of a diverse public without the pressure to be populist. Indeed, the UK has a public service system that has been the envy of the world for many years. This includes a number of commercial broadcasters who provide public service programmes, including two national channels (ITV and Channel 5) and the specialist Welsh language public service provider, S4C, along with public service broadcasters (Channel 4 and S4C) that are wholly or partially commercially funded. At its core stands the BBC, a not-for-profit public service broadcaster funded exclusively by a licence fee imposed on all households receiving broadcast television according to the terms of a charter agreement negotiated every 10 years with the government of the day. This arrangement aims to ensure that the BBC is protected from undue government interference and that its funding is guaranteed – an important consideration since public service broadcasting needs government support to guarantee its funding, but it must be independent of government control if it is to deliver its remit. In return, the BBC acts in the public interest and offers a universal service aimed at educating, informing and entertaining the public, as its first Director General John Reith famously declared.

By the time of the Communications Act 2003, the media and communications landscape was clearly changing, with public service broadcasting under strain across Europe and around the world due to globalisation, digitisation and the convergence between old and new media (Iosifidis, 2010; Raboy, 2008). Public service broadcasting was still – and remains – a central part of the UK media system, much valued by the public for its cultural and democratic role as well as for providing a complement to advertising funded and subscription broadcasting. But the future prospects for public service broadcasting were attracting widespread attention, and critical commentators in the UK and around the world were becoming increasingly concerned about its ability to compete – if that was what was required of it – in a fast, globalising and ever more commercial environment. Further, the fine balance between public service and commercial broadcasters, as well as between the independence and accountability of the public service broadcasters, was becoming increasingly controversial (Born, 2004). As the centrality of the BBC in particular came to be increasingly questioned, it is intriguing that arguments for a diversification of public service providers may have originated in both the market liberal and social democratic positions. Then Senior Partner for Strategy and Market Developments at Ofcom, Ed Richards, reflected the former position when arguing that:

> Any public action to influence the broadcasting system must accord with the aim of ensuring consumer sovereignty. In other words, people should be free to watch what they want to watch, without 'guardians' of the public interest imposing their views on others. As Professor Peacock put it: 'the onus of proof is placed on government to show that the consumer interest is best achieved other than by the choices of listeners and viewers themselves.' (Richards and Giles, 2005: 73)

But many across the political spectrum, including social democrats, believe that a more participatory democracy would be supported if the public service media system were opened up to greater diversity of content, a wider range of voices and alternative forms of production (e.g. Keane, 1991). This context of debate and periodic controversy was hardly reduced by the introduction of a new and powerful regulatory agency into the mix. Independent broadcasters that delivered public service content were regulated by Ofcom's Content Board, but the BBC, as a self-governing, independent public service broadcaster and centrepiece of the system, still had considerable independence. Ofcom was given the responsibility of reviewing public service television provision, including the BBC, thereby introducing a new level of accountability within the BBC to a quasi-government agency and potentially compromising independent self-government as set out in the BBC Charter. Many watched eagerly to see where Ofcom would stand on the challenges of competition, plurality, innovation and diversity in reviewing public service television. However, since the BBC was self-governing, Ofcom was given only limited regulatory powers in the remit for this review, focusing on consulting, researching and reporting more than regulating. Indeed, given the charter agreement between the BBC and the government, the widespread support for public service broadcasting in general and the BBC in particular, and periodic parliamentary scrutiny of public service broadcasting, Ofcom is arguably only a minor player in the broader social and political debates concerning the status, funding and future of public service broadcasting. Our interest in its work in this area, therefore, is because it illustrates Ofcom working as an independent regulatory agency, using its expertise in market analysis, audience research and consultation to review the performance and analyse the conditions under which public service broadcasting operates.

Public service broadcasting in the 1980s and 1990s

Throughout the twentieth century, the British model was hugely influential, with many countries across Europe and the rest of the world following or adapting this approach in developing their public broadcasting systems. Until the 1980s, sufficient European countries had monopoly public service systems with direct government control or a licensing arrangement, as in the UK, leading some commentators to refer to the European model of public service broadcasting (Blumler, 1992; Iosifidis, 2010). However, during the 1980s the European nations moved away from public monopoly ownership to allow the development of media and communications markets. At the European policy level, as we saw in Chapter 2, a hybrid approach emerged in a protocol that was part of the Amsterdam Treaty of 1997. This combined market harmonisation across the region with provision for individual countries to determine their own level of public service broadcasting. However, public service broadcasting has also been much contested, not only for the relation between competition and pluralism, but also in terms of fundamental questions about the social, cultural and democratic role of the media and, in consequence, the nature and scope of public service broadcasting.[1]

The European history contrasts markedly with that of the USA, where, as McChesney (1999) notes, the country saw a vociferous debate in the early days of radio about whether part of the radio spectrum should be reserved for not-for-profit stations, many of which were based at universities. The regulator responsible for allocating licences, the Federal Radio Commission (FRC), under pressure from private interests, favoured commercial broadcasters at the expense of publicly-funded or community media, and for some European commentators, there is now a danger that Europe appears to be heading towards a similarly deregulatory future, with decreasing public ownership and the development of commercial media (see de Bens, 2007). However, for others, the UK is instead witnessing a more gradual shift in which growth of the commercial sector means that public service broadcasting is reducing its 'market share' but maintaining its levels of funding and provision (Iosifidis, 2010). Normatively, the debate is hardly resolved: for those who see the future in terms of neoliberalism or corporate liberalism, the dismantling of the patrician remnants of the welfare state is an economic and ideological necessity. By contrast, there are many who would prefer to preserve or even increase the contribution that public service broadcasting makes to democracy, culture and civil society, while also acknowledging that the role of public service broadcasting will have to adapt to the information age.

The particular history of public service broadcasting in the UK has witnessed many twists and turns in the debates over the role of broadcast media in public life and as a market. While the initial Reithian tradition was grounded in elite democracy, high culture and the dissemination of expertise, it was soon challenged by calls for populism and the commercialisation of the media, arguably calls for the democratisation of culture (Crisell, 2002). Thus Scannell and Cardiff (1991) document the gradual shift during the 1930s away from the high-minded notions of founding father Lord Reith towards the embracing of popular music, regular schedules, and new radio genres such as series and soaps. Similarly, Lewis and Booth (1989) chart the impact of exposure to foreign radio stations during the Second World War, which provided the impetus to the popularisation of the BBC as a monopoly public service broadcaster. Curran and Seaton (2010) emphasise the importance of the Second World War in stimulating something of a social revolution, such that the nature and role of public service broadcasting was rethought alongside the emergence of the post-war welfare state. And, in parallel to the unfolding story of the BBC, the clamour for the development of a commercial media system resulted, in 1955, in the granting of a commercial broadcasting licence to ITV. Significantly, ITV's licence was granted at an advantageous price, given the potential revenue from advertising, in return for a range of public service commitments including national and local news, factual broadcasting and high-quality drama. This introduced a duopoly, with one public broadcaster and one commercial broadcaster, an arrangement that lasted for 30 years and represented a balance between economic growth and social policy as part of the post-war welfare state (Curran and Seaton, 2010).

Although the Labour government in the late 1970s had already begun to question the sustainability of the welfare state and the viability of state ownership as a mechanism of state control and the regulation of markets, it was the Thatcher government of the early 1980s that instigated a radical shift in the relationship between the state and the economy. Both public ownership and the proliferation of quasi-governmental bodies came under attack and a range of public utilities was privatised as part of the creation of a 'share-owning democracy' in which the public interest was to be guaranteed by shareholders rather than public ownership. In the case of the privatisation of telecommunications, the large-scale public monopoly British Telecommunications (BT) was not broken up but retained as a virtual private monopoly (Baldwin and Cave, 1999). When the Thatcher government turned its gaze towards broadcasting, therefore, it was through the lens of welfare reform and privatisation, with both the BBC and the public service requirements on commercial broadcasters seen as illustrating inefficient public intervention in the market and a repository of liberal thinking that was no longer representative of the diversity of public interests in a complex plural society. However, the anticipated frontal attack on the BBC did not come, and although public service broadcasting was subject to a new level of scrutiny, it seemed that the Thatcher governments were looking to reform rather than dismantle the system. Perhaps this was in deference to the widespread public support enjoyed by the BBC, possibly because support for public service broadcasting was spread across party lines to include members of the Conservative party. Nevertheless, the Thatcher government made two moves that had important though contrasting effects on public service broadcasting: the creation of Channel 4 and S4C and the appointment of the Peacock Committee to investigate the financing of the BBC.

The Communications Act 1982 established Channel 4 as a not-for-profit commercial public service broadcaster carrying advertising initially on behalf of ITV, which financed it through a levy on advertising revenues from both Channels 3 and 4. Later it was able to sell its own advertising slots. Channel 4, in contrast to the BBC and ITV, was permitted only a limited in-house production capability and instead commissioned programmes from independent media production companies. At the time, however, commissioning from the independent production sector was more ideal than real and there was concern that many of the commissions would be from ITV.[2] Channel 4 also had a different remit from the BBC and ITV – to meet the needs of citizens not well provided for by the existing duopoly and to be self-consciously innovative in programming content and form, and in its early years it experimented with the aesthetic form and engaging social and cultural difference. Born (2004) documents how this level of innovation gave way over time to more popular programming, such as reality television. However, at least in the beginning, the establishment of Channel 4 was a critical move because it encapsulated the argument that the BBC (and to some degree ITV) represented an out-dated model of public service broadcasting and that innovation was more likely to result from changing the terms and conditions of public service broadcasting (beyond the BBC) rather than looking to reform the existing institutions.

The second key intervention by the Conservative government in the mid-1980s was to commission a review of BBC funding by the Peacock Committee (see O'Malley and Jones, 2009) in the hope that it would recommend that the BBC be allowed to generate income from advertising and so would become, as was already the case for public service broadcasters in France, Germany, Italy and elsewhere, a not-for-profit public service broadcaster funded through advertising revenue. However, the Peacock Committee came to a different conclusion, arguing that subscription was the most efficient form of funding for all broadcasters and that if it were adopted, then public funding could be reserved for relatively minor instances of market failure. The thinking was that the consumer would then be in a position to exercise choice in a more open media market delivering a range of content including public service broadcasting. Although the Thatcher government did not implement many of the recommendations of the Peacock Committee, its report influenced how the debate over public service broadcasting was conducted.

Public service broadcasting has traditionally 'addressed the nation', but the proliferation of channels and platforms means that the idea of broadcasting drawing the audience together is being displaced by a more dispersed audience (Abercrombie and Longhurst, 1998). Indeed, the very idea of national broadcasting is under pressure from the ever higher proportion of programme content produced abroad and the rise of transnational media (Chalaby, 2009). Increasingly, the proliferation of channels has emboldened those who believe that the expansion of commercial media would, in and of itself, deliver content that meets public purposes. The advent of mass broadband internet access has compounded the pressures on public service television, for it means that public services once provided exclusively by television and radio are now available online – such as educational material, news from independent and press websites, information about markets, and information from similar sources around the globe (Moe, 2010). In combination, these dramatic changes to the market, the audience and the technological mode of content delivery challenged the established policy of incremental change, seemingly pushing for a radical re-conceptualisation and reform of public service broadcasting (Jakubovitz, 2010). However, the counter-position – that the BBC has always been capable of adapting to changing times and meeting challenges to its legitimacy (Seaton and McNicholas, 2009) – retains its adherents too.

Ofcom's remit in reviewing public service television

The context within which Ofcom began its work on the review of public service television was, clearly, complex and contested, with different views expressed regarding the role and continuing relevance of public service broadcasting. Also contentious was Ofcom's role in this matter, since Ofcom is purportedly a convergent media regulator but the BBC is a self-governing public service broadcaster.[3] On its formation, Ofcom took over some of the regulatory powers of the BBC in the regulation of programme standards (harm and offence) but the BBC (through the BBC Trust) retained control over the regulation of impartiality and accuracy. Also, although the BBC Trust retained the power to set quotas for news and current affairs and for national and regional programming, it was required to consult Ofcom about these quotas; in particular, the BBC Trust had to gain Ofcom's agreement to any reduction in these quotas (Danby and Hart, 2010).[4] Unsurprisingly, then, while Ofcom was supposedly required to act in the interests of the ministry (DCMS) in gathering independent evidence to inform the periodic review of the BBC Charter, critics asked whether Ofcom could remain neutral in debates concerning the provenance, funding and scope of public service broadcasting.

From the outset, Ed Richards, then Senior Partner for Strategy and Market Developments at Ofcom, moved to calm nerves and expectations in a speech to the Royal Television Society in December 2003 (Richards, 2003). Acknowledging that the first review came at a critical moment in the history of public service broadcasting, Richards argued that a review would reflect what he referred to as a 'liberalising and reforming Act', while its timing would allow the review to inform the government's work on the BBC Charter and Ofcom's own work on the digital switchover at a time when households were increasingly accessing multiple channels, potentially reducing the historical dominance of the market by traditional broadcasters. The operating principles of the new regulator were clearly laid out – the review would reflect Ofcom's commitment to furthering the interests of both citizens and consumers, to transparency and accountability, and to public and stakeholder consultation and the generation of a substantial body of evidence. It would also bring to bear Ofcom's strategic analysis of the converging media sector, centred on managing potentially competing commitments to competition, plurality and diversity and promising fresh thinking in an area that was of importance to society.

Ofcom's first review was to be conducted as soon as possible after the Communications Act 2003, with subsequent reviews at least every five years thereafter. Specifically, the Communications Act 2003 (Section 264 (3a)) gave Ofcom 'an obligation to carry out a review of the extent to which public service broadcasters have, during that period, provided relevant television services which (taking them all together over the period as a whole) fulfil the purposes of public service television broadcasting in the United Kingdom'. Remembering that the remit of Ofcom's Content Board includes the delivery of public value for non-BBC broadcasters while the BBC Trust is responsible for this for the BBC, Ofcom was required to report its review publicly, including recommendations on how to maintain and strengthen the quality of public service television (radio, for reasons that remain unclear, was omitted from the Act, although the relations between community radio, public service and commercial radio were addressed by Ofcom; see Chapter 8).

The 2003 Act specified that the core purposes of public service broadcasting were to inform, educate and entertain by stimulating its audience and encouraging them to reflect, and by supporting the range and diversity of cultural activity in the UK through a variety of genres, including drama, comedy, music, film, and the visual and performing arts. According to the Act, public service television should also provide services aimed at 'facilitating civic understanding and fair and well-informed debate on news and current affairs in, and in the different parts of, the United Kingdom and from around the world' (Section 264, 6(c)). In addition, public service television should provide a wide range of sporting and leisure programming and a suitable variety and range of educational programmes. Sufficient factual broadcasting should be produced so as to cover a range of topics, including science, belief, social issues, international events and special interests. The provision of programmes on religious beliefs was expected to cover religious news and the history of different beliefs in addition to broadcasting acts of worship.

Framed by an account of changes in the provision and delivery of public service television during the reporting period, Ofcom's remit, then, was to form a view on whether public service broadcasting, taking the system as a whole, was meeting its public purposes through the delivery of high-quality accessible programmes and services. A series of additional judgements were also required. Are sufficient high-quality and original children's programmes available? Are communities, cultural interests and traditions from different locations and regions in the UK adequately represented? Is sufficient public service television programming produced in the UK, with a reasonable proportion of it outside London? And, finally, what could be done further to strengthen and enhance public service broadcasting? In what follows, we argue that Ofcom shaped the agenda for the review in two significant ways. It relied heavily on audience research in the evaluation of the performance of existing public service broadcasters rather than on regulatory judgement and it focused more on scenario modelling of future market conditions for non-BBC public service broadcasters than on how to strengthen and enhance the performance of the existing system. The spirit of the Act was to support public service broadcasting while making it more accountable and to look for incremental improvements in the system. Ofcom, by focusing on the changing market conditions for media and communications and looking towards the longer term, adopted a more radical stance.

Ofcom's first review of public service television

Ofcom conducted its first review of public service television in three phases. Phase one was focused on definitions of public service broadcasting (PSB), market analysis and audience research. Phase two provided analysis of possible future scenarios for public service television. Phase three presented Ofcom's recommendations for the future.

Competition for Quality (Ofcom, 2005b) summarised the work of the first PSB review. Starting by attempting to define what we, as a society, want from public service television, Ofcom focused on the purposes and characteristics rather than the institutions of public service broadcasting. Since both Parliament (in the 2003 Act) and the BBC itself (BBC, 2004) had already examined these issues, it is unsurprising that their approaches overlapped. Ofcom chose four purposes: to inform, educate, produce original national programmes and to reflect cultural diversity, arguing in addition that public service broadcasting should be characterised by programmes of high quality that were original, innovative, challenging, engaging and widely available. Reflecting, perhaps, the continuing influence of the Peacock Report and its emphasis on reducing the structural constraints that PSB creates for competition, this specification was detached from any mention of broadcast institutions and anticipated a future in which public service content would be produced by a range of providers with different remits, funding arrangements and delivery platforms.

Complementing this conceptual work in framing the nature of public service values, Ofcom's audience research examined public support for public service television, revealing a high public regard for the quality and range of programming, the broadcasters, the funding model and the regulation of public service broadcasting. However, while public support for public service broadcasting was an essential part of its legitimation, the Communications Act 2003 had asked not for an analysis of public opinion (although in section 14 it does require public opinion research for other reasons) but for Ofcom to make an in principle judgement about the quality and fitness for purpose of existing provision. Gibbons (2005: 48) criticises Ofcom's use of opinion research as a proxy for the public interest, arguing that 'success in providing quality is not judged by mass appeal but by independent criteria of value'. While it is surely fair to include public opinion to compensate for the relatively rare contributions of the audience to public consultations, the point is that a reliance on public opinion may provide only an unstable legitimation for public service broadcasting, one that evades a principled assessment of the content and services provided by the public service broadcasters and whether this meets the communication rights of citizens.

More influentially in terms of the ensuing public debate, Ofcom's analysis of market trends pointed up the risks to the institutional structures, funding arrangements and technological infrastructure of public service television posed by the dynamic and interactive models emerging in the realm of digital new media. The main problem that Ofcom stressed was quite specific, namely the unsustainable basis for advertising-funded public service broadcasting given the increased competition for advertising revenue from digital platforms. Ofcom's projections, based on extrapolations from the falls in revenue in the preceding years, suggested a looming crisis. However, making such projections is hazardous, and one might instead expect that over time advertising spend would find a level that balances broadcast and online advertising without deserting the former altogether. Indeed, a mixed portfolio of broadcast, online and other forms of advertising may prove advantageous, with broadcasting remaining an effective locus for certain types of advertising.

Ofcom's recommendations in the short term (leading up to the digital switchover, i.e. for 2005–12), included maintaining the existing levels of public funding for the BBC along with ideas on how to support public service broadcasters funded by advertising given the increased competition for advertising revenue – such as government grants, industry levies and realising greater value from licensing. Ofcom also considered possible changes to the remits of the public service broadcasters, taking into account their changing technological and financial circumstances. The BBC would remain as the cornerstone of public service broadcasting, funded by the licence fee and with a remit to deliver content that would provide public service values for all. ITV was to focus on its strengths, providing news and high-quality drama and regional news and current affairs but also reducing the scale and scope of its regional and children's programming. Channel 4 would remain a not-for-profit public service broadcaster funded through advertising with a special remit for innovation. Channel 5 would focus on original UK production.

For the longer term, however, based on its combination of a risk-based analysis of future technical and market trends and concerns about the immediate funding problems facing those public service broadcasters funded by advertising, Ofcom advanced an agenda of radical change in the public service system – in contrast with the more gradualist approach typical of the UK context hitherto. Its most innovative suggestion was the idea of a public service publisher. Publicly funded to commission public service content that had been especially created for digital and online platforms, the funds of the public service publisher would be open for competition from any agency except the BBC. Arguing that the existing broadcasters should not dominate new media as they had during the era of terrestrial broadcasting, the intention was to stimulate the digital and online delivery of media content that would meet public purposes, thus providing an alternative to the traditional broadcasters. Channel 4 was one intended recipient for funding through this mechanism, as were local and community media and a range of cultural outlets such as galleries, educational institutions and small-scale production companies that were able to innovate in drama, comedy and factual content.

Ofcom further recommended that public service television should prioritise the representation of nations and regions, local communities and special interest groups – through out-of-London production for both the BBC and ITV, the protection of language services, and the production of local content by the proposed public service publisher. Ofcom also recommended that the BBC be asked to develop new proposals for local and regional programming. Finally, Ofcom recommended changes in the regulation of public service television, supporting a separation of the roles of governance and management of the BBC, increasing the competition for the production of public service content, and extending its own powers to test the implications for the media and communications market of innovations by the BBC. The argument, widely debated, was that the BBC had become too big, too protected from competition, not properly accountable, and likely to continue this dominance into the new media age. By providing valuable market and audience research, by revitalising the debate over the purposes of public service broadcasting and its future, and by drawing attention to the challenges of the new media age, Ofcom acted as a catalyst for public engagement in this important area of media policy. The gist of its specific recommendations was to limit the capacity of the BBC so as to take advantage of technical and market changes to open up new possibilities for an alternative delivery of public service programmes and services.

A public service for all

In its first review, Ofcom adopted a vision of a future in which technological and market innovation would transform the media and communications environment. In some ways regarding the BBC as more of a constraining legacy than a partner in innovation, Ofcom's argument was that in the future online and digital services would increasingly provide much of the public service content traditionally delivered by broadcasting. In some respects, this is now already underway, although with public service broadcasters proving themselves to be far more innovatory than a brake on this future. It may be argued here that Ofcom's sense of dramatic change just around the corner is undermined by the history of media and communications – for successive waves of technological innovation have not necessarily eradicated previous technical forms. More notable is the way that existing institutions can adapt, often becoming more specialised in their aims, as part of a more complex and more gradual process of change. As if to illustrate this, by the time of the final phase of Ofcom's first review the BBC had already committed itself to a clearer definition of its public purposes, increased public accountability and reform of its governance (BBC, 2004).

The idea that the internet could provide public service content that meets many if not all of the purposes of public service media remains questionable. It is notable that Ofcom did not subject online content to a robust analysis of its ability to meet public purposes. Blogs, social media and the websites of educational and public institutions offer exciting new forms of content, but do they deliver the same things as broadcast public service content, and do they satisfy all the public purposes of public service media? Certainly, access to the internet, especially broadband, remains highly unequal – in terms of broadband speed, use and digital literacy, with nearly a third of households still lacking access (Ofcom, 2009a, 2010c). However, it is important to distinguish between new media as a sphere of production, where its public service value remains uncertain, and as a carrier of information and media content. To be sure, the internet will increasingly become a means of conveying content from existing producers: the BBC website is the third most visited site in the UK precisely because it complements and enhances rather than displaces broadcasting; BBC iPlayer, as a way of viewing programmes for seven days after broadcasting, demonstrates how the internet extends public service broadcasting's ability to meet its public purposes.

Commentators were not slow to critique the proposals contained in *Competition for Quality* (Ofcom, 2005b). For Gibbons (2005), Ofcom did not give sufficient weight to arguments against its own premise, namely that competition was the best way to promote quality and a diversity of content in public service broadcasting.[5] As signalled by the title of the consultation document itself, competition was seen from start to end as the favoured route to quality, with social and cultural issues cast in economic language, notwithstanding the critical responses received during the consultation. Arguing that it was already broadly accepted that quality was a case of market failure (i.e. it was not necessarily generated by market competition), Gibbons suggested that Ofcom confounded institutional diversity with content diversity, measuring the former more confidently than it reflects on the latter. So, while the difficulties of commercial channels threaten to position the BBC as a monopoly provider, this need not result in a lack of content diversity or a lack of innovation. Channel 4, which undoubtedly adds to this diversity, was at the time regarded by Ofcom as about to fail economically, though since then it too has flourished.

More generally, Ofcom glosses over the considerable disagreements among economists about how to define and measure quality other than through popular appeal. And it seems to lose sight of the distinction between quality programming and quality public service broadcasting in advocating the need for competition for the BBC. But it is not quality *per se* that public service broadcasters must provide, but rather quality programming that meets the specific purposes of public service broadcasting. As Freedman (2008) and others add, high-quality public service broadcasting drives up expectations of quality across the market more generally, not through competition but by setting high production and content standards and thereby enhancing provision of all kinds. In contrast, commercial media corporations produce quality programming mainly or only where this is profitable – usually sport and news, sometimes drama, but rarely in the genres of documentaries, current affairs, the arts and music, or educational and children's programming. In short, there are reasons to contest any assumption that public value across the range of public service broadcasting will increasingly be delivered by commercial broadcasters and online services. It remains possible, even likely, that innovation in key areas of public value will be driven, as they have been historically, by public service broadcasters.

During the final phase of Ofcom's work on the first public service broadcasting review, the Department for Culture, Media and Sport began its own review of the BBC in preparation for a charter renewal, resulting in the White Paper *A Public Service for All: The BBC in the Digital Age* (DCMS, 2006). Four features of the new charter settlement between the government and the BBC were relevant to Ofcom's work on the review: the BBC was required to change its governance arrangements from a board that combined executive control and public accountability to a trust with oversight of the BBC management team; it had to become more explicit and accountable about the public value delivered by its services; it would become subject to public value analysis and market impact assessment for its new media content and any innovations in programming, with Ofcom and the BBC Trust responsible for conducting these; and finally, the emerging consensus from the charter renewal work of the committees in both Houses of Parliament and DCMS was that the BBC should remain the cornerstone of the public service broadcasting system, with its funding maintained (Gibbons, 2009).[6] These changes were significant and were accompanied by a generous financial settlement for the BBC, suggesting that while through its various reviews Ofcom was publicly visible in debates over the nature and future of public service broadcasting, the key acts were taking place in negotiations between the government and the BBC. Collins sees the positives in these new arrangements:

The separation of the Trust from the Executive, the explicit definition of objectives and the regular assessment of BBC performance together with other important changes such as the requirement for the Trust to 'regularly discuss' BBC efficiency with the National Audit Office and the strengthening of both the BBC's fair trading obligations and Ofcom's powers in respect of BBC trading practices mean that the governance regime under which the BBC henceforth will operate is both more independent and more stringent than that which preceded it. (Collins, 2007: 166)

A critical question is whether these changes represent less an innovative way in which public services can justify themselves in a mixed market and more the creep of market or corporate logic into public service broadcasting. The strategic application of public value management to all the BBC's activities complements market impact tests for innovations in services, thereby optimising reach, impact, quality and value for money (Collins, 2007). Thus for Collins, a reasonable compromise has been reached that does much to orient the BBC to the 'realities' of public service delivery and strategy in the context of a globalising market, even if it does not satisfy those who would advocate either the traditional model of public service broadcasting or an entirely commercial broadcasting sector. Alternatively, this 'corporate' direction in the governance of the BBC can be interpreted as an extension of managerialism, which Born (2004) and Freedman (2008) see as inimical to public service. The government's approach, here, is not specific to media and communications but rather is grounded in work conducted in the Cabinet Office under New Labour on public value management (Kelly et al., 2002). This established as principles for the management of public bodies the importance of developing strategies that would enhance public or user involvement, the focus on satisfaction rather than outcomes, the emphasis on enhancing trust in the service provider, and the value of treating consumers of public services fairly.

This stress on public involvement reshapes the BBC, as we have argued for Ofcom, as an institution in the public sphere – a branch of public administration that engages citizens and other stakeholders in an extended and ongoing dialogue between the public and the providers of public services. In practice, however, as we have claimed of Ofcom and as Collins claims of the BBC, public value management generally gets watered down so that the ways that these institutions 'take account' of public concerns and preferences fall short of the ideal of a deliberative partnership between government agencies, public services, the public, civil society bodies and commerce.

Ofcom's second public service television review

The charter agreement and the work of the DCMS and the BBC on public value had put fundamental questions about the purposes of public service broadcasting back on the public agenda. Given this context, combined with the negative impact of the economic recession on the revenues of public service broadcasting providers funded by advertising, Ofcom brought forward its second review of public service television. Having previously analysed both market and technological changes, we would expect Ofcom to evaluate whether public service broadcasting as a system was meeting its objectives and how it could be maintained and strengthened in the future.

While regulators may expect that government will not adopt all their recommendations, Ofcom's aims regarding the second review lacked the confidence of the first review, which gave an impression of driving the agenda. The reasons for this shift were not evident, but the growing political consensus over the future of the BBC and public service broadcasting in general, the response of the BBC to the challenge to reform governance, continuing public support for PSB and the growing confidence of the existing broadcasters in the online environment all contributed to a sense that Ofcom's underlying agenda was not gaining support even though its work on PSB review was widely valued. For the second review, Ofcom describes its role more modestly as providing evidence about audiences, citizens and consumers, stakeholder views and analysis of market trends in order to support the policy decisions to be taken by government and Parliament:

Ofcom's task in the current review is to provide the analysis and the ideas which will allow government and Parliament ultimately to decide whether and how public service should be re-invented for the digital age. (Ofcom, 2008b: 3)

Ofcom began its second review in 2008 by publishing *The Digital Opportunity* (Ofcom, 2008b). Although the policy context had changed, events had borne out Ofcom's prediction that public service broadcasters funded by advertising would find the new competitive market very difficult and that they would therefore have to try to rein back on their public service obligations. Also, the market share of the main public service broadcasters had fallen by 17 per cent, although it still accounted for two-thirds of all television viewing. The experiences of ITV and Channel 4, if anything, brought into question the idea that in the future the market would provide public service media. As Gibbons (2009: 4) put it: 'Despite two decades of multi-channel broadcasting, investment in high quality UK content other than sport is overwhelmingly by the current public service broadcasters.' Ofcom's own data add film to this short list of genres but it acknowledges that beyond this, the 'overall level of market investment in original UK content has reached a plateau' (Ofcom, 2008b: 3). In short, subscription services deliver only a small part and only some dimensions of the public value expected of public service broadcasting.

Nonetheless, in *The Digital Opportunity*, Ofcom reiterated its view that 'the regulatory and funding model which supports today's public service broadcasting framework has had its day' (Ofcom, 2008b: 3). Since the same report showed that public support for public service broadcasters remained high,[7] Ofcom argued against, rather than, as before, relying on public opinion. Now it claims a lag between structural market changes and public opinion, predicting that support will reduce in the future. However, an alternative reading is that the public is not convinced that subscription, digital and online services are delivering viable alternatives to public service broadcasting.[8] In adopting a clear and authoritative style, it may be argued that here, as elsewhere, Ofcom's approach to interpreting public opinion lacks the interpretative flexibility or recognition of data ambiguity that one would expect in social science, giving fuel to the idea that their approach to audiences is grounded more in market than social research methods.

In conducting its audience research, Ofcom asked people to rate the importance of the four purposes of public service broadcasting defined in its first review (namely, informing our understanding of the world; stimulating knowledge and learning; reflecting the cultural identity of the UK; and representing alternative viewpoints). Irrespective of demographic distinctions, everyone judged these purposes to be important, and minority ethnic groups particularly valued the role of television in supporting social identity. Interestingly, television was regarded as the medium most likely to meet these purposes, particularly by comparison with the internet. This latter was valued more for its individual contribution to matters such as learning and pursuing personal interests (Ofcom, 2008b). These findings surely help explain why support for public service broadcasting is holding up in the age of new media. The public recognises the differences among media in terms of delivering public purposes, and acknowledges the continuing capacity of broadcast media to meet citizenship needs and concerns.

However, Ofcom points to the changes underway among young people's media use, notably their rapid adoption of the internet, to support its replacement hypothesis that the heyday of television is over. Yet young people seem to find more hours than there are in the day, for although the internet occupies a growing amount of their time television viewing has dropped far less than expected among those same youth. This instead supports the supplementation hypothesis – that new media supplement older ones while older ones are remediated, adapting to their changing circumstances (Livingstone, 2002). Moreover, while young people now consider the internet more important than television, this is not to say they no longer value or rely on television. To compare and contrast media is, in any case, incompatible with the convergent media environment. Television is increasingly watched online, and the delivery of broadcast content through the BBC's iPlayer and related services means that the boundary between public service broadcasting and the internet is increasingly blurred. Thus it may be that for the public, at least, the key distinction is not delivery platforms but the distinction between the products provided by public service broadcasters and other sources of content. Indeed, Ofcom's own (2008b) research found that the public places a high value on UK-originated programmes that reflect the everyday lives of citizens in all their diversity. Overwhelmingly, people value news, current affairs and other forms of factual broadcasting. Other genres appear less popular but this is an artefact of the method:

Ofcom used a forced choice format for people to rank the five most important genres (unlike the use of importance ratings for judging the purposes of public service television reported above). Consequently, film, comedy, religious programming, the arts and classical music were lower down the list, and it is likely that these judgements reflected viewing preferences more than perceived value.

Ofcom (2008b) also found that people value a plurality of producers, particularly for genres such as news and current affairs. This was supported by 'contingent valuation' research, in which people indicated how much they were prepared to pay, in principle, to guarantee a range of providers. For Ofcom, this showed that people support its idea of competition for quality, but it need not mean that they think multiple providers will, in and of itself, drive up quality. Rather, and put more simply, it is likely that people think different channels and sources offer different perspectives and this is worth paying for. This also requires careful interpretation, for while people say they want choice this may not mean they wish personally to engage with a wider range of content but instead that they wish for sufficient range that their own particular niche interests are represented, which is quite a different argument from that concerned with the conditions for ensuring quality. Finally, it may be that people value plurality for societal reasons, that they believe multiple opinions should be expressed in a democracy rather than that multiple providers should operate in a market. Being prepared to pay for plurality may be the audience's way of expressing support. It need not necessarily mean they wish for public service content to become paid for; on the contrary, their intention may indeed be to support inclusive rather than exclusive access to content. In short, it is difficult to say from this research what exactly people are endorsing – public sphere values or Ofcom's conception of plurality as choice leading to competition.

Turning to the question not of audience preferences but of market trends, Ofcom also examined changes in the period leading up to its second review in 2008. Four out of five households had digital television and the rapid increase in use of diverse digital media and on-demand platforms was striking. Accordingly, the public service broadcasters were developing new digital channels (e.g. ITV3 in 2004, ITV 4 in 2005, E4 in 2005 and Film 4 in 2006), although these tended not to have the same level of UK original content as the mainstream channels. Since new digital channels are not bound by public service obligation, the result is that some public service channels carry less public service content than on their mainstream channels while some non-public service broadcasters provide digital channels that contribute to some public purposes (e.g. Sky News, Discovery, Yesterday, and the History Channel carry news and documentary programming; Channel M in the Manchester area for a time addressed local needs; and specialist channels such as Teachers' TV are separately funded by the government to deliver aspects of public value; Ofcom, 2008b).

As the system diversifies, new questions arise. Is this the competition for quality that Ofcom sought in its first review? Should the growing scope for commercial channels to carry recognisably public service content be welcomed or criticised for their conservative reliance on tried-and-tested formulas? Since it is still unclear that innovation in digital platforms produces innovative and high-quality public service content, it cannot be assumed that a plurality of providers will necessarily reproduce, let alone enhance, the existing public service offer. On the one hand, Ofcom (2008b) documents the reduction in spending on UK-originated content by both public service broadcasting and non-public service broadcasting.[9] On the other hand, the increasing adoption of broadband services is enabling the growing availability of public value information from public and commercial bodies online. The future, Ofcom admits, is difficult to predict, but it suggests three broad trends: there will increasingly be new opportunities in both digital television and online for the delivery of public service content; the share of public service content on traditional broadcast channels will decline; and as the competition intensifies and the media audience continues to fragment, innovation and original UK content will decline.

Ofcom's consultation on the second review

In place of the first public service review's confident prediction that these developments would provide competition for quality for the BBC, the second review called for a new model for the structure and funding of public service broadcasting in the UK. Ofcom identified four contrasted models for consultation: evolution of the current system; only the BBC would survive; the BBC plus Channel 4 would bear the responsibility; and a broader competitive funding model would be established. Ofcom offered *The Digital Opportunity* for public consultation between 10 April 2008 and 19 June 2008. The consultation attracted a huge amount of material, including 270 formal responses plus various contributions from online debates and submissions of research evidence from the public service broadcasters and the Satellite and Cable Broadcasting Group (SCBG). In addition, Ofcom received postcard petitions from two campaigns: 13,000 supporting the campaign for Border TV's *Look Around* news programme and 2,500 postcards and 700 emails objecting to any move to share the licence fee with broadcasters beyond the BBC. Although Ofcom asked some specific questions, providing an online questionnaire as a guide, many contributors chose their own format or presented extensive documentation. Responses from the existing public service and commercial broadcasters and key stakeholders such as The Voice of the Listener and Viewer (VLV) were in the form of substantial documents.

As with the public opinion evidence, responses to the consultation were generally strongly supportive of the purposes and characteristics of public service broadcasting, although some responses differed from Ofcom's account of these in emphasising the importance of particular institutions, programme genres or services, such as community-based media projects, ethnic media, media with broader international appeal and film (Ofcom, 2008c). On the issue of declining UK original content, Ofcom reported audience support for the importance of such content for public service broadcasting, although views varied about the relative weight that should be given to community, local, regional or national content or, differently, about the relative importance of UK-originated content for 'core' genres such as news, current affairs, quality drama or children's programming. Views on the potential of online services to deliver public service purposes were split between the optimists who saw enormous potential and the sceptics who believed that online services would only ever partially deliver on their public service purposes. Commercial enterprises expressed concern that their contribution to public service values should be acknowledged (Ofcom, 2008c).

Views on the regulatory solutions proposed in *The Digital Opportunity* were more mixed, though many agreed with Ofcom's view that the market, even in the context of increasing opportunity and the proliferation of channels and online services, would not deliver on many of the purposes of public service broadcasting. Consequently, there was also broad support for Ofcom's analysis that a new funding model was needed. However, some thought that Ofcom was overplaying the threats to advertising revenues for ITV and Channel 4 in the longer term and urged Ofcom to extract greater value from spectrum releases. Some – notably the BBC – questioned Ofcom's account of the relation between pluralism and competition, offering alternative conceptions of plurality focused on diversity of content and on niche or community-based media rather than competition for the BBC. The most contentious issue was whether the licence fee should be 'top sliced' so as to extend its use beyond the BBC, with many voices against this, although there was some support for the idea that Channel 4 should somehow be included in the public funding net. On the models proposed by Ofcom, there was strong support for the gradual evolution of the current system and virtually no support for the BBC-only model. The idea of the BBC and Channel 4 as jointly publicly funded was seen as a possible alternative should the evolution of the current model not prove possible. There was little support for a model in which there was open competition for public funding for public service content delivery (Ofcom, 2008c).

Criticisms of top slicing dominated the academic responses to Ofcom's second public service review (Harvey, forthcoming; Iosifidis, 2010; Seaton and McNicholas, 2009). For most, top slicing would establish a precedent for allocating possibly growing portions of the licence fee to other, even commercial broadcasters in return for public service content. Notwithstanding the threat this would pose to the BBC, whose success, quality and innovativeness rely – many have argued – on its scale, resources and reach, this could be just the kind of incremental change that has often occurred in the UK media system. Whether it would really undermine the BBC's position as 'the cornerstone of public service broadcasting' would be hard to determine. Similarly, whether competition really aids or hurts the BBC was unclear. Iosifidis (2010) has contested Ofcom's assumption that competition is the norm in public service systems elsewhere, arguing that in systems with more than one publicly-funded public service broadcaster (e.g. Germany) collaboration or complementary aims and objectives are the norm. Others, however, point to cases where competition from commercial broadcasters has driven innovation in the BBC (e.g. Lewis and Booth, 1989).

Conclusion

Ofcom's reviews have been impressive in the depth and quality of their market analysis, the numbers and quality of participants in the consultation process, and the production of original audience research. The consultation process and the impact of the reviews on the public debate have confirmed that Ofcom has very quickly become an important agent in media and communications in the UK – it has become an institution in the public sphere. Ofcom is not, however, a neutral player. Both reviews attracted considerable criticism for their focus on economic matters at the expense of social and cultural policy, as was evident in the use of economic concepts and metaphors to explain social and cultural aspects of policy even in the domain of public service broadcasting. And the relative importance attached to research compared to consultation was also criticised, raising some interesting questions about the value of different voices – expert or lay, directly expressed (as in consultations) or 'collected' through opinion polling or other social scientific methods. What seems impossible to achieve, not only by Ofcom but by many civic and political institutions, is the diverse and direct participation of ordinary voices in public deliberation. In this, we need to distinguish between Ofcom as an institution that creates an opportunity for different perspectives and voices to be heard and contribute to media policy and the idea of Ofcom as an institution that, albeit on the basis of its engagement with stakeholders, fixes on a position as a consensus or a summary of opinion. In a sense, Ofcom took the second position in the first PSB review, in which a clear Ofcom line emerged, but in the second review acted more as a means of gathering evidence and opinion on behalf of government.

Beyond creating a space for (qualified) debate, Ofcom developed a discernable 'line' on public service broadcasting, having established through detailed analysis the challenges facing the existing arrangement for public service broadcasting in its first public service review. In the first review, the idea of the public service publisher, designed to establish alternative, competitive funding for existing public service broadcasters, caught the imagination and was widely debated. In the second review, this was replaced by a mapping of alternative funding models that, again, provided the terms for public debate, with much discussion of models 1–4 and much speculation about the preference of Ofcom and, more importantly, the government. The notion – indeed for some, the spectre – of top slicing the licence fee has been a common theme throughout both reviews. In fact, top slicing is not new, as the government has allocated portions of the licence fee for non-BBC activities periodically since the inception of the licence fee in the 1920s.[10] Moreover, a version of top slicing is what came to pass, though not until after the 2010 General Election. But this is to get ahead of the story

What is clear is that stakeholders had taken the opportunity to make a range of relevant and informed points, express different views, experiences and perspectives on the current and future state of public service broadcasting and, thereby, engage in critical policy deliberation as invited by the regulator. Moreover, the responses confirm both public support for the importance of public service broadcasting and fairly widespread public understanding of and concern about the pressures on the system. However, a number of critical questions remain. Did the consultation really enable deliberation or merely provide an opportunity for the venting of opinions? A consultation permits the expression of different views but this is not the playing out of argument and counter-argument. Although alongside the formal consultation process, many events – public and otherwise – were the site of heated argumentation, the question must remain: did consultation affect Ofcom's policy decision making? And was the result to bring us closer to resolving the key issues facing the public service broadcasting system? Ofcom had fulfilled its obligations, but to what effect? One interpretation was that Ofcom's evidence of continuing public support for PSB contributed to a political climate which favoured arguments for retaining the existing system, with appropriate modifications for changing market pressures and to deal with digitisation and the development of online services. Ofcom's radical agenda was not followed up. However, Ofcom's proposals, even the public service publisher, also received strong support, setting in train the idea that public funds could be legitimately and productively deployed beyond the BBC. This combined with Ofcom's findings that stakeholders were in favour of a role for regulation and accountability to reinforce moves to make the BBC in particular more open and accountable to the public.

Finally, what of the fraught question of Ofcom's relation to government? It is difficult to determine how far the hand of government was evident in Ofcom's reviews of public service broadcasting, though it would be naïve to imagine no political influence on the conclusions reached and the options set out (or those that were sidelined along the way – such as the prospect of raising funds through industry levies). To be sure, Ofcom contributed evidence, conceptual and market analysis, public consultation and original research to a wider political and social debate. However, a number of issues emerged in Ofcom's management of the reviews that pointed to regulatory creep or an attempt to capture the agenda, particularly in the first review; Ofcom's broad interpretation of the remit given to it by the Act; the imposition of a view of radical change on public service television; focusing over much on the issues facing markets to the detriment of social and cultural issues; not giving sufficient weight to the way that public service broadcasting was adapting and driving the delivery of innovation in digitisation and new media.

The differences between the two reviews reflect changing economic conditions and the shifting political climate surrounding charter renewal. The focus of the reviews switched from searching for a future in which a plurality of competing providers would co-exist to a system with the BBC at its heart, diversity being provided by Channel 4 and competitive tendering for innovative digital and new media material. Paradoxically, the reviews demonstrated both the effects of a regulator able to influence the agenda and process of the review and, at the same time, a regulator that was vulnerable to political and market agendas. The wide participation in the process was encouraging, but the impact of the consultation on Ofcom's final recommendations was arguably less important than Ofcom's policy position and the views of the government of the day. In the case of the public service broadcasting review, Ofcom perhaps illustrates the fate of regulatory agencies charged with particular responses by Parliament which gather momentum as events (and, in this case, markets and technologies) change, and so the regulator finds itself using its expertise and flexibility by being tasked to respond to these events, engaging stakeholders and making recommendations as government policy is itself in flux.

Notes

1 Thanks to Greg Lowe for this point.
2 Thanks to Sylvia Harvey for this point.
3 As a self-governing public enterprise, the BBC is governed along the following lines: 'The Trust will act as the BBC's sovereign body and have ultimate responsibility for the licence fee. It will be responsible for outlining and monitoring the BBC's performance, in addition to approving the highest-level strategies and budgets, and holding the Executive Board to account for delivery of services. The

Executive Board will be responsible for the day-to-day management of the BBC, developing programme strategies, delivering the BBC's services and taking all detailed financial and operational decisions within the framework established by the Trust. It will be chaired by the Director General or, at the discretion of the Trust, a non-executive. It will contain a significant minority of non-executives who will support the executive members as "critical friends"' (Danby and Hart, 2010: 3).

4 Thus collaboration between the two bodies would be needed in certain cases. Danby and Hart (2010) illustrate the interaction between the regulatory powers of the BBC Trust and Ofcom by using the infamous case of Russell Brand and Jonathon Ross insulting the actor Andrew Saks in 2008, which led to 1,900 complaints being made to Ofcom: Ofcom invoked its Broadcasting Code to fine the BBC £150,000; the Trust then asked the BBC to issue an apology; Ofcom and the BBC Trust then agreed a Memorandum of Understanding to guide their mutual response to such cases in future (BBC, 2007).

5 Ofcom defines the competition for quality as a competitive marketplace, a plurality of both the production and commissioning of public service content and greater flexibility in the public service broadcasting system to cope with the changes that lie ahead in technologies and markets.

6 A significant aspect of the financial settlement given by charter renewal was the provision for an increase in the licence fee to cover the costs of the digital switchover (to enable all households to switch their televisions from analogue to digital sets). This put the BBC in the vanguard of digitisation, against the grain of Ofcom's first review, which recommended that this role be taken by the public service publisher, with the BBC as a lesser partner in the digital age. It was also significant for assigning part of the licence fee to a time-limited task required by government, thereby confusing the independence of the relation between the BBC and licence-fee payers.

7 Ofcom's qualitative research confirms its survey findings that people continue to trust the established public service broadcasters and value the quality and range of programming available. Both the survey and the qualitative research indicate that people distinguish between the personal and social value of media and that they place importance on both (Ofcom, 2008b).

8 Ofcom's research also indicates that the public continues to value public service broadcasting institutions. Perhaps this reflects what in behavioural finance is called mental accounting, whereby the public believes that choice is good yet also values tradition.

9 There has been a steady decline from 2004 (£3,025 million) to 2007 (for which Ofcom's estimate is £2,070 million). However, the fall is mainly due to reductions in the levels of production by public service broadcasters and the level of UK-originated production in non-public service broadcasters has remained at a similar level (8–10 per cent of the total). This raises questions about the capacity and intentions of commercial broadcasters to increase their spending on original UK content, although it also raises important questions for the BBC as its funding increased by 63 per cent between 1997 and 2010.

10 Until these events, governments had not taken portions of the licence fee for non-BBC activities, although from the 1920s to the early 1960s there were precedents for varying amounts of the licence fee to be so used. Therefore it is too strong to claim that top slicing is unprecedented, but reasonable to claim that recent governments have avoided this. Thanks to Richard Collins for this point.

6

MEDIA LITERACY

A new lease of life for an old policy

Increasingly, the media mediate between public and government, business and consumers, teachers and pupils, even among family members (Livingstone, 2009a). As work, education, commerce, social relations and leisure rely ever more on the media for their everyday functioning, greater attention is being paid to the ways in which the public could be enabled to undertake an effective, critical and creative engagement with the media and, thereby, the wider world. The convergence and diversification in media and communications technologies and services open up new opportunities for individuals, and yet these same changes also expose individuals to new risks. Given the pace, complexity and globalised nature of technological change, many would argue for a flexible co- or self-regulatory regime, central to which is the devolution of risk management to individuals, albeit one that is often couched in the discourse of 'empowerment' and 'consumer choice'. Indeed, from a citizen and consumer perspective, the same changes that spur the shift in regulatory burden from the state or firm to the individual are also those that increase the potential harms that individuals must work to avoid. In the new regulatory regime, individuals are expected to inform themselves, make their own choices in a complex technological environment, and bear the cost of any mismanagement of personal risk. They may also become, in a positive move, more positively, more responsible for creating their own opportunities.

The expectation that ordinary people can and will become informed decision makers, competent in maximising their opportunities and minimising their risks, is widely promoted in terms of 'literacy'. Each sector of society, it seems, has its own literacy – health literacy, financial literacy, environmental literacy, and also, media literacy. Each sector, too, is moving away from a reliance on the supposedly benevolent state authorities who traditionally have determined what is 'good' for people and from what they should be protected. Instead we are witnessing an emphasis on consumer education (often at point of sale), transparency in information provision (such as educational or hospital league tables ranking outcomes) and privatised customer care services (from helpdesks, call centres and insurance schemes). The parallel provision of mechanisms for independent oversight, accountability and redress is more variable and, following the UK's 2010 so-called 'bonfire of the quangos',[1] ever less certain in the future.

In relation to media and communications policy, the argument for media literacy runs as follows. We are witnessing the emergence of a complex consumer landscape that promises more opportunity and choice, whether or not this is delivered in practice, and that simultaneously affords more risk if poor decisions are made. To navigate this landscape, the public must become literate in the specific knowledge requirements of each sector. In a subsequent discursive twist, literacy is linked to citizenship: for instance, in the media and communications sector, there is growing emphasis not only on media literacy but also on 'digital citizenship', for people must not only navigate, evaluate and select from a digital array of information, but they also act, connect and participate in a digitally mediated society, and this invites a rethink of the familiar rights and responsibilities that have been long associated with citizenship.

Although 'media literacy' has become widely spoken about by multiple stakeholders from industry to civil society and from government ministers to global content providers, the term is far from being recently invented. Given a growing de- (or re-) regulatory shift in the media and communications sector, media literacy has become a shorthand way of pointing to the array of policies and initiatives that have been designed to bridge the gap between what people know about and what they may need to know about media in an increasingly liberalised and globalised environment. Does that make its promotion simply a neoliberal policy for media markets, or can media literacy have some wider and more positive implications for citizens?

Of course, media literacy has long referred to the public's knowledge of and competence in relation to the media, drawing on a field of study and a diverse arena for educational and community initiatives spanning print literacy, film literacy, advertising literacy and visual literacy, among others. Media education has been taught in schools in many countries for some decades, sometimes as part of a protectionist agenda (teaching children to critique and be wary, all the better to defend themselves against mass culture), sometimes as part of a creative agenda (teaching children to appreciate the cultural forms and genres, all the better to extend their aesthetic and critical understanding), and more recently as part of an empowerment agenda (teaching children to use the technical tools of self-expression, all the better to participate in modern society). The value of media literacy is also recognised by critical scholars and civil society advocates as part of a wider citizenship agenda, as a form of participation and inclusion, as a means of overcoming disadvantage, as a means for community empowerment or, more tactically, as a preferable alternative to technical or regulatory content restrictions.

Moreover, the history of media literacy has not been without contestation. Indeed, there is a lively legacy of struggle over definitions, methods and purposes (Bazalgette, 2001; Buckingham, 1998; Hobbs, 1998). Hobbs (2008) observes that the convergence of media and information technologies acts to make *more* rather than *less* evident the long-standing differences among advocates of the different approaches.[2] In the late 1990s, 'the "great debates" in media literacy centred on the tensions between *protectionist* educators concerned about the toxicity of media's cultural environment and others who emphasized student *empowerment*' (Hobbs, 2008: 437, emphasis added). Today, while the theme of protection persists among child psychologists, parenting groups and some content regulators,[3] most academic and policy commentators emphasise empowerment over protection, prioritising a view of the media as affording an expressive, cultural and participatory opportunity which brings significant benefits to those who are able to 'read' its codes and conventions and to use its tools and technologies.

Thus, although the mass media's power to (mis)represent the world to their audiences continues, there is increasing interest not only in their representational role but also in their mediating one. Once, everyday knowledge could be partitioned into distinct spheres relevant to school, work or home. Now it is converging in ways that challenge publics and public policy. The task of information searching, for instance, once addressed by providing access to public libraries (and associated experts) now intersects with teaching people to manage a computer interface (previously a rather specialised skill for the few). This task is undertaken in private at home (necessitating home-school or informal learning/lifelong programmes to reach into the home), and it must contend with a vastly expanded array of possible search results that are not pre-filtered according to editorial standards, commercial agendas or political biases. Take another example: the activity of creating communication was once taught to children in school as a matter of curricula knowledge (reading and writing) and regarded as sufficient for a lifetime. But today's adults must continually learn to communicate in new ways, though they are unlikely to return to school to do so and cannot be reliably reached in other ways – hence the haphazard reach of adult media literacy campaigns and the unequal take-up of e-government initiatives to submit online tax forms or blog with political candidates.

What people know about the media has become significant, not only in terms of the benefit of such knowledge to them as individuals. This knowledge is also being discursively and materially embedded in the principles, funding and practices of the private, public and third sector organisations that shape the media and communications environment. Furthermore, positively promoting this knowledge has become a policy priority. In a fast-changing digital environment, it can no longer be assumed that a formal childhood education plus adult experience of the world is sufficient to provide the skills and knowledge for a flexible, engaged, participatory and competitive society. The world, put simply, is changing too fast, and so policy makers concerned with public and private sector innovation require adults to be encouraged, if they are not already motivated, to commit to a process of continual learning and the updating of their skills and competences.

A puzzling task for the new regulator

Section 11 of the Communications Act 2003 accorded Ofcom a particular and, in the history of media regulation, an unprecedented, responsibility to 'promote media literacy' among the general public, and the consequences are being widely watched by governments around the world. Given rapid convergence across digital platforms, the focus of media literacy is widening to include not only the knowledge of audiences of audiovisual media but also the public engagement with a burgeoning range of information and communication technology (ICT). It was incorporated into the New Labour government's *Digital Britain* agenda, with the appointment of a Minister for Digital Inclusion and a Champion for Digital Inclusion, the review and development of schools' media education curriculum, and a greater requirement placed on broadcasters and content providers to educate the public in the emerging conventions of digital representation, persuasion and meaning creation.[4]

When first instituted, the requirement placed on Ofcom to promote media literacy was unclear to many within and beyond the regulator. As Ofcom's then Communications Director, Matt Peacock, put it in 2005:[5] 'It's a very diffuse concept. It's really hard to nail it down.' Not only was the concept difficult to explain to the public, the requirement to promote media literacy was also said to be unwelcome to the regulator, perhaps because it would be an unachievable task. Can a population really become truly media literate? And how much media literacy is enough? Complicating matters further, EC rules prevent the charging of the telecommunication companies for any activity beyond the basic cost of regulation also restricted the regulator. Thus initially, a half a million pounds per year were provided separately as a grant-in-aid to Ofcom by the DCMS, an amount that Ofcom subsequently added to significantly (from income derived from broadcasters) as media literacy ascended in Ofcom's ranking of its priorities.[6] Whatever the early history, since 2003 media literacy has been a visible strand of the regulator's activities, and with some success, for a period at least.

It is striking that statements about media literacy by Ofcom and many other organisations begin with matters of definition, given their surprisingly casual regard for, say, the distinction between citizen and consumer or self-regulation and co-regulation. At first, it seemed that for Ofcom, the government departments to which it is responsible[7] and the stakeholders with which it engages, the simpler the definition the better. Perhaps to ward off the ridicule of the press, in a 2002 parliamentary debate MP Kim Howells summarised media literacy in layman's language simply as a policy designed 'to help everyone manage the new media environment more safely'. Unsurprisingly, in the days when the Communications Act was being formulated, the nature of media literacy had been little debated outside academia and educational circles. The term hardly tripped off the tongue and in early policy discussions eyebrows were often raised when it was introduced. Moreover, Section 11 of the Act did not define media literacy, seemingly leaving it to the regulator to shed light on its meaning. However, the Act did state that media literacy should, to paraphrase a little,

> ... bring about or encourage others to bring about ...
>
> 1 a better public understanding of the nature and characteristics of material published by means of the electronic media;
> 2 a better public awareness and understanding of the processes by which such material is selected, or made available, for publication by such means;
> 3 the development of a better public awareness of the available systems by which access to material published by means of the electronic media is or can be regulated;
> 4 the development of a better public awareness of the available systems by which persons to whom such material is made available may control what is received and of the uses to which such systems may be put; and
> 5 the development and use of technologies and systems for regulating access to such material, and for facilitating control over what material is received, that are both effective and easy to use.[8]

According to the Act, media literacy encompasses understanding the nature of content and the selections that publication entails, plus an awareness and provision of effective tools by which to manage personal access to content. A protectionist agenda drives such a conception of media literacy, contrasting with the ambitions generally held for print literacy, namely, that people should be able both to read effectively and critically – whether to complete their tax form, to critique an election manifesto or to appreciate Shakespeare – and to write creatively so as to participate fully in society.

However, as befits an institution operating in the public sphere, Ofcom's first action in 2004 was to hold a public consultation on the definition of media literacy, receiving 94 responses from industry, public bodies, academics and diverse others. Ofcom's initial ideas (as set out in the consultation document) were rather unambitious:

So media literacy is a range of skills including the ability to access, analyse, evaluate and produce communications in a variety of forms. Or put simply, the ability to operate the technology to find what you are looking for, to understand that material, to have an opinion about it and where necessary to respond to it. With these skills people will be able to exercise greater choice and be able better to protect themselves and their families from harmful or offensive materials. (Ofcom, 2004b: 4)

In the first sentence, Ofcom restates the simple yet effective definition framed by the National Leadership Conference on Media Literacy a decade earlier (Aufderheide, 1993) and widely adopted since – the ability 'to access, analyse, evaluate and communicate messages in a variety of forms' (Livingstone, 2003: 3). However, the restatement waters this down considerably. Ability becomes 'a range of skills' (a translation that enables a quantitative evaluation of policy effectiveness). Access (which could include complex navigational competences) is reduced to 'operate the technology'. Communicating is qualified as 'responding' to an externally initiated message and only 'where necessary'. Last, the purposes of media literacy are radically scaled back to centre on consumer choice and protection from harm. However, the many consultation responses received urged a more ambitious approach, and although the definition that emerged combined 'analyse and evaluate' into 'understand', it nonetheless captured the importance of the critical and creative dimensions of media literacy more effectively than the Act. Ofcom (2004c) thus concluded that 'media literacy is the ability to access, understand and create communications in a variety of contexts'.[9]

Also consistent with the new regulatory regime, Ofcom then commissioned an academic literature review on theory and evidence for media literacy among adults (Livingstone et al., 2005) and children (Buckingham, 2005). There followed a series of 'audits' – repeated national surveys to assess the extent of adult and child media literacy – that were made available on their website. Compared with the previous dearth of media literacy-related research or activities, especially regarding adults, and compared with the low esteem in which children's media education was often held, Ofcom's actions brought a welcome prominence to the media literacy agenda. Most positively, in its review of its media literacy work from 2004 to 2008, Ofcom (2008d) moved away from the protectionist logic of the Act to support the empowerment approach, stating that:

Ofcom's work to promote media literacy is intended:

- to give people the opportunity and motivation to develop competence and confidence to participate in digital society; and
- to inform and empower people to manage their own media activity (both consumption and creation).

The contrast with the definition of media literacy from the DCMS – which has funded Ofcom's media literacy work from the outset – is interesting, for this offers possibly the least ambitious expectations of the public:

> Media literacy is the ability to use a range of media and be able to understand the information received. At a higher level, it includes the ability to question, analyse and evaluate that information. (DCMS, n.d.)

Here the complexity of the digital network society is reduced to a one-way information resource; only two of Ofcom's three elements (access/use and understand/evaluate, but not create or communicate) are included; and only those (unspecified) who attain a 'higher level' are expected to gain the necessary critical literacy to judge the authenticity or trustworthiness of information obtained.[10] All are reduced to passive mass audiences, in short, and those at the lower level will also remain uncritical audiences. At a time when commercial influences over content are increasing (via product placement, advertising, sponsorship, advergames, marketing to children, etc.), the political influences over content are diversifying, and public input into content is threatened, such low expectations for public levels of media literacy stand out.

However, the promotion of media literacy is an international trend, and it is by no means for the UK alone to define it. In the USA, the Federal Communications Commission recognised a lack of digital literacy, along with economic disadvantage, as a barrier to the adoption of new technologies, making the promotion of literacy in the digital age as important to national economic competitiveness as print literacy was to the industrial age (Horrigan, 2010; see also Clyburn, 2010). Internationally, UNESCO published a Media Education Kit (January 2007) and is developing information literacy indicators for cross-national evaluations (Frau-Meigs, 2007; Frau-Meigs and Torrent, 2009). Mention of digital, information or internet literacy has begun to appear at the Internet Governance Forum, with a dynamic coalition on media and information literacy being formally established in 2009, as well as in the more or less developed activities of many countries (e.g. ACMA, 2009; Media Awareness Network, 2010). Now instantiated in Europe's 2010 Digital Agenda (European Commission, 2010), the argument that everyone must become literate in new media in the information society also took some establishing in Europe.

Definitional diversity in Europe

> Media, especially new digital technologies, involve more Europeans in a world of sharing, interaction and creation ... However, people who cannot use new media like social networks or digital TV will find it hard to interact with and take part in the world around them. We must make sure everyone is media literate

so nobody is left out. Citizens are being talked to all the time, but can they talk back? If they can use the media in a competent and creative way we would take a step towards a new generation of democratic participation. (Viviane Reding, European Commission Information Society and Media Commissioner, European Commission, 2009)

Media literacy came to prominence as part of the Lisbon Agenda, the European strategy for a globally competitive information society adopted in 2000 and re-launched in 2005 with the aim of getting European citizens and businesses online by 2010. Sceptical voices suggest that the Lisbon Agenda has failed,[11] but it is noteworthy that, given considerable contestation among public, private and civil society actors, 'media literacy' emerged as a useful point of consensus – or, it may be argued, compromise – between consumer protection (and market restriction) and empowerment (and market liberalisation). For its critics, the concept is sufficiently vague and open in its talk of empowerment to please everyone while scarcely tying down any particular, expensive or restrictive requirements. For its advocates, media literacy is the only sensible way forward for a converged media environment in which a skilled workforce, a competitive market, and an empowered citizenry are all crucial.

Building on the work of the High Level Expert Group on Media Literacy, the European Commission conducted a public consultation on the definition of media literacy and the means of implementing policy to advance it, in autumn 2006 (European Commission, n.d.). The definition proposed in that consultation questionnaire bore a notable resemblance to that of Ofcom (and the earlier USA's National Leadership Conference) but downplayed the element of creating messages, positioning communication as a personal rather than a collective or civic matter:

... the ability to access, analyse and evaluate the power of images, sounds and messages which we are now being confronted with on a daily basis and are an important part of our contemporary culture, as well as to communicate competently in media available on a personal basis.

However, revealing the potential of public consultation processes to widen public debate, the conclusion fairly drawn from the 106 formal responses received from 26 countries was the importance of adding 'the ability to create and communicate messages as it is considered essential in enabling people to make effective use of media in the exercise of their democratic rights and civic responsibilities' (European Commission, 2007).[12] It was then written into the Audiovisual Media Services Directive (European Parliament and the Council, 2007), which was notable since the regulatory framework it replaced contained no reference to media literacy. The Television without Frontiers Directive (European Commission, 1989) addresses consumer matters, especially for children, through top-down rule making:

Member States shall take appropriate measures to ensure that television broadcasts by broadcasters under their jurisdiction do not include any programmes which might seriously impair the physical, mental or moral development of minors, in particular programmes that involve pornography or gratuitous violence. (Article 22)

Although this Article survives intact (as Article 27) in the Audiovisual Media Services Directive,[13] the revised Directive also refers to media literacy, particularly in its treatment of converged and future audiovisual services (European Parliament and the Council, 2010). Nonetheless, media literacy was defined rather narrowly, certainly by comparison with Ofcom's statement on Strategy and Priorities for the Promotion of Media Literacy which included critical and creative literacies (e.g. Ofcom, 2004b, para. 14):

Media literacy refers to skills, knowledge and understanding that allow consumers to use media effectively and safely. Media-literate people will be able to exercise informed choices, understand the nature of content and services and take advantage of the full range of opportunities offered by new communications technologies. They will be better able to protect themselves and their families from harmful or offensive material. (European Parliament and the Council, 2007, para. 37)

As the same paragraph continues, as regards the internet, it is responsible (protectionist) rather than emancipatory (or empowerment) uses that are of concern:

Internet training aimed at children from a very early age, including sessions open to parents, or organisation of national campaigns aimed at citizens, involving all communications media, to provide information on using the internet responsibly.

Critics might observe that, notwithstanding the mention of 'citizens', media literacy here seems individualised, prioritising consumers and consumer choice over citizens and citizens' rights, and prioritising protection over participation. This significantly protectionist conception contrasts with the empowerment focus advocated by UNESCO, which states that:

Empowerment of people through information and media literacy is an important prerequisite for fostering equitable access to information and knowledge, and building inclusive knowledge societies. Information and media literacy enables people to interpret and make informed judgments as users of information and media, as well as to become skilful creators and producers of information and media messages in their own right. (UNESCO, n.d.)

Interestingly, more recent pronouncements from the European Commission have taken an increasingly wide approach, possibly influenced by the

European Media Literacy Charter (Bachmair and Bazalgette, 2007), the Council of Europe's human rights-focused Recommendation on Empowering Children in the New Information and Communications Environment (2006) and related initiatives. The European Commission's Recommendation (20/8/09) on 'media literacy in the digital environment for a more competitive audiovisual and content industry and an inclusive knowledge society' (Europa, 2009a) reiterates Ofcom's definition (and that of the USA's National Leadership Conference before it):

Media literacy relates to the ability to access the media, to understand and critically evaluate different aspects of the media and media content and to create communications in a variety of contexts. (Europa, 2009a: para. 11)

But in explaining why media literacy matters, an ambitious set of purposes is outlined, going significantly beyond the definitions of both Ofcom and the Audiovisual Media Services Directive and combining public and private sector interests and emphasising:

- The ability of European citizens to make informed and diversified choices as media consumers would contribute to the competitiveness of the European audiovisual and content industry (para. 10).
- How these contribute to 'the objectives set for the European Union at the Lisbon European Council and in the i2010 initiative in particular regarding a more competitive knowledge economy, while contributing to a more inclusive information society' (para. 6).[14]
- This includes 'enhancing awareness in the European audiovisual heritage and cultural identities and increasing knowledge and interest in audiovisual heritage and recent European cultural works' (para. 14).
- Further, it 'is a matter of inclusion and citizenship in today's information society. It is a fundamental skill not only for young people but also for adults and elderly people, parents, teachers and media professionals ... Media literacy is today regarded as one of the key pre-requisites for an active and full citizenship in order to prevent and diminish risks of exclusion from community life' (para. 15).
- Thus media literacy enables 'the expression of diverse opinions and ideas, in different languages, representing different groups, in and across societies [and so] has a positive impact on the values of diversity, tolerance, transparency, equity and dialogue' (para. 16).
- And, most grandly, 'Democracy depends on the active participation of citizens to the life of their community and media literacy would provide the skills they need to make sense of the daily flow of information disseminated through new communication technologies' (para. 17).

These wider ambitions are, we suggest, coming to the fore not only in Europe but also in Britain, challenging the narrow endorsement of media literacy as the 'sweetener' for consumer advocates of an otherwise neoliberal and deregulatory policy.

Today our viewers and listeners are far more empowered. Digital television, the internet and increasingly broadband is putting more choice in the hands of the user. As a regulator, we will reflect that, welcome and encourage it. There can no longer be a place for a regulator ... determining what people 'ought' to have. (Carter, 2003b)

Although it is possible to state an ambitious policy in simple terms, promoting media literacy is no simple undertaking. However, the political payoff is substantial: in so far as a media-literate public is attainable, it may become defensible to support a policy of market deregulation, cutting the bureaucratic 'red tape' of consumer protection, content labelling, customer redress, child safety, data privacy protection and platform-specific content regulation.

As viewed by Ofcom's first Chief Executive, Stephen Carter, the value of media literacy was that it permitted the regulator to roll back interventionist market regulation, encouraging a voluntary stakeholder collaboration in the interests of consumer choice. Such a neoliberal policy was held to be important to protect the UK's creative industry in relation to broadcasting, as was evident in Britain's attempts to reduce the regulatory strictures built into the Audiovisual Media Services Directive. It was also held to be vital in relation to the internet not only for reasons of freeing the market, but also for practical reasons – the global internet is certainly hard to regulate at a national level (Livingstone, 2011). As the UK's then Secretary of State for Culture, Media and Sport, Tessa Jowell, stated: 'if people can take greater personal responsibility for what they watch and listen to, that will in itself lessen the need for regulatory intervention' (*The Daily Mail*, 21/1/2004, p. 23). Ofcom concurred: Robin Foster, Ofcom's Partner for Strategy and Market Developments in 2005, said: 'We will have to learn to rely more on markets than ever before. And we need to rely more on individual consumers and on companies exercising responsibility in those markets, with increasing emphasis on self-regulation and co-regulation.'[15]

Reliance on individuals means that they must become more responsible, and more informed. In its public consultation on media literacy, Ofcom (2004b: 5) stated: 'With increasing complexity of technology and wider media choice people will have to take more responsibility for what they and their children see and hear on screen and online ... We will all become gatekeepers for content coming into our homes.' In its response to the 2006 European Commission consultation on media literacy, Ofcom stated that 'Media literacy is increasingly becoming a fundamental component of European and national regulatory policy agendas in the communications sector, especially as developments in the creation and distribution of content challenge current approaches to regulation in this area'. Media literacy, one may conclude, is being co-opted by a neoliberal politics for reasons that are quite distinct from those for which academics and educators have long advocated it. For the particular challenge of managing online content too, media literacy shows a viable way forward:

The independent regulator, Ofcom, does not regulate content on the internet, but does have a statutory duty to promote media literacy under the Communications Act 2003. In pursuit of that duty, Ofcom has been working to raise people's awareness of how to use web browsers, electronic programme guides and other tools in order to navigate safely and effectively. (David Lammy, Minister for Culture, Media and Sport, in Hansard, 2007)

In short, it can be argued that media literacy has risen to prominence on the policy agenda because increasing consumer knowledge and awareness advances the goal of economic competition by legitimating the reduction of top-down regulatory intervention in a converging and globalising media market (e.g. by relaxing the restrictions on product placement) while simultaneously sustaining a promise (little evaluated in outcome) of 'empowerment' to the public.

A newly responsible, self-regulating audience is, it appears, being called for in these proclamations (Ouellette and Hay, 2008), a key new player (albeit more spoken for than heard) in the emerging multi-stakeholder regime regulating twenty-first-century media and communications policy. This implied audience represents a vital component of efforts to reduce state regulation and increase industry self-regulation (e.g. through the promotion of codes of conduct, editorial principles, technical solutions for the user, access controls, notice and take down procedures, etc.). The costs for the individual in this regime shift are little articulated, although Ofcom's 2006 European Commission consultation response (Ofcom, 2006c: 4) does acknowledge that, 'these schemes rely for their effectiveness on consumers actively taking measures to protect themselves and their families'. But if they do not – if people do not become dutiful and sensible consumers – it is unclear who will bear the responsibility for any adverse consequences. It seems likely, from previous research on knowledge gaps, the digital divide and cycles of disadvantage that the burden of risk will fall most heavily on those who are least able to bear it. As Beck (1986/2005) argues, the adverse risk consequences of deregulation, surely including those of digital illiteracy, fall unevenly.

That media literacy offers a rationale for deregulation may be demonstrated by widening the lens to encompass other forms of literacy. It is not just media literacy that has risen up the policy agenda. A search of the UK press revealed references to print literacy, financial literacy, scientific literacy, ICT/computer literacy, emotional literacy, spatial literacy, Gaelic literacy, political literacy, technical literacy, film literacy, media literacy, Catalan literacy and theological literacy; a little further searching added ethical literacy, environmental literacy, information literacy, health literacy and critical literacy. Often, an explicit link is made between individual responsibility and market liberalisation (Livingstone, 2008a). It seems that literacy policies enable the broader shift from direct control by government to governance through 'action at a distance' (Rose, 1990). Countering this with a call for more government or regulation may not seem a promising alternative. However, one critical response could be to resist minimal or reductive definitions of (media) literacy, as the more readily people are shown to have sufficient media literacy (if this can be specified), the more readily deregulation is legitimated. Moreover, the more ambitious the definition, the more public (or commercial) resources must be devoted to ensuring all segments of the population meet that definition (since a policy that embeds inequality or penalises the already vulnerable will always lack credibility).

The politics of media literacy

Looking back over decades, research and policy regarding media literacy can be characterised by three main features. First, except to those involved, it has been marginal even in relation to media production and regulation, let alone in wider societal debates regarding employment, inclusion or democracy. Second, it has been focused primarily on the needs of children and young people and, since these are best addressed in school, media literacy has been closely tied to media education, with the latter providing the means of implementing the aspirations of the former. Third, it has never transcended a fundamental polarisation between the protectionists (who regard media literacy as a defence against the harms of the media) and the empowerment advocates (who regard media literacy as a domain for creative self-expression, communal action and cultural heritage).

Today, none of these three features defines the agenda, though the legacy of each persists. First, media literacy is prominent in the speeches of ministers, included in a wide array of national and international policy statements concerning the economy, democracy and 'the information society'. Most significantly, media literacy is not regarded solely as a tool by which to understand the media themselves but, as with print literacy before it, as a tool with which to engage the world at large. Second, while children and young people are still important to media literacy policy and practice, Ofcom has devoted considerable resources to promoting the media literacy of the population more generally. Moreover, children's discursive position has shifted from that of the vulnerable in need of protection to that of the pioneer, the digital native leading the way into the future (Helsper and Eynon, 2010). Furthermore, although supporting children and ensuring equality of opportunity remains a priority for many governments, the new challenge is to include the entire adult population, especially groups such as older people and people on a low income, within the scope of media literacy activities.

Third, the polarisation between protection and empowerment no longer maps on to the political division between right and left, or in terms of communication theory, onto Lazarsfeld's (1941) distinction between administrative (using knowledge to support established interests) and critical (i.e. independent of established interests) scholarship. Critical and administrative agendas have converged on prioritising an empowerment discourse, at times leaving it ambiguous as to just why media literacy is being advocated. For example, a charity-funded centre to encourage diasporic communities to use the internet may intend to further a social democratic agenda and yet be co-opted by a neoliberal government promoting competitive workforce skills or a 'self-help' ethos. The adoption of critical ambitions by administrative discourses makes these lines hard to draw. On the other hand, the enthusiastic adoption of the language of digital literacy or digital participation by community activists working with disadvantaged or minority ethnic young people has surely attracted new attention and funding sources to some long-marginalised initiatives. And, in the face of government or regulator advocacy for a minimal, functional definition of media literacy, critical scholars are proving successful in countering with more ambitious expectations for informed and participatory citizens, expectations which it is discursively hard for a government to disavow (e.g. Bazalgette, 2001; Buckingham, 2007; Hobbs, 2008; Jenkins, 2006; Kress, 2003; Snyder, 2007).

For government policies on media literacy, the already widespread array of bottom-up and community initiatives represents a fortunate basis on which to build. But this means that critical researchers and third sector bodies must ask whether their co-option in this manner represents an equally fortunate chance for increased funding and visibility or, instead, a risk that their agendas will become distorted while, inadvertently, they may find themselves supporting a deregulatory policy that, in turn, individualises risk (Beck, 1986/2005). This risk leads some political economists of communication apparently to refuse support for media literacy. For example, McChesney (1996: para.5) regards media literacy as distracting cultural critics from questions of power, for what matters more than what people do with the technology is 'who will control the technology and for what purpose?', hence the absence of media or digital literacy from McChesney's Media Reform Movement's public interest agenda (Freepress, 2009). Since emancipatory purposes are now claimed on all sides, and activities developed for one purpose are readily re-described in the interests of another,[16] we would still ask: can this work both ways, so that the undoubted increase in public and private sector resources and effort mobilised by media and digital literacy policy can be harnessed to achieve outcomes on the critical agenda?

From media literacy to digital participation

> The necessary education, skills and media literacy programmes to allow everyone in society to benefit from the digital revolution will be a central part of the Digital Britain work and key to our success. (DCMS and BERR, 2009: 5)

Nothing stands still in the discourses of either policy or academia. Along with the emergence of discourses of digital natives, digital inclusion and *Digital Britain*, it seemed – at least for the remainder of the New Labour government – that digital literacy was overtaking media literacy, and that digital participation was overtaking both. Long-standing ambivalence about literacy (as a difficult term, and as elitist in so far as it stigmatises its polar opposite as 'illiterate') encouraged an alternative – participation and, additionally, citizenship (as in the phrase, 'digital citizenship'). Both these alternative terms are simultaneously ordinary and yet ambitious: they are in everyday use, inclusive rather than exclusive, and yet exciting – democracy's very hopes rest on the participation of its citizens. At a European level, Commissioner Reding marked this discursive transition, from media literacy to digital participation, in a speech in August 2009:

> We must make sure everyone is media literate so nobody is left out. Citizens are being talked to all the time, but can they talk back? If they can use the media in a competent and creative way we would take a step towards a new generation of democratic participation. (Quoted in Europa, 2009b)

And in her first speech as European Commissioner for the Digital Agenda, Neelie Kroes put digital literacy as the second of three key points (along with high-speed internet access for all and the removal of barriers to demand) for the period 2010–15 in her plan to 'keep Europe at the forefront of twenty-first century economic and social developments' (Kroes, 2010).[17] In the USA also, the discourse was changing. Launching the National Digital Literacy Programme as part of the National Broadband Plan, Federal Communications Commissioner Mignon Clyburn's speech (Clyburn, 2010) opened by stressing the importance of the market agenda of widespread broadband adoption, within which digital literacy – identified as a barrier – was defined rather narrowly as an individual and instrumental skill: 'Many Americans lack the basic understanding of how to locate trustworthy content, how to protect personal information, and how to safely interact online' (Clyburn, 2010: 2).

Yet throughout her talk and, especially, by the end, imperatives of inclusion and democratic participation came to the fore (as guided by the ambitions of the print literacy agenda): 'Nothing can open more doors for a person than literacy. But knowing how to read is no longer sufficient to be "literate" in the 21st century. Basic literacy must be supplemented with digital literacy' (Clyburn, 2010: 4).

In the UK, the government's report on *Digital Britain* (BIS and DCMS, 2009), led by Lord Stephen Carter[18] after he stepped down as Ofcom's CEO, made a key move away from media literacy by observing, with some validity, that media literacy was 'a technocratic and specialist term understood by policy makers but not really part of everyday language' (p. 40). The *Digital Britain* report argued that 'it is now vital to move away from media literacy as a discrete subject and term and to move towards a National Plan for Digital Participation' (BIS and DCMS, 2010: 40). Echoing the early difficulties in defining media literacy, digital participation was then defined, unfortunately, in tautological terms as:

Increasing the reach, breadth and depth of digital technology use across all sections of society, to maximise digital participation and the economic and social benefits it can bring. (BIS and DCMS, 2010: 41)

Nonetheless, the proposal was to support 'the formation of a Consortium of Stakeholders, led by Ofcom, to drive Digital Participation. Funding would be made available of up to £12m over three years from the Universal Service provision announced in Budget 2009' (BIS and DCMS, 2010: 42), this representing a very considerable increase on Ofcom's original media literacy budget. Subsequently taken forward in the *Digital Britain* White Paper, the national plan was proposed in March 2010 and built on the coincidence of interests in maximising use of the internet across government, industry and the public. For citizens, this interest was described as inhering in 'financial savings, access to formal and informal learning opportunities, employment potential, improved salary prospects and the many other advantages – economic, social and cultural' (BIS and DCMS, 2010: 5). But such instrumental purposes were supplemented by the recognition of the value to individuals of 'civic and democratic engagement activities, self-publishing and content creation ... the growth of online communities of interest, cultural understanding and social capital, formal and informal learning opportunities and employment opportunities'(ibid.: 8).

However cynical one may be of government, this appears to be an acceptable list and arguably it now behoves academics to make the effort to amplify it. After all, surely the grandest vision for media literacy would encompass, first, equality of opportunity in the knowledge society, which requires overcoming digital inequality and exclusion; second, active and informed participation in a revitalised democracy which requires critical engagement with the mediated public sphere; and third, self-actualisation for individuals and communities, achieved through enabling the lifelong learning, cultural expression and personal fulfilment that is everyone's right in a civilised society (Livingstone, 2003). Nonetheless it is disheartening that, when launched by the Digital Inclusion Minister, Stephen Timms, the emphasis was more on e-government (i.e. the top-down electronic delivery of state objectives to individuals) than participation by citizens:

> Being online is crucial for participation in the 21st century society – the internet unlocks a wealth of information and services, giving people more choice in life and access to a range of education, health and financial opportunities. (BIS and DCMS, 2010: para. 6)

This reading of the plan has been reinforced by European developments. For example, at the same time as the above (spring 2010), the Internal Market and Consumer Protection Committee (IMCO) of the European Parliament called for a European Charter of users' rights and obligations in the information society. Further, the draft Opinion on the Digital Agenda (to replace the Lisbon i2010 Agenda from 2010) focused on matters of copyright, privacy and vulnerable users' rights in relation to digital content, also calling on the European Commission to 'promote digital literacy and work towards making as many government online services as possible available to consumers' (European Parliament, 2010). Again, an official, top-down vision for consumers emerges rather than a participatory, alternative or bottom-up vision of 'participation' for citizens.

From principles to practice

In fieldwork conducted at the end of 2008, Ofcom (2009a) reported that only 41 per cent of UK citizens had registered to vote, 26 per cent had signed a petition, 13 per cent had contacted a government department or local council, 7 per cent had contacted an MP or councillor, and 2 per cent had taken part in a protest or demonstration in the past year. Having internet access at home would make all of these activities more likely, suggesting that digital participation, itself resting on digital literacy, can enhance wider civic participation. Encouragingly, Ofcom's Adult Media Literacy Audit conducted in 2006 and repeated in 2008 (Ofcom, 2006b, 2008d, 2009b) found media literacy to be on the increase. Not only did basic access to digital media increase, but so too did use of online information sources (e.g. for health). Further, more people than before checked on the reliability of a website and more were critical of the quality or trustworthiness of broadcast and online content. However, while only a minority lacked the confidence to use creative tools on digital platforms, the majority still had not done this in practice.[19] Interestingly, although young adults (so-called 'digital natives') had the greatest confidence and use of digital media, their critical knowledge of media funding sources was the lowest, and by comparison with their knowledge of the broadcast environment, people of all ages were unclear about how online and mobile content was regulated.[20] Moreover, from the subsequent Media Literacy Audits conducted in 2010 and 2011, evidence of increasingly levels of media literacy is now less clear, even suggesting that a plateau has been reached (Livingstone and Wang, 2011).

Can media literacy for an entire population be achieved at the level hoped for? As with any other form of public education – from print literacy to health education or financial understanding or scientific knowledge – media literacy policy generally is under-resourced in its delivery and uneven in its implementation, while media literacy itself is unequal in its adoption by those of differential social status (and so risks exacerbating rather than reducing knowledge gaps), inconsistently translated by individuals into everyday practices (the traditional 'attitude–behaviour' problem), and, intriguingly, still unproven as a strategy for either empowerment or protection. At present, these difficulties are positioned by stakeholders on all sides as challenges – providing a rationale for increasing investment, especially by leveraging private sector and media industry input as well as that from the public sector, and justifying a strategy that targets resources more on socially and/or digitally disadvantaged than advantaged groups.[21]

As a result the challenge remains to identify what media literacy the public needs, across all segments of the population and all sectors of society, a challenge that has been exacerbated by rapid technological and social change. Crucially, the next step – namely, instituting initiatives to address these needs – has proven to be extraordinarily expensive, highly contested and, as yet, largely unevaluated in terms of outcomes. To delimit its task, Ofcom's (2004c) Statement on *Strategies and Priorities for the Promotion of Media Literacy* originally stated:

We will work with stakeholders to help focus on the present and future media literacy needs of all members of society. There are many stakeholders who have a key role to play in the promotion of media literacy skills, knowledge and understanding in both adults and children. These include content producers, broadcasters, platform and network providers, educators, government departments, parents, children's charities and other organisations. Our principal role will be to provide leadership and leverage to promote media literacy. (Ofcom, 2004c: 2)

Leadership and leverage, while perhaps all that Ofcom could undertake, hardly met the agenda of expectations building up. Thus media literacy initiatives remained what the (Labour) government's *Digital Britain* report of 2009 described as: 'very fragmented', notwithstanding 'a large amount of resources being dedicated to this work ... They lacked a higher strategic vision or indeed the appropriate aligning of the initiatives to ensure that they were being efficiently delivered and that they were complementing each other' (BIS and DCMS, 2009: 40). Furthermore, it is unclear that the subsequent vision of digital participation could offer an improvement, even had it been taken up by the Coalition government. Notably, *Digital Britain* advocated the affordances of digital media as a solution by which to right many wrongs in society, from civic apathy to a low-skilled workforce, conflicted communities, an impoverished underclass, a struggling education system, and a decline in the competitive standing of UK plc. Yet while the ambitions of media literacy advocates were often substantial, the ambition of delivering all of the above on £4 million per year was surely always unrealistic.

From individual skills to social capabilities

The Audiovisual Media Services Directive not only requires member states to improve media literacy among their national populations, but also to report every three years on the levels attained (Article 33). This has necessitated the development of an assessment tool and associated indicators, as reported by the European Association for Viewers' Interests (2009). As with many policy statements in this field, their report begins with the definitional issues, notwithstanding the risk of 'paralysis by analysis' (2009: 6). Reflecting on its authors' intellectual, critical and third sector expertise, it then distinguishes individual competences from environmental factors, arguing that both are central to media literacy. While individual competences form the focus of all the policy definitions above, the inclusion of environmental factors (such as media education, media literacy policy, media industry, civil society, communication rights, availability of media, freedom of expression and degree of pluralism) fits with the critical analysis of media literacy not as an inert skill or the property of an individual but rather as a social, contextualised capability (Garnham, 1999; Mansell, 2002).

First, literacy depends on legibility – one can only read, or contribute to, a 'legible' environment, with rules and conventions understood by users. As Woolgar (1996) and others have argued, technologies are also text, and the institutional purposes and culture, organisational norms and structures, and communicative design and intent are all embedded in the very construction of the interface, as is also an implicit conception of the user – what they know, don't know, can and cannot do, take for granted or need to learn. The more impenetrable, opaque or ill-designed the text or interface – for example, if trust markers (e.g. source, date, funding, purpose) from the content, or distinctions between types of content (public/sponsored, edited/ unedited) are blurred – the more users will struggle (Livingstone, 2008b). To point the finger at users for lacking literacy when it is the texts that are illegible is, surely, inappropriate.

Second, literacy depends on the social context. As Buckingham puts it, 'literacy is a phenomenon that is only realized in and through social practices of various kinds, and it therefore takes different forms in different social and cultural contexts' (2007: 44). Indeed, the environmental approach echoes the critique from New Literacy Studies (Gee, 2003; Kress, 2003; Snyder, 2007; Street, 1984) of purely 'autonomous' models of literacy, those which assume literacy skills can be defined independent of any context, as the universal properties of individuals. Looking back over this chapter, such a critique helps us understand why media literacy – conceived as an individual skill – has proven so hard to define, since the imagined contexts of use, though generally unstated, are diverse. As should be equally clear, in seeking to omit, or include, such elements as critical evaluation or creative communication, such definitions are political – they rely on ideological assumptions about how people ought to act in the world, including in and through a mediated world. Should that be receptive or productive, acquiescent or critical, individualised or collective?

Definitions, clearly, are far from neutral. Hence Street challenges the autonomous model with an alternative, 'ideological model' that 'offers a more culturally sensitive view of literacy practices as they vary from one context to another' (Street, 2003: 77), and for whom the normative goal is rather a media-literate society in which collective capabilities to use media technologies underpin critical judgements, inclusive participation and concerted action in the public interest. It is, Street argues, 'not valid to suggest that "literacy" can be "given" neutrally and then its "social" effects only experienced afterwards' (2003: 78). Indeed, literacy, as with all forms of knowledge, is:

… always embedded in social practices, such as those of a particular job market or a particular educational context and the effects of learning that particular literacy will be dependent on those particular contexts. Literacy, in this sense, is always contested, both its meanings and its practices, hence particular versions of it are always 'ideological', they are always rooted in a particular world-view and in a desire for that view of literacy to dominate and to marginalize others. (Street, 2003: 77–8)

In this chapter, we have sought to identify the particular worldview prioritised by contemporary media literacy policy, characterising it as driven primarily by a neoliberal desire to promote competitive markets and roll back regulation (Mansell, 2011); hence the focus on digital access, workplace skills and skills than reduced state costs, say, for e-government or e-health. Increasingly, however, we have also seen the very openness of the conception of media literacy permits efforts to enhance some critical skills (especially if these facilitate individual protection against content harms or commercial messaging, in turn enabling reduced content regulation) and some participatory or creative skills as part of a wider shift towards digital participation. Whether the attention and resources to be devoted to digital participation and digital citizenship policies will really enhance levels of social inclusion and participation remains unclear, especially as a culture of severe financial restraint is increasingly characterising public policy.

As Street also implies, it behoves us, finally, to ask what kinds of literacy are being marginalised in current policy. Here there are many candidates – Watkins (2009) calls for a recognition of young black men's 'literacy' in relation to music, using lyric writing and rap music to counter – or at least express anger regarding – the marginalisation of their identity. Gee (2003) advocates games literacy to provide alternative routes to learning for those who have been failed by the formal education system. Seiter (2005) challenges teachers to recognise the media-imbued knowledge with which children first enter school, only to have this knowledge scathingly rejected as invalid. At a grass-roots level, this critical or social approach to literacies, plural, is not without influence. Indeed, it is often exactly at the moment when top-down governmental initiatives must be translated into local practices (online centres, classrooms, communication activities) that a more diversified and contextualised approach to literacy will be recognised as necessary. But at the level of national and international policy statements, the 'autonomous' model prevails.

This makes it all the more interesting, then, that the European Commission study proposed assessment criteria for member states so that they may meet the reporting obligation imposed on them by the Audiovisual Media Services Directive that includes environmental factors. The study finds (European Association for Viewers' Interests, 2009: 78) that 'there is a discernible correlation between media literacy levels in individuals and media policies and measures implemented by institutions' and, further, that 'many of the best performing countries are highly developed in terms of democracy, infrastructure, and social and economic welfare'. In other words, public provision in general supports the environmental resources for media literacy and these environmental resources in particular support individual skills. Empirically, as well as theoretically and ideologically, therefore, there is reason to broaden the focus on media literacy beyond that of individual skills. As the report concludes:

The relationship between an individual's skills and Environmental Factors is two-way – a more favourable environmental context enhances individual media literacy levels, and the existence of media literate citizens compels the development of coordinated policies and actions. However, the role of individual inclination becomes determinant probably only after a certain threshold of support for the advancement of media literacy has been reached. (European Association for Viewers' Interests, 2009: 78)[22]

Conclusion

Governments and regulators in other countries have observed Ofcom's forays into the field of media literacy with interest, for the Communications Act 2003 made media literacy a matter of media regulation instead of, as has been more usual in countries where it is actively promoted, a matter for ministries of education to address as they think fit. Thus a critical gaze at Ofcom's practice was merited – especially given its tendency to subordinate emancipatory to protectionist objectives on the one hand, and deregulatory objectives on the other. This chapter has traced how Ofcom's work on media literacy was shaped by its operating principles as a regulator. This included an emphasis on consultation, on the conduct of research into public attitudes and understanding, and on debate and engagement in relation to communication issues that affect the public. In the process, Ofcom has provided a forum for researchers across the academy, industry and third sector to debate media literacy issues, and it has also conducted a substantial body of new and valuable empirical research.

However, Ofcom has paid more attention to the access and usage elements of its definition than to evaluation or creation, and it has tended to frame media literacy as a matter of overcoming individual barriers to access or choice in the media environment rather than one of enhancing individual or, especially, collective opportunities to use media platforms for creation, participation and critique. This is consistent with the expectations held of a largely economic regulator, as is Ofcom's evident preference for easily quantifiable measures of media literacy – for example, do people use the interactive functions on their digital television set, can they check the provenance and date of a website, or do they know who to complain to if content offends them? But it is disappointing for those who hoped for a more ambitious conception of media literacy; those who might ask, for example, whether the use of digital media means that more people are scrutinising government, that global misunderstandings are being renegotiated or that marginalised identities can now be expressed and valorised?

Public policy struggles face two tasks: one is to effect change for the better; the other – King Canute-like – is to hold back change for the worse. If, for the moment, one defines 'better' and 'worse' as perceived by actors themselves, one might conclude that, thus far, the emancipatory approach to media literacy has achieved moderate success in defining and extending policy definitions of media literacy and in critiquing, if not holding back, some of the most reductionist approaches. One may also conclude that, irrespective of the implicit political agenda, there is considerable value in efforts to research public understanding of the changing media environment or in developing initiatives to overcome the barriers to equal adoption of new technologically mediated opportunities or in pushing commercial providers to collaborate on codes of conduct that will deal fairly and transparently with their customers.[23]

Although, as we have suggested, it seems that the British debate initially influenced the European one closely following on its heels, we now discern a reverse influence, with Britain's initially instrumentalist approach being reconceived in light of the wider European debate, which was itself shaped by diverse and critical stakeholders capitalising on the interpretative flexibility of the concept as well as the complex and at times conflicting forces driving it further up the policy agenda. Thus we have traced how, in debates over media literacy, the emancipatory language of public empowerment was early employed, co-opted even, to advance a neoliberal agenda of market deregulation. From the insertion of media literacy into the UK's Communications Act, Europe's Audiovisual Media Services Directive and its Digital Agenda, it would seem naïve to interpret the broad political intent in any other way.

So where next for media literacy? Notwithstanding the signs, especially in Europe, that the media literacy agenda is widening to encompass positive, even emancipatory though perhaps over-ambitious objectives, these continue to run counter to the deregulatory objectives often expressed by public and private sector stakeholders. More concretely, however, the protectionist approach has done better – parents and teachers are now largely aware of online risks, many consumers use technical tools to control their access to potentially harmful or offensive contents, signposting commercial and offensive content is on the industry's agenda, self-regulatory content codes are being negotiated, and some efforts are underway to extend digital literacy to the young, the poor and older people.[24] However, the UK's present Coalition government is harder to read. Explicit statements on media literacy are few and far between, and pronouncements on digital participation have been reframed, arguably watered down in terms of digital access and inclusion. Still more pessimistically, with major public sector cuts, and a renewed interest in deregulation, media literacy policy may be foundering, at best surviving as, merely, a means of overcoming the digital divide in the race to get online.[25] Will media literacy, as a plank of the Coalition's media policy, disappear as quickly as, in retrospect, it flourished in the UK under the New Labour government? At the time of writing, Ofcom's media literacy endeavour is being 'restructured', with its scope significantly reduced and its future uncertain.

And yet the arguments for promoting media or digital literacy among the general population are as strong as ever, especially for children and the disadvantaged or marginalised, but also, given the pace of technological change and market complexity, for everyone.[26] Given this continued imperative that the public has a critical understanding of and a capacity to engage with a fast-changing media and communications environment, we have resisted the temptation to read any and all media literacy initiatives in terms of the onward march of a neoliberal or deregulatory agenda. Instead, we have argued that the definitional hiatus introduced by the rush to build media literacy into the new regulatory regime, even if initially conceived as a rationale for deregulation, has allowed for a widespread public debate from which a far more complex and ambitious solution is emerging. In short, what began – and what survives in some quarters – as a rather technocratic policy to ensure consumers have the necessary minimal skills to get online, press the 'interactive' button on their remote control or avoid getting exploited by has phishing or phone scams, has grown into a policy that has, and could further, strengthen, the infrastructure of democratic societies. Cynics might argue that media literacy became the policy window through which all kinds of interests were temporarily squeezed, but it is equally plausible to argue that the mediation of everything (Livingstone, 2009a) means that media literacy is indeed a prerequisite for doing anything, even though this vastly amplifies the challenges of delivery and evaluation.

Notes

1   In the Public Bodies Bill (House of Lords, 2010), one of the early acts of the Coalition government was to close, cut or redirect the activities of a large number of quasi-autonomous bodies ('quangos') working to promote and protect the public or consumer interest in diverse sectors.
2   Hobbs (2008) distinguishes between media literacy, information literacy, critical literacy and media management (broadly, a public health approach to counteract media-induced harms).
3   Here the view is of media as substantially if not fundamentally harmful, necessitating defensive responses (critical, cognitive, social) on the part of individual recipients if they are to discriminate among contents and so stave off any of the ill-effects of exposure. With widespread access to diverse and at times extreme forms of online content, debates are once again rife over whether matters of harm and offence are best addressed through education or regulation.
4   For example, the UK's National Plan for Digital Participation, a strategic, state-led, multi-stakeholder initiative, designed 'to ensure that everyone who wants to be online can get online, do more online and benefit from the advantages of being online' (2010: para. 6), was launched by the Department for Business Innovation and Skills in March 2010. This included multiple references to literacy, including a definition of 'digital media literacy' as 'the ability to use, understand and create digital media and communication' (BIS and DCMS, 2010).
5   Author interview with Matt Peacock, Communications Director, Ofcom, 13/07/05. This is not to say that Peacock did not think media literacy was important.

As he went on to say: 'It's actually about the thing that separates what we have now, which is the ability to prevent a very powerful, the most powerful medium in history, from tipping what can sometimes be very fragile … you know, into chaos. But they're separated by 60 years of learned behaviour and regulation rules and the rest of it.'

6 Thanks to Robin Blake for clarification of this point.

7 The Department for Culture, Media and Sport plus the Department for Trade and Industry, later renamed the Department for Business, Enterprise and Regulatory Reform and, then, the Department for Business, Innovation and Skills.

8 Section 11 of the Act also specifies that 'references to the publication of anything by means of the electronic media are references to its being – 1. broadcast so as to be available for reception by members of the public or of a section of the public; or 2. distributed by means of an electronic communications network to members of the public or of a section of the public'.

9 Since then, the website has replaced 'access' with 'use' in order to emphasise the cultural and cognitive dimensions of access rather than hardware issues.

10 In fact, this definition from the DCMS represents a summary of one provided by Ofcom in its 2006 Adult Media Literacy Audit (Ofcom, 2006b: 7). However, in subsequent statements, including its Adult Media Literacy Audit 2008, there is no explicit assumption that critique can be postponed for 'advanced' use, and the more inclusive definition (access, understand and create) is employed.

11 As Wyplosz (2010) argues, one reason for the failure was that 'peer pressure turned into mutual congratulations'. The European Community does not agree that the agenda has failed, unsurprisingly (see Commission of the European Communities, 2009).

12 In its decision, the Commission cites the contributions of a number of media scholars as well as the 'best practice' evinced by Ofcom.

13 Approved by the European Commission in 2007 with the expectation of being incorporated into the laws of member states by 2009.

14 Upcoming challenges for Digital Europe were raised in a public consultation launched by the Commission in October 2009, initiating the new European ICT strategy that the Commission presented in 2010 as part of the next wave of the Lisbon Agenda.

15 Author interview with Robin Foster, Partner, Strategy and Market Developments, Ofcom, 09/06/05.

16 The protectionist agenda, by contrast, remains less open to flexible reinterpretation; indeed, it remains hotly contested between market liberal (and libertarian) versus conservative (or communitarian) perspectives. Perhaps because of this history of controversy, the protectionist interests behind media literacy policy often remain unstated, marginalised by the excited rhetoric of new opportunities for citizen empowerment. Nonetheless, they have not disappeared, re-emerging when the media literacy agenda is spelt out, even though – revealing a dilemma within the right-wing agenda – they conflict with the deregulatory push behind national and international efforts to liberalise markets.

17 However, in so far as media literacy is dealt with under the rubric of 'education', it is subject to the subsidiarity principle, leaving its promotion to national governments rather than being actioned on a pan-European level.

18 Lord Carter was appointed to the new post of Minister of Communications, Technology and Broadcasting on 3 October 2008.

19 Little change was observed in terms of the demographics of those reluctant to use the digital functions of various media – older people, women and those of lower socioeconomic status showed lower levels of awareness, interest and confidence.

20 Similar findings hold in other countries – for example, in the USA even among so-called 'digital natives' there is considerable variation in digital skills (Hargittai, 2010).

21 Though many resources – online and broadcast materials, education in schools, UK online centres – are open to all.

22 The study's recommendations (pp. 13–14) are also noteworthy: '1. To identify critical understanding as the key factor in the development of policies for promoting media literacy. 2. To promote citizen engagement as an essential component of full and active European citizenship. 3. To encourage national governments and media regulatory authorities to include in their remits the monitoring and enhancement of media literacy; to promote intra- and international exchange of good practice. 4. To facilitate and extend access to ICT, with specific focus on the internet. 5. To promote public debate and awareness of media literacy. 6. To encourage the integration of media education in educational curricula both as specific goals and cross-curricular subjects. 7. To sustain the role of civil society organizations and related media literacy initiatives in order to foster a democratic culture and shared values. 8. To encourage an active involvement by the media industry, especially audiovisual media.'

23 In another example of critical approaches influencing state policy, we await the outcome of Buckingham's current project to develop the progression criteria by which to assess children's media education in schools at different ages. While such concepts of targets, attainment, progression criteria and testing seem entirely opposed to the ethos of a social and contextual approach to media literacies, it is also the case that without these – without any means of evaluating or assessing whether resources and educational efforts to teach soft skills or learner-centred notions of literacy have been effectively expended – such resources will quickly cease.

24 Moreover, there is a rising clamour for strengthened consumer protection, safety nets for the vulnerable, personal data and privacy regulations, new forms of content regulation, online advertising rules, a rethink of copyright and intellectual property laws – it being increasingly recognised that individual consumers cannot be expected to navigate such complexities, nor that it would meet human rights nor other civilised expectations that they should take on such burdens.

25 As implied, for example, in Minister for Culture, Communications and Creative Industries Ed Vaisey's speech on the subject of libraries in the digital age, July 2010. See http://www.culture.gov.uk/news/ministers_speeches/7223.aspx. However, the Digital Participation site has been taken offline, asking visitors to refer to Race Online 2012, which has a 'Manifesto for a Networked Nation' set forward by the Coalition government. See http://raceonline2012.org/press-coverage (including a press release from the Cabinet Office).

26 For example, the parallel initiative to promote financial literacy might also seem doomed but in early 2011 the news reported that 'Over 100 MPs [are] to fight for financial education in schools'. Possibly the costs to the nation of a financially illiterate public attract greater concern than the costs of a public struggling with the media environment. See http://www.moneysavingexpert.com/news/family/2011/01/over-100-mps-to-fight-for-financial-education-in-schools (31 January, 2011).

7

ADVERTISING REGULATION AND CHILDHOOD OBESITY

Introduction

Children's media – both the media produced specifically for children and the much wider category of media they engage with in practice – periodically occasion a particularly fraught struggle between the market-oriented policies of competition and deregulation on the one hand, and the cultural or citizen-oriented policies designed to meet children's needs and interests and to protect them from harm, on the other. In this struggle, policies for competition and deregulation are positioned as generic – they apply, ideally, to all media markets and within this, children tend to figure as a special case, grounds for making an exception, if they figure at all. Policies for cultural and citizen needs, however, are specific to the constituency at issue – children, in this case, but in other contexts older people, minority ethnic groups, rural populations, and so forth. Although guided by general principles (of universal service, fairness of redress, right to privacy, value for money, etc.), these policies cannot themselves be applied in a manner that is uniform across the population. Managing the balance, struggle even, between the generic principles of the market and the specific needs of particular constituencies of citizens is difficult, and for a largely economic regulator such as Ofcom, it can seem easiest to prioritise the former, so that meeting the needs of the market becomes 'the rule' over the latter, where meeting the needs of children becomes 'the exception'.

Children, despite being a sizable segment of the population, risk being treated as a rather difficult minority, seemingly more trouble (given the often-contested public, moral and regulatory agendas that surround them) than they are worth (in terms of advertising or other revenues, even in terms of political capital), notwithstanding the populist rhetoric that celebrates children as 'the future'. Contrast, for instance, the abundance of political statements and journalist column inches along with the vast volume of expert academic journal articles devoted to this 'special audience' (Dorr, 1986) with the fact that Ofcom, like other regulators before it and like those in many other countries, devotes no special department or unit to regulating children's media or media use. Thus children are easily sidelined: for example, policies for fairness or objectivity or privacy struggle to accommodate the particular concerns that arise for child audiences or users. Indeed, the general invisibility of the child audience supports policy makers' complacency in referring, over and again in their pronouncements, to 'the population' when what is meant is 'adults only'.

However, in some areas of media and communications policy, children implicitly dominate, despite lacking a formal department or champion. For example, media literacy policies in many countries are often, in practice, policies for children's media literacy or media education, to the neglect of adult media literacy requirements (including those of 'vulnerable' or 'excluded' adults). In this respect, Ofcom's approach to media literacy – as discussed in Chapter 6 – was ground-breaking in its even-handed focus on adults as well as children. In the case of broadcast content, children occupy a special place – in Ofcom's *Broadcasting Code* (2005c), most notably, and also in the strong UK legacy of the 'watershed', a broadly accepted time-based restriction on programmes that can be scheduled according to the needs of children in the audience (before 9pm on terrestrial channels and 8pm on digital/satellite channels). But in some cases, regulating in the interests of children may be seen to clash directly with the interests of adults – whether and how pornographic content should be broadcast is a case in point (Helsper, 2005).

In what follows, we explore the unfolding events in one particular case in which the interests of the market and the needs of children clashed, with Ofcom as the referee charged with the task of an evidence-based and fair adjudication. This case concerned the question of restricting television's advertising to children of 'unhealthy' or 'junk' food (formally referred to in the health debates over obesity as food 'high in fat, sugar or salt' or HFSS). In relation to advertising, it has long been accepted that special rules apply regarding the child audience. Going beyond the concerns already addressed by the *Broadcasting Code*, namely, that children are held to be particularly vulnerable to media images and messages about violence, sex and sexuality, gender or other stereotyping (Millwood Hargrave and Livingstone, 2009), the argument in relation to advertising is also that children are distinctively susceptible to planned persuasion – not only are they likely to absorb the gender stereotypes embedded in a toy advertisement, but also they are easily persuaded to want the toy too (Kunkel, 2001).

Our concerns in this chapter are threefold. First, Ofcom's approach to food advertising on television illustrates the difficulties faced by a dual regulator required to balance market and citizen imperatives. While the former demands a lighter touch approach to regulation, the latter reveals how such an approach may produce adverse, long-term effects on citizens who are external to the market. Thus from the first day of its operation in 2003, Ofcom found itself as 'pig in the middle'. Second, in operational terms, this case also shows how Ofcom, as a public-facing regulator, desirous of promoting dispersed rather than centralised governance, necessarily became engaged in a consultative process with other agencies, government and the public, this in practice revealing some of the real difficulties of a multi-stakeholder deliberation, especially that which was (at least partially) conducted in public. Third, the case illustrates the particular difficulties of ensuring that regulation is evidence-based, for although evidence-based policy has become an important principle in contemporary regulatory regimes, achieving this is far from straightforward. As we shall show, evidence is produced within external fields of expertise that have their own agendas, which are internally contested, and which may produce evidence that is ill-suited to the requirements of regulatory decision making.

Regulating advertising to children

Using a mix of state and self-regulation, countries have long intervened in the advertising market, both in general and in relation to children in particular. Regarding the children's market, food advertising, along with toy advertising, has always figured highly (Kunkel, 1990), as has the wider question of the 'Commercialisation of Childhood' (Buckingham, 2009a; Nairn and Fine, 2008). But it was only with the recent 'discovery' of rising obesity levels across the developed world that, as Hawkes (2007) observes in her review of international changes in regulation for the World Health Organisation (WHO), the issue of food marketing to children attracted widespread attention at national, regional (especially European) and international levels. The past decade has seen a chequered history of regulatory intervention, formal challenge and, often, a subsequent relaxation of initially tough restrictions, followed in due course by more debate and renewed calls for further regulation on the part of the state or, increasingly, by self-regulatory bodies. For an overview of the present 'tangled web' of state, co- and self-regulatory bodies regulating marketing to children in the UK, see Pitt (2010), and for an international perspective, see Hawkes (2005, 2007).

Before the establishment of Ofcom in 2003, the UK advertising market was regulated by the Advertising Standards Authority (ASA) for non-broadcast advertising and by the Independent Television Commission (ITC) for broadcast advertising. Both were conducted in accordance with the European framework – the Television without Frontiers Directive (1989) and, since 2007, the Audiovisual Media Services Directive, a directive that explicitly encourages opportunities for co-regulation (European Parliament and the Council, 2007). Once formed in 2003, Ofcom's *Broadcasting Code* (Ofcom, 2005c) took over advertising regulation in the UK in terms of amount, placement, political advertising, the distinction between advertising and programming, and so forth. However, Ofcom made an early decision – in tune with its avowed principles of lighter-touch regulation and the promotion of co-regulation – to pass the regulation of advertising content to the thereby-expanded ASA (as from November 2004). The ASA thus regulates television advertising under contract from Ofcom, funded by a levy on advertising airtime costs. It addresses public complaints and enforces the Broadcast Committee of Advertising Practice (BCAP) code that, along with the CAP code (for non-broadcast advertising, now including some online content), draws heavily on the codes of practice of the International Chamber of Commerce.

Consequently, as regards the advertising of junk food to children on television, while matters of timing, placement and amount remained the responsibility of Ofcom, the content of such advertising became a matter for the BCAP code. Today, paragraph 7.2.1 of the code states that, 'Advertisements must avoid anything likely to encourage poor nutritional habits or an unhealthy lifestyle in children', and paragraph 7.2.4 states that, 'Licensed characters and celebrities popular with children must be used with a due sense of responsibility. They may not be used in HFSS product advertisements targeted directly at pre-school or primary school children'. But these rules represent a recent strengthening of the regulations in this area, following the activities of Ofcom, the Department of Health, the Food Standards Agency (FSA) and other organisations lobbying for change in the nature and amount of advertising promoting HFSS foods to children. They are, indeed, a consequence of the events outlined below.

The initial stimulus for change came just as Ofcom was first established in December 2003, triggered by a request from the then Secretary of State for Culture, Media and Sport that Ofcom should consider strengthening the rules on HFSS advertising to children on television. This request was, in its turn, a response to the growing concern in the Department of Health and elsewhere regarding the growth in obesity among the general population, including among children. The Foresight report, 'Tackling Obesities: Future Choices' (Government Office for Science, 2007: 2), warned that:

By 2050, Foresight modelling indicates that 60% of adult men, 50% of adult women and about 25% of all children under 16 could be obese … The NHS costs attributable to overweight and obesity are projected to double to £10 billion by 2050. The wider costs to society and business are estimated to reach £49.9 billion per year (at today's prices).

Although such projections have been criticised as excessive (see the Technical Appendix to Buckingham, 2009a), WHO was already calling for 'urgent action' in 2000 (WHO, 2000), and by 2002 they had described the rise in obesity 'the major public health problem of our time' (WHO, 2002). As Ofcom noted in its first report, *Childhood Obesity – Food Advertising in Context* (2004d), 10 per cent of England's 5 to 9 year olds were obese and a further 20 per cent were overweight, these figures having steadily increased over the previous decade. By 2006, 16 per cent of 2 to 15 year olds in England were classed as obese (NHS, 2008).

In the UK, whether one reads government concern as focused on the public's well-being or on the present and future costs to the NHS of an unhealthy population, or both, the government's White Paper, *Choosing Health* (DH, 2004), identified 'a strong case' for advertising restrictions, thereby setting in train the debate that constitutes the case study for this chapter. As Ashley et al. commented in *The Guardian* (2003: para. 10), although wary of 'charges of running a nanny state ... there is a growing mood in Downing Street that better preventive measures are vital to cutting health inequalities, curbing an escalating NHS budget and producing a healthier society'. In relation to food advertising, Ofcom found itself under ministerial instructions as soon as it opened for business, exactly when it sought to establish itself as a supporter of lighter-touch self-regulation at arm's length from government.

The challenges of evidence-based policy

Two lines of evidence have long underpinned the regulation of television advertising to children. One concerns children's vulnerability to persuasion, part of the wider literature on media's effects on the attitudes, desires or behaviour of its audience. This has long shown that children's preferences, and sometimes also their behavioural choices, are influenced – to a statistically significant though generally rather small degree – by exposure to particular persuasive messages. The other, part of a wider literature on children's socio-cognitive development, asks more specifically about their understanding of techniques of persuasion in order to judge the fairness or deceptiveness of advertising to children. This research suggests that children follow a developmental path from an early ability to distinguish advertising from programming (at around two or three years old) to the recognition that advertising is trying to sell something (at around eight years old), even using techniques that may exaggerate, mislead or deceive, to, by around 12 years old, a mature ability to weigh and possibly reject such messages so that behaviours are not affected (Kunkel, 2001).[1]

More recently, the convenient assumption that these lines of evidence are complementary has been critically examined, questioning whether it is really the case that children who are sufficiently cognitively mature to recognise advertising techniques will be able to defend themselves against the persuasive messages that they convey. To put the challenge more simply, the notion that advertising literacy undermines the effects of advertising turns out to be remarkably little supported by empirical evidence. Indeed, since there is plenty of evidence that older teenagers and, indeed, adults, are also influenced by advertising (at least, to a similarly modest degree that young children are), it can hardly be that achieving advertising literacy prevents advertising effects (Livingstone and Helsper, 2006).[2] It may still be argued that advertising directed at those too young to understand its intentions is unfair, even deceptive (Kunkel, 2001), but this is a different argument, one that is focused on the right to recognise when one is being persuaded rather than on a distinctive vulnerability to persuasive messages.

As the foregoing illustrates, it may be far from straightforward to ground regulatory decisions in the evidence base. In the case of Ofcom's regulation of food advertising on television to children, the regulator was faced with taking into account – indeed, taking its lead from – the agenda, arguments and evidence from not one but two fields of expertise quite outside the normal scope of the regulator's own specialist knowledge of media and communications. The first, as already noted above, concerned expertise on child development. Content regulation for children has often relied on children's socio-cognitive development as the basis for age regulation implemented via restrictions on marketing or scheduling, and/or via parental rules. But if it is unclear that children's vulnerability to persuasion is reduced when advertising (or media) literacy is increased, Ofcom could hardly point to younger children's distinctive vulnerability to influence in support of restrictions on advertising to children below a certain age or for the promotion of media literacy intervention as a regulatory solution.

The second field of expertise important to its remit but beyond Ofcom's scope concerned the dramatic rise in obesity rates in the world's wealthy countries, most notably in the USA and, following close behind, the UK. The evidence base that informed the White Paper, *Choosing Health* (DH, 2004), stemmed from the work of health epidemiologists internationally, and had been established by the WHO in 2000 (WHO, 2000), among other organisations. The argument that obesity is rising among all age groups but especially among children in developed countries has been broadly accepted, although the recency and scale of the problem remain somewhat contested (Buckingham, 2009a). The questions, then, were how to explain such a rise, for it could hardly be ignored, and what could be done to redress the problem, this being the more contentious issue. This is, undoubtedly, a difficult problem, and one that goes beyond the immediate expertise of a communications regulator. As Livingstone and Helsper (2004) reported to Ofcom, there is evidence for multiple causes, working at four distinct levels (cf. Story et al., 2002: 3):

> (1) Individual (intrapersonal) – psychosocial, biological and behavioural factors. (2) Social environmental (interpersonal) – family, friends and peer networks. (3) Physical environment (community) – accessibility, school food policy and local facilities. (4) Macrosystem (societal) – mass media and advertising, social and cultural norms, production and distribution systems and pricing policies.

However, notwithstanding the continued emphasis in health circles on the many causes of this complex problem (Harrison et al., 2011), in public perception, advertising is a popular target. It was hard to discount the fact that in 2003, UK annual spending on advertising for food, soft drinks and chain restaurants was £743 million, with £522 million spent on television advertising, including £32 million on children's airtime. Most of this expenditure was on breakfast cereals, confectionery, savoury snacks, soft drinks and fast-food restaurants (Ofcom, 2004d). Unsurprisingly, then, advertising was widely positioned discursively as a key factor in the rise of obesity among children, threatening to obscure the many other putative causes of obesity. From a health perspective, media messages appear to be a tractable target for policy intervention, arguably more so than several of the other causes of obesity. From a communication perspective, however, the evidence base is at times problematic, since the many, often rigorously conducted population surveys of obesity levels too rarely include precise measures of advertising exposure. In the main, health epidemiological surveys identify a small to moderate correlation between obesity and a general measure of television viewing.[3] But as critics have observed, this correlation might reflect the fact that television viewing is a sedentary activity that reduces metabolic rates and displaces physical exercise. Or it might be because television viewing is associated with frequent snacking, pre-prepared meals and/or fast-food consumption. Or indeed, the correlation might occur because television viewing includes exposure to advertisements for HFSS food products.

Such uncertainties in interpreting the evidence rarely find their way into popular – and political – discourses regarding obesity. This is not least because the counterfactual claim – that watching hours of advertising has no effect – seems implausible as well as contra some of the recent evidence (Institute of Medicine of the National Academies, 2005). Thus for Ofcom, the 'problem' of childhood obesity arrived in its in-tray already packaged as a problem of food advertising when Ofcom began operations in late 2003.

Policy responses to childhood obesity were focused on advertising at an early stage by a highly publicised report by the FSA published in September 2003 (Hastings et al., 2003) that linked food marketing to childhood obesity. This argued that 'Food promotion is having an effect, particularly on children's preferences, purchase behaviour and consumption. This effect is independent of other factors and operates at both a brand and category level' (2003: 3). Although the report was scrupulous in noting the limits as well as the strengths of the evidence and, appropriately given the methodological limitations of the research, cautious in its claims regarding cause and effect, the government made a stronger reading. The then Secretary of State for Culture, Media and Sport, Tessa Jowell, called on Ofcom in December to tighten up the 'inadequate code' on advertising 'in the light of the emerging evidence about the impact of advertising' and given the media's reporting of a 'growing crisis of obesity in children' (quoted in Ashley et al., 2003: paras 2–3). Behind this request lay the threat of tougher regulatory action and the FSA's call for a ban was regarded with some sympathy by government, the public and, certainly, the health lobby. In public discourse, there appeared to be a compelling case that junk food advertising was making children fat.

The industry was faster in its response than the regulator, and before Ofcom could respond, in December 2003 the Food Advertising Unit (the research centre of the industry's Advertising Association) published an apparently devastating refutation of Hastings et al.'s claims (Paliwoda and Crawford, 2003). In January 2004, Ofcom then commissioned this volume's second author (Sonia Livingstone) to write an independent commentary on the disagreement between the FSA report and that of the Food Advertising Unit (Livingstone, 2004). This was part of an attempt by the regulator to adjudicate fairly on a highly contested clash between market and citizen interests where the terms of the debate were fought out in the language of evidence (research design, statistical effect sizes, validity and reliability, etc.) more than in the language of regulatory principles.

The disputed points could be summarised as follows (Livingstone, 2004; see also Buckingham, 2009a, 2009b, 2009c; Millwood Hargrave and Livingstone, 2009). First, the problem of methodology. Is there enough evidence regarding the effect of advertising on children's diet, and is that evidence of sufficiently high quality, conducted recently, and in the UK or relevant to the UK? Also, have the confounding factors been controlled for? Has television advertising been distinguished from other forms of advertising? Does it matter if the dependent measure is only children's food preferences rather than actual diet or weight? And, tapping into a long history of contention, can the results of experiments be generalised to real-life situations? Second, the problem of explanation. How can the multiple putative causes be disentangled, identified and weighed? Are there other causal factors with greater effects that could or should be tackled instead? Third, a question of scale. Does the evidence point to an effect whose size is large enough to merit policy intervention (a point on which evidence reviews are oddly silent[4])? Relatedly, is there evidence that a ban on advertising would significantly improve children's health (this being surprisingly difficult to establish)? Last, the question of consequences. Does the responsibility for any effects of advertising lie with the advertisers or with the consumers who choose to watch advertising and who arguably could reject its messages? If consumers became more advertising literate, could they then bear more responsibility, reducing the regulatory burden on marketers?

As is often the case with a complex body of evidence, produced for diverse reasons in several countries over a period of decades, there are few clear-cut answers to these questions. But this is not to say there was no case to answer, and Ofcom's task was to reach a proportionate decision, even if this included recourse to the precautionary principle in the absence of a consensual conclusion (Klinke and Renn, 2001). Hastings et al. (2003) reviewed the evidence that advertising was likely to affect children's food choices and, therefore, obesity. Reporting to Ofcom, Livingstone argued that there existed 'a modest body of fairly consistent evidence demonstrating the direct effect of food promotion (in the main, television advertising) on children's food preferences, knowledge and behaviour' (Livingstone, 2004: 28) and, further, that indirect effects (e.g. advertising influencing parents or peers who then influence a child) were likely to exist, although these had been little investigated.

In the USA, similar or even higher figures for rising childhood obesity were emerging, and a parallel investigation into the potential role of advertising in worsening the problem was undertaken first by the American Psychological Association (Kunkel et al., 2004) and then by the Institute of Medicine of the National Academies (2005). The latter observed that US$11 billion was spent on advertising in 2004, including US$5 billion on television advertising, and it reviewed 123 of the strongest relevant articles on the influence of food advertising on young people. Its key conclusion was that:

> ... among many other factors, food and beverage marketing influences the preferences and purchase requests of children, influences consumption at least in the short term, is a likely contributor to less healthful diets, and may contribute to negative diet-related health outcomes and risks among children and youth. (Institute of Medicine of the National Academies, 2005: ES-9)

In short, although the evidence did not show a large effect, and although the methodologies used were not without their problems, there was sufficient evidence both nationally and internationally that television advertising played a significant role for Ofcom to take action.

Regulatory action and reaction

Following the initial argument between Hastings et al.'s (2003) report for the FSA and the Advertising Association's highly critical response, and given the pressure from government, Ofcom set in train a series of responses that included further reviews of the literature (Livingstone, 2004, 2006; Livingstone and Helsper, 2004), conducting its own primary research, both qualitative and quantitative (Ofcom, 2004c), and working with the FSA in support of its nutrient profiling scheme, a scheme that aimed to label food according to a traffic light system of green (i.e. can eat plenty of this as part of a healthy diet), amber (eat only some of this) and red (eat only a restricted amount of this). Although ultimately this latter scheme failed, the promise was that the same colour coding could provide the basis for advertising restrictions (more for 'red' products and less for 'amber' ones, while positively promoting 'green' ones).

On the basis of such work, and following a public consultation (Ofcom, 2006d) on the regulatory options, Ofcom sought to build consensus by conducting negotiations with all the parties. In this way, and in the face of several authoritative literature reviews of the evidence, the advertising industry came to acknowledge that advertising had some 'modest' and possibly adverse effects on children's food choices (not least because it wished to acknowledge that, by the same token, the promotion of healthy food options could be equally, if modestly, influential, thereby benefiting children). Meanwhile, the health lobby recognised that, since the evidence for advertising effects varied only in so far as it showed them to be small or absent, but never large, other causes of childhood obesity should also be considered and, possibly, regulated (Story et al., 2002). Examples included calls for regulating the promotion of unhealthy foods in schools and supermarkets, addressing the insufficient provision of health facilities or intervening in the considerable influence on children of 'unhealthy' parental habits in relation to shopping, cooking and eating.

In November 2006 Ofcom reached its decision, announcing a ban on HFSS advertising not for all programming, or all programming before the 9pm watershed (as health campaigners wanted), but a ban specifically during children's programming (i.e. when programmes made for children or of particular appeal to children were scheduled, including all programming on dedicated children's channels). Children, as for most if not all of Ofcom's regulations regarding the child audience, were defined as 4–15 years old. Ofcom's 'final statement' in February 2007 explained the restrictions, to be phased in partially from April 2007 and with the full restrictions applying from January 2009. In parallel, as noted above, the ASA also revised its BCAP code, restricting the techniques (e.g. use of celebrities) by which food and drink could be advertised to children.

While possibly a response to government demand to take action, this decision was nonetheless evidence based. Ofcom recognised, on the basis of several literature reviews and its own empirical research, that advertising played a noticeable if modest role in influencing children's food preferences, choices and diet. However, regulators have long faced the difficulty that self-regulatory codes can restrict unfair or offensive advertising but not 'the *cumulative* effects of perfectly legal, truthful marketing campaigns' (Hawkes, 2005: 380, original emphasis). In reaching their decision, it may therefore be considered that Ofcom made much of the handful of longitudinal studies which supported such a cumulative effect[5] to take a step beyond the usual actions associated with self-regulation (Pitt, 2010).

Further, Ofcom appeared to have accepted the view that younger children could not be singled out for special treatment since, first, the evidence for advertising effects applied as much for adolescents (and, indeed, for adults) as it did for young children and, second, there was little evidence that increased media literacy (as applies to older teenagers and adults) reduced advertising effects (Livingstone and Helsper, 2006). Another way of putting this dilemma would be to say that the public policy goals at stake were often confused. If the public policy goal was that advertising should be fair, then indeed it should be more regulated for younger children (whose literacy is less) than older ones. But if the public policy goal was that advertising should not exacerbate levels of obesity, then it should be recognised as one influence among many and, since all ages are affected by both advertising obesity, it should be restricted across the age range. In the USA, it is often the former argument that holds sway (Kunkel, 2010).[6] On this occasion, in the UK, the latter seems to have won out. Indeed, following the conduct of a series of retrospective interviews with stakeholders on all sides, Buckingham (2009b) observed that, although initially Ofcom seemed minded to restrict junk food advertising for children under 9 years old only, these arguments were much cited as having tipped the argument in favour of extending the restrictions on advertising across the age range.[7] Certainly, Ofcom's decision to extend the restrictions to cover children up to 16 was received with surprise.[8]

Any other ingredients contributing to Ofcom's decision – political pressure, industry pressure, internal judgements – were less clear. But it might be surmised that, contrary to the general shift towards softer governance strategies, this decision was significantly influenced by old-fashioned, top-down, behind-the-scenes state intervention, pushed by the powerful health lobby for whom this was a triumph, notwithstanding their calls for yet further restrictions.

Regulatory effectiveness?

How should Ofcom's intervention in the regulation of food advertising to children be evaluated? In its 'final review' of HFSS advertising restrictions in July 2010 (Ofcom, 2010b), Ofcom presented its own account of developments, evaluating the effectiveness of its regulatory strategy in terms of, first, changes in the advertising seen by children and, second, the impact on broadcasting revenues. Significantly, Ofcom did not seek to evaluate its policies in terms of any measurable benefit on children's diets or health, although this was, after all, the driving purpose behind the government's injunction for policy action.

Did restricting the advertising of junk food to children on television result in their reduced exposure to such advertising? Ofcom's answer has been an unequivocal yes. Comparing 2005 and 2009 viewing data, children watched the same amount of television (including the same amount of commercial television) before and after the ban. This finding still holds, even taking into account the other changes between 2005 and 2009 – notably, a shift in children's viewing from the main public service to digital channels, and a rise in advertising, including growth in the number of advertisements for HFSS products. Consequently, in 2009 compared with 2005, 'children saw around 37% less HFSS advertising (i.e. a reduction of 4.4bn impacts); younger children (4–9 years old) saw 52% less' (Ofcom, 2010b: 3).

So even though children watch programmes designed for general audiences (in which advertising in general and HFSS advertising in particular rose over the period), the absence of HFSS advertising during children's airtime and on children's digital channels resulted in a substantial reduction in exposure to HFSS television advertising. Not only did Ofcom (and the ASA) restrict the scheduling (and nature) of advertising to children but, it appears, the industry also complied, with few, if any, reported breaches of the new rules. Consequently, in so far as exposure to junk food advertising contributes to children's poor food choices and, therefore, their likelihood of becoming obese, Ofcom's interventions may be judged effective.

However, a reduction in exposure to advertising on television may not mean a reduction in exposure to advertising overall. Ofcom's (2010b: 24) review also shows that, as regards food and drink advertising, 'advertising spend on television declined to a low of £527m in 2009, while spend on press, outdoor and cinema advertising increased between 2005 and 2009'. Moreover, 'advertising spend on food and drink products across the internet increased from £1.9m in 2005 to £8.7m in 2009' (Ofcom, 2010b: 26). Since Ofcom did not assess children's exposure to these other media, the balance of exposure to HFSS advertising across the media cannot easily be determined. But it seems likely that, as is often the case, restrictions on television advertising have had the unintended consequence of stimulating advertising in other media.[9]

The unintended consequences of the Ofcom ban go yet further. Advertising not only serves the interests of marketers and the food industry, but it also brings in revenues to the commercial channels. In announcing the ban on junk food advertising to children, Ofcom estimated the loss in advertising revenue to commercial broadcasters at some £30 million per year (Ofcom, 2006d). Its announcement was soon followed by another from the main commercial public service broadcaster, ITV, that it had ceased to commission new children's content and would no longer meet its quota of eight hours per week dedicated children's programming. Although before and, arguably, since, revenues from advertising in children's airtime have not been explicitly hypothecated to the production of children's programming, the timing of a reduction in the former and the announcement of major cuts to the latter seems more than coincidental.[10] There followed a year-long flurry of public and political concern at the apparent demise of most or all indigenous children's television production other than that of the BBC. In December 2007, Janet Anderson, MP, proposed an Early Day Motion in the House of Commons that recognised the crisis by stating that:

> ... this House ... believes that public service television for children plays a hugely important role in contributing to the educational and cultural development of children; and therefore calls on the Government to ensure that UK children of all ages, races and faiths have a genuine choice of high quality, UK-made children's programmes that reflect the diversity of UK culture and children's lives ... on a choice of channels. (Anderson, 2007)

Civil society groups argued that Ofcom should have held ITV to its quota, a requirement of its broadcasting franchise, while Ofcom argued that little could be done when revenues were so undermined. Some observers added that, since children were switching their attention to the internet, the days of children's television were numbered. Yet, Ofcom's *Future of Children's Television Programming* report (Ofcom, 2007b) instead predicted a slight rise in children's viewing of programmes specifically made for them – from 30.5 per cent of their viewing in 2007 to 31.5 per cent in 2012 (see Ofcom, 2007b: 182). Interestingly too, when in 2010 Ofcom sought to assess the impact of the advertising restrictions on broadcasting revenues, it proved unclear that the advertising restrictions were responsible for the loss of new commissioning. Ofcom's conclusion is worth quoting:

> For the final review, Ofcom sought views from broadcasters on whether they were able to provide adverting revenue data for 2008–9 that would shed light on the impact of the advertising restrictions. All of the broadcasters that responded indicated that it would not be feasible to disentangle the impact of the restrictions from other factors, such as the economic downturn. (Ofcom, 2010b: 5)

ADVERTISING REGULATION AND CHILDHOOD

In addition to the consequences for children's exposure to advertising, and the unintended consequences of, first, advertising moving to other media and, second, the costs to children's broadcasting production, two further consequences of these events are relevant to our present inquiry – what can be learned for the practice of evidence-based policy and the viability of self-regulation? We turn to these questions now, before concluding this case study. It should be noted, however, that the real purpose of these regulatory efforts – the potential health benefits for children – has not, it seems, been examined, although a positive sign may be discerned – health statistics showed that the three-year moving average for childhood obesity was 'flattening out' by 2008 (NHS, 2010: 20), suggesting that the long-term upward trend had perhaps been halted.

Reflections on evidence-based policy

Policymakers may be sceptical about recommendations from researchers who fail to grasp the political necessity of forging consensus among rival constituencies, whereas researchers may see policymakers as too quick to compromise on issues where such tactics are not supported by empirical findings. (Kunkel, 1990: 116)

A rational regulator must identify and weigh the available evidence, contextualising it in relation to other factors (economic, political, practical) in reaching a proportionate judgement. A public-facing regulator must, additionally, make its rationale for regulation both transparent and accountable. The case of television advertising of junk food to children opened up wider public anxieties about childhood – and anxieties about the family, authority, technology, tradition, morality and the future, thereby throwing a very public spotlight on to Ofcom's actions. In this contested domain of multidisciplinary expertise, Ofcom found itself debating the evidence with a diverse array of experts from the medical and health professions – psychologists, consumer researchers and cultural analysts – as well as with parent and community groups, child welfare organisations, religious organisations, journalists and more. Notwithstanding Ofcom's early decision to delegate the regulation of advertising content to the ASA, it could not delegate the entire responsibility for such regulation (as accorded to Ofcom by the Communication Act 2003). Thus it was to Ofcom that the government turned for action, and it was Ofcom that the health lobby criticised when public and expert opinion concluded that significant blame for rising childhood obesity lay with television advertising.

Ofcom's response, closely watched by regulators worldwide, exemplified the actions of the new regime, as this chapter has reviewed. Ofcom conducted a sizable body of new research. It held deliberative meetings with diverse stakeholders, including attempts to bring the antagonists together. It sought to assess the proportionality of policy options and held public consultations on these options. With considerable, often adverse, publicity and threatened litigation attacking the regulator both for being too lenient and too tough on the advertisers and commercial broadcasters, Ofcom perhaps could not win. What, then, may be learned regarding the potential of evidence-based policy?

Six models of evidence-based policy making are in common use, as summarised by Nutley et al. (2007). Two are long-established, one 'push' and one 'pull' model, from an academic point of view: (1) in the *knowledge-driven model*, research is disseminated to policy makers to inform decisions or actions, while (2) in the *problem-solving model*, policy makers seek out research findings to address a specific question or problem. Both of these, Kunkel (1990) claims, have long shaped the US regulatory environment as implemented by the Federal Communications Commission in the 1970s and a parallel case could be made for the UK at that time. However, two models make academics very cautious about engaging with policy making: (3) the *political model* uses research findings as ammunition when decision making is adversarial, and (4) the *tactical model* treats research findings as a resource for applying or deflecting pressure, supporting or rejecting a decision, as desired. The last two models represent minimal and maximal versions of, surely, an optimal approach: (5) the *interactive model* is less linear, centring on a sustained interaction between research and policy, and (6) the *enlightenment model* seeks to transcend any instrumental use of research in order to gain a more thorough insight and understanding of a given situation, recognising that research is not a pre-given but is partly developed and certainly interpreted through a process of constructive engagement with the policy landscape.

As Nutley et al. (2007) go on to argue, given the range of relevant expertise and the diversity of stakeholders concerned with a particular policy issue, 'there is real scope here for the creation and reinvigoration of a variety of partnerships aimed at fostering a growth in research-informed dialogue' (2007: 266). Perhaps this represents an ideal for regulators and academic researchers alike, but such partnerships, if they do occur, tend to be instrumental, lasting the duration of a project, and are far from developmental in renegotiating the potential of research. They are also further than one might wish from challenging 'preconceptions of research findings as fixed and immutable' or of 'favouring instead the idea that the value of research is revealed through dialogue, contextualisation and assimilation with other forms of knowledge' (2007: 268). For all stakeholders except those in academia, the flexibility of research 'findings' is regarded as either a failing of the research process or as an opportunity for tactical negotiation. Yet, 'as anyone working in the field of research use knows, a central irony is the only limited extent to which evidence advocates can themselves draw on a robust evidence base to support their convictions that greater evidence use will ultimately be beneficial to public services' (2007: 271).

What clarity does this throw on Ofcom's claim to be evidence-based in its decision making? Academics, undoubtedly, favour the first and last of these models: they wish the work they conduct autonomously to be noticed and attended to by potential research users, but they also would hope to improve understanding and even enlightenment. Since neither often happens, this encourages a degree of cynicism about 'evidence-based' policy. The first model lends itself to the regulator-commissioned literature review: academic research, it is assumed, proceeds for its own reasons, published in academic journals as it is completed, and may subsequently be mined for insights that are relevant to regulatory decisions. The problem is that the academic research may not fit the regulatory objectives.

In the field of children's advertising, for instance, most research does not distinguish product category from brand advertising, yet this is a key distinction for the industry which holds that while brand advertising works (i.e. consumers can be persuaded to prefer brand X over brand Y), category advertising does not (i.e. consumers cannot be persuaded to prefer an unhealthy product over a healthy one) (see, for example, Eagle and Ambler, 2002). The advantage of such an argument (which is not accepted by the FSA and others) would be that the industry could contemplate some restrictions on brand advertising but that there is no need to limit the free market for the latter. Faced with evidence that advertising persuades children to select unhealthy snacks over healthy fruit options, the industry tends to declare that, first, it does not produce advertisements with such an intention (i.e. the experiments lack ecological validity), and second, the researchers have confounded categories and brands in their research design, rendering their findings irrelevant or misguided.

In another example of a mismatch between research and policy, the regulator tends to divide children according to established age groupings on the assumption that the child audience is aged between 4 and 15 (the parent is presumed to be present and responsible for those under age 4, scheduling is presumed to manage the programme exposure of those under 15). But again, academic research might divide children in other ways, producing findings for 'teenagers' (including those both younger and older than 15) or it might produce findings that argue for a developmental shift in cognitive understanding of advertising intent around 7 or 8 years old, thereby foregrounding an age that regulators have no policy tools to address.

Since Ofcom has been generally instrumental in its use of research, it would doubtless claim to follow the second, problem-solving model, certainly in the case of advertising foods to children, though in some areas, such as media literacy, it has also sought a more sustained interaction with academic researchers as its media literacy policy has developed.[11] Critics fear, however, that the political and/or tactical models are more often employed, in which case researchers are co-opted as a *post hoc* justification for a policy decision taken elsewhere (Buckingham, 2009b). Although in order to ensure maximal applicability and benefit from research, Nutley et al. (2007) favour the interactive model, this risks the independence of researchers who must, as a community if not as individuals, both engage with research use but also critique this process from a disinterested vantage point. It might be anticipated, then, that the more engaged some researchers become, the more conflict will arise within the research community itself. Ironically, the more academic researchers take different positions here (as they rightly should), the more the credibility of the evidence is undermined in the eyes of the policy makers. Arguably, it is reasoning such as this that led Ofcom to invest so heavily in building up its own, supposedly authoritative, certainly expensive, research expertise, an enterprise since reduced in the comprehensive spending review of the Coalition government in 2010–11.

Conclusion

Looking ahead is an uncertain business. In relation to generalised public concern that childhood is becoming commercialised, parenting groups and other civil society actors representing children's interests have long lacked the power of advertisers, marketers and broadcasters in representing their case, and it works against them more than against industry that researchers have struggled to document, through sufficiently consistent and rigorous evidence, the conditions under which regulation would be justified. Still, in the case of junk food advertising, unlike that of 'commercialisation', the evidence that kick-started Ofcom's actions pointed to a substantial problem, that of childhood obesity. Thus it is not just parenting groups and consumer organisations that are complaining to government about excessive or inappropriate advertising to children – it is also the very powerful health lobby, including the government ministers responsible for health budgets.

In consequence, and unexpectedly for a regulator concerned to reduce and not increase restrictive regulation, Ofcom instituted a junk food ban on television programmes aimed at children, drawing on an independent evidence base to guide it, having conducted substantial multi-stakeholder and public consultations, and in the face of considerable industry protest. Although judging the value of Ofcom's interventions is not straightforward in terms of either process or outcome, its very considerable resources have undoubtedly been game changing, and it is hard to imagine that the process would be either sufficiently evidence-based or focused on the public interest without such efforts. This is not to say that the process was easy or that the outcome was satisfactory to the public or health experts – indeed, the latter continue to complain that Ofcom has been weak in its actions and thus ineffective in its consequences.[12]

The changing media and communications landscape continues to pose new regulatory challenges. One such is the regulation of product placement. In 2009, the then Secretary of State for Culture, Media and Sport, Andy Burnham, argued against the use of branded alcohol, junk food or gambling in programme making, in the interests of children, but his replacement, Ben Bradshaw, subsequently ruled to allow such product placement, in the interests of broadcasting revenues. In February 2010, Andy Burnham overturned this policy, now in his role as Health Secretary acting in the interests of children's health.[13] Another challenge is the regulation of advertising and marketing to children on the internet, one that has been compounded by the twin difficulties that global players produce content for, but not necessarily within the jurisdiction of, the UK, and that neither content providers nor regulators can know whether a 'user' is an adult or a child (Fielder et al., 2007; Montgomery and Chester, 2009; Pitt, 2010). In relation to neither of these challenges, as yet there is much reference to the evidence base, although this gives cause of concern regarding the liberalisation of both product placement and online marketing. One can only hope that the incoming regulatory regime will accord some weight to the empirical evidence, although, to be sure, this cannot determine the value judgements that, ultimately, direct policy decisions.

At the time of writing in 2011, Ofcom is reviewing its budget and commitments in the context of a new Coalition government, and a new Communications Act is proposed. Provision for indigenous television programming for children seems no longer a high priority on the public agenda, although concerns about obesity continue to hit the headlines on occasion. The media and communications landscape also continues to change, with online and converged platforms becoming ever more central to children's daily experiences, raising new challenges for advertising, sponsorship, product placement and other forms of marketing. Pressures for change continue as well – both from the health lobby and from the public. One among many headlines reads, 'Top doctors call for "fat tax" and warnings on junk food' (*The Observer*, 11/7/10). As parents walk into MPs' constituency offices, worried about commercialisation, sexualisation, online risks and more, government wishes to take action. Following on from the previous Labour government's review of the Commercialisation of Childhood (Buckingham, 2009a) and the Sexualisation of Youth (Papadopoulos, 2010), the 2010 Coalition government announced a Task Force on Childhood (Cabinet Office, 2010) as one of its very first acts in

June 2010. This resulted in the Bailey Review (2011), which called for a range of self-regulatory restrictions to curb the perceived commercialisation and sexualisation of childhood, thus revealing for the present a swing of the pendulum towards citizen protections.

Notes

1   For example, Roedder (1981) designed and tested a developmental model proposing three stages of advertising literacy: (i) Limited: children have no knowledge or sophistication in judging the intentions of advertisers. This applies to children roughly under 6 to 8 years of age. (ii) Cued: children have the knowledge to counter-argue advertising claims, but do not use this knowledge spontaneously. This stage is commonly found in children between 8 and 12 years old. (iii) Strategic: children have both the knowledge and the ability to use this knowledge without being cued. Most children over 12 years old are able to use this strategic advertising literacy.

2   We would not wish this to be taken as an argument against the value of media literacy. Kunkel (2010) seeks to rescue the case for media literacy by arguing that adolescents as well as younger children lack media literacy, hence they do not show the lesser effects of advertising. Buckingham (2009c) takes a different tack, arguing that the purpose of media literacy is not to prevent media effects, and hence its value must be evaluated in different terms entirely. Both arguments have their merits.

3   For example, a 34-nation study of 10 to 16 year olds in 2001–02 found that, in 22 of the 34 countries (including the UK where obesity figures are relatively high), there was a significant positive relationship between BMI (body mass index) classification and television viewing time (Janssen et al., 2005). See Livingstone (2006) for related studies.

4   This may be because they are difficult to estimate from already published research, and also because they are difficult for policy makers to interpret. For example, although effect sizes are estimated in this domain to account for 2–5 per cent of the variation across the population in terms of BMI, such small effects may add up to a substantial effect on the population. In one estimate, for every additional hour of daily television viewing, in the USA, an additional 1.5 million young people would fall into the 'obese' category (McGinnis et al., 2005).

5   For an overview of these studies, see Livingstone (2006). Few such studies exist because of the considerable expense and planning involved in setting up an experiment that follows up the effects on children through to when they are adults.

6   On the other hand, if the fairness argument is reframed not as a question of evidence (do children understand the persuasive intent of advertising?) but as one regarding the fairness of advertising to those with the legal status of 'children', then the United Nation's Convention on the Rights of the Child would also legitimate advertising restrictions to teenagers, indeed to all those up to the age of 18.

7   As Buckingham (2009c: 225) concludes from his stakeholder interviews, 'the arguments in Livingstone's 2006 report ... seem to have played a crucial role in swaying the regulatory balance'.

8   Although for Buckingham, this is far from an evidence-based decision since no researcher has ever found either literacy or effects to change markedly at age 16; rather, 16 is the age at which broadcasters and regulators have traditionally defined the start of the 'adult' or 'general' audience, defining children as 4 to 15 years old. Meanwhile, Pitt (2010) observes that the age bar in regulating marketing to children varies considerably among the many regulatory bodies, with cut-off ages ranging, without apparent justification, from 12 to 18 years old.

9   Measures to restrict online advertising to children have since been incorporated into ASA's self-regulatory CAP/BCAP (Committee of Advertising Practice, n.d.), and concerns regarding advertising to children have been flagged by Fielder et al. (2007). See also Montgomery and Chester (2009).

10   In the US context, Kunkel (1990: 110) assumes just such a policy of hypothecation underpinning the Federal Trade Commission's recognition that, 'because stations were obligated to offer at least some children's programs, they would be allowed to present advertising to generate revenues associated with the costs of providing such content'. While acknowledging the key difference – that in the UK, children's content has been part of a public service obligation even for ITV – it does appear that the reduction in revenues from children's advertising legitimated the consequent reduction in production of children's content.

11   As evidenced by its Media Literacy Research Forum, the monthly *Media Literacy Newsletter* and the International Media Literacy Conferences held in 2008 and 2010.

12   Notably, in 2006, the British Heart Foundation threatened legal action against Ofcom after it omitted the option of a total ban on advertising junk food to children after the 9pm watershed from its consultation options (Hardy, 2008).

13   'Climb down over TV product placement', Denis Campbell, health correspondent, *The Guardian*, 4/2/10.

8

COMMUNITY RADIO

Introduction

Community media are an important means of empowering citizens and encouraging them to become actively involved in civic society, [...] they enrich social debate, representing a means of internal pluralism (of ideas), [...] an effective means to strengthen cultural and linguistic diversity, social inclusion and local identity. (European Parliament, 2008: 5–6)

Community radio uses the medium by non-professional broadcasters in a way that directly benefits a target audience that is not well catered for by mainstream professional radio. (Gordon, 2005: 15)

Although a key feature of community radio is its diversity of forms, it is generally driven by a positive vision of media produced by the people for the people. The question is how to achieve this. Since the past few years have seen an extraordinary blossoming of community radio, one answer lies in regulation. For Stoller (2010), Chief Executive of the Radio Authority until 2003 and then Ofcom's External Relations Director, enabling the expansion of community radio has been one of Ofcom's primary achievements. In this chapter we explore the relationship between regulation and community media, focusing on Ofcom's work on community radio, which built on the work of the Radio Authority, one of its legacy regulators. Does community radio demonstrate a clear-cut success for regulatory intervention? As an area of regulatory focus, community radio – in common with our other case studies – has its own particular stakeholders, history and politics. It has also attracted a distinctive body of academic scholarship, which we draw on for an alternative account of the significance of community radio and Ofcom's role in shaping this in the UK.

Community radio is not-for-profit radio produced by and for communities. Different from both commercial and public service radio, each of which flourishes in a local form, it is socially embedded in particular ways. These include specific locales (towns, cities or rural areas), or dispersed groups with a common interest or identity (often, ethnic or linguistic minorities), or short-lived channels developed for particular purposes (e.g. Radio Ramadhan, radio stations for music festivals) or, last, a specific institution such as a hospital or university. With specific ties to community, it offers an explicit and demonstrable alternative to the mainstream, forming part of civil society and significantly networking individuals and social groups together (Carpentier et al., 2001). Community radio may be motivated by the educational aim for communities to educate themselves, the political aim of communities having control over the conditions for free and open discussion of issues that matter to them, or, as part of the human rights agenda, the effort to instantiate communication rights for communities and interest groups (Lewis, 1993). It also differs from both commercial and public service radio in the commitment and engagement of the community members who volunteer to run the station or contribute to the production process. This, it is often argued, gives community radio its creative edge and connects it to the community it serves, by contrast with mainstream institutions that deliver content to a remote, even unknown audience (Carpentier, 2011). Community radio, therefore, may provide the infrastructure for communities of practice (Wenger, 1998) and, more widely, for civil society.

As with other forms of alternative and community media, its recent history draws from the radical politics of the 1960s and 1970s, with their counter-cultural attack on corporate culture, resonance with life political movements and support for the importance of community and rights (Rennie, 2006), although the history of alternative media is far longer (Atton, 2002; Carpentier, 2011). Since the involvement of enthusiastic volunteers, 'ownership' by the audience and engagement from the user community are all critical to the ethos and the success of community media, one might argue that community radio should be wholly separate from mainstream media. However, as Lewis and Booth (1989) argue, alternative media may positively influence the mainstream, stimulating innovation and so diversifying forms of expression for a broader public. For example, they trace how pirate radio stations in the 1960s were in the vanguard of a movement that resulted in significant changes to the BBC's policy on popular music broadcasting. Indeed, during that time the BBC was developing local radio, spearheaded by Frank Gillard, who had been impressed by observing community radio stations in the USA. However, Stoller (2010) argues that although those ideals of community radio inspired the early days of BBC local radio, its strategy became increasingly corporate, leaving community radio to find new forms and outlets. Independent (i.e. commercial) local radio might have provided one route, and there was some support from the regulator in the 1980s, the Independent Broadcasting Authority (IBA). But, according to Stoller, the IBA lost patience with the left-wing activist stance of community radio advocates and matters drifted until 1984, when the Thatcher government looked anew at the idea of experimenting with community radio.

A right-wing government might appear an unlikely quarter for such an initiative, given the character of alternative and pirate radio, but it fits well with the Conservative focus on community (now the 'big society') and, as an added bonus, offered a way of thinking through the idea of public service media beyond the BBC. Furthermore, something had to be done about the pirate stations, and making them legal could be the solution. Although the experiment was not realised, Stoller (2010) identifies a subtle shift in the perception of the potential of community media as being both popular and of value to local communities. However, the potential difficulties for regulating and funding what would effectively be a 'third tier' of the broadcasting system (the first two being national and local) are indeed daunting. Community radio stations are diverse in their structure, organisation, scale, purposes and audiences, so a healthy community radio sector should reflect this diversity and be distinguishable from both commercial and public service broadcasting local radio (Bailey et al., 2007; Carpentier et al., 2001; Charles, 2010; Lewis and Booth, 1989). Still, by the end of the 1980s, despite some advance in the community media cause, nothing further had happened:

> For those who hoped for a separate third tier of not-for-profit radio in the UK, pretty much all seemed lost with the passage of the 1990 Broadcasting Act. (Stoller, 2010: 313)

Nonetheless, today there are over 200 licensed community radio stations in the UK, in striking contrast to the impoverished community media of the 1990s and before, as well as a flourishing situation in some other countries.[1] So how did this change come about? Since 11 million people can now receive community stations in the UK, a substantial increase over the past few years, is community radio 'a genuine success story', as CEO Ed Richards claims (Ofcom, 2009c)?

The community radio order 2004

Following its formation by the Broadcasting Act 1990, the Radio Authority took the view that some commercial local radio stations were to all intents and purposes community media meeting the needs of local communities (Stoller, 2010). Doubtless this view was not shared by the community media movement, for whom this was a frustrating time. Nonetheless, the Radio Authority was minded to support the development of community radio, having inherited a mixed bag of stations that were neither commercial nor public service broadcasting. These included hospital and student stations, cable services established in a number of 'New Towns' (e.g. Milton Keynes), a range of special event licences and a number of pirate radio stations. Stoller (2010) describes how members of the Radio Authority instigated a 'quiet revolution' by granting restrictive services licences to community stations, effectively creating a community radio sector albeit on insecure regulatory foundations. Making sure to grant such licences only to highly localised stations that used low power transmitters, the Radio Authority granted 178 licences in 1991, 241 in 1992, and by 2002 were granting over 400 a year. Although these licences were temporary (only 28 days), they were taken up with alacrity, demonstrating the varied demand for community radio services among local communities, institutions and special interest groups.[2]

The Radio Authority also sought to influence government, particularly the New Labour government after 1997, to support the sector. In 1999 it instigated a trial of what it called 'access radio' to grant longer-term licences to community radio stations. As part of its attempt to overcome opposition from commercial radio to this innovation, the Radio Authority strategically distinguished community radio from both commercial local radio and BBC local radio stations, and formalised the idea that a key and salient feature of community radio was its potential to deliver social gain to its community. While this idea is strategically valuable, it was not easy to defend. Both commercial and public service stations claim that they offer social gain, and both have an established funding mechanism that sustains them. Not all were convinced that a 'third tier' was needed to sit 'outside' the market and the public service system, complementing them both while purveying its alternative values and its grounding in communities and social groups.

Nonetheless, the Community Radio Association (which later incorporated community television and became the Community Media Association or CMA) continued to campaign and organise, also contributing to initiatives to join community media across Europe (AMARC-Europe). Interestingly, the stations that formed part of the Radio Authority's original trials joined the CMA, and the case for community radio was also supported by the CMA's research comparing community media in six different countries (Australia, Canada, France, the Netherlands, Ireland and South Africa). The engagement of the CMA first in the work of the Radio Authority and then of Ofcom suggests that a civil society body can gain momentum and focus through its relationship with a regulatory agency. Nonetheless, the relationship between regulators and civil society groups is often impeded by frustrations on both sides, as one might imagine when a branch of public administration sits down to work with a loosely organised civil society group.

Following the campaigning of the CMA and the trials conducted by the Radio Authority (which had been subjected to an independent academic review; Everett, 2003), community radio was included in the Communications Act 2003, thereby allowing the Secretary of State to introduce secondary legislation on community radio. The DCMS's 'Community Radio Order' created the framework for Ofcom to license community radio stations under certain conditions, thereby moving away from the mixture of temporary licences and pirate stations towards a situation that permitted groups a licence to run a community radio station based on '… a description of services to be provided primarily for the good of the public of a particular community (rather than for commercial reasons)' that would 'confer significant benefits on the public or on the communities for which they are provided' (DCMS, 2004). Significantly, the Order defined 'community' as people living, working or being educated in a locale or people with common interests or characteristics even if they did not live in the same geographical location. Community radio was defined as a not-for-profit 'social enterprise', which resulted in social gain, while social gain was in turn defined as provision for those under-served by existing services (addressing social exclusion), facilitating discussion and the expression of opinions (promoting the public sphere), providing training opportunities to members of the community (skills enhancement), and affording an opportunity for the relevant community to reflect on itself and get to know itself better (social cohesion). The stations should give members of their community the opportunity to participate in managing and staffing the station in a way that is accountable to the local community. Perhaps in response to concerns from commercial broadcasters and government about competition for local radio, Ofcom was to conduct a review after two years of the first licences being granted, focusing on:

> The delivery of social gain and impact on the target communities, funding matters, including the level of advertising and sponsorship revenue and the economic impact on the commercial radio sector. (Ofcom, 2004e: 5)

The Order also addressed issues of media ownership by disqualifying existing broadcasters from holding community radio licences, by limiting ownership of community radio stations to one per group, and awarding licences to groups not individuals. Beyond these requirements, community radio offered the prospect of enhancing economic and social development in a community locale by providing information about local authority social services, promoting economic development, employment and social enterprise, providing workplace opportunities and promoting social inclusion, cultural and linguistic variety, civic participation and volunteering. As a wish list, this is extensive; as a set of requirements on community radio, it is daunting. Some resources were made available, however, and Ofcom became responsible for allocating the Community Radio Fund of £500,000 per year granted by the DCMS (reduced to £440,000 in 2010).

Regulating community radio

Taking on this legislative framework, Ofcom acted quickly. It conducted a consultation, commissioned research, and reflected on the Community Radio Order itself along with Radio Authority reports on previous community radio trials (Everett, 2003). Based on all these sources, Ofcom drafted a statement called *Licensing Community Radio* (Ofcom, 2004e), which outlined its regulatory approach. The consultation process confirmed general support for the development of community radio in the UK, although some small-scale local radio stations expressed their concern about potential competition. Partly in response to such concerns, Ofcom concluded that there was more support for a supervisory approach than for the lighter-touch regulation that applied to commercial radio. Here as elsewhere, Ofcom's approach was to avoid giving a competitive advantage to community radio stations and to enact a clear distinction between community radio and existing commercial and public service radio stations. The result was a cautious approach to granting licences, combined with periodic reviews of market impact, social gain, and financial audit.

Ofcom's approach to spectrum allocation was to secure for community radio those parts of the spectrum that were unable to support commercial stations, arguing that transmitters with a range of 5 km were adequate for the needs of community radio except in cases of a dispersed community where the possibility of two transmitters was considered. Even this rather minimal expectation proved difficult to meet, given that the AM and FM spectrum was already crowded in urban areas. Consequently, Ofcom engaged in a technical review of spectrum availability and the possibilities for flexibility in its allocation, with the BBC supporting the idea that parts of its FM spectrum be made available to community radio in addition to the usable spectrum allocated by Ofcom. One hope was that pirate stations would feel encouraged to take advantage of the new opportunities and become licensed, although Ofcom warned that it would continue to take enforcement action against pirate stations.

An interesting feature of Ofcom's approach to licensing was the degree to which the process was applicant-led in terms of defining the location and community to be served (Ofcom, 2004e: 10). Notably too, Ofcom made it clear that it would not adjudicate between overlapping or competing applications. Instead, based on the Community Radio Order 2004, Ofcom's eligibility criteria included a profile of characteristics for the proposed community radio station, identification of the relevant community, concrete articulations of potential social gain, the financial capability of the applicant to deliver the service as well as its mechanisms for accountability and potential for engagement and education/training and, last, whether the station was competing with existing local radio services.

The question of potential economic impact on local commercial radio ('economic testing') had provoked concern during Ofcom's consultation process, by contrast with the proposals for testing fitness for purpose and potential public value. Whether community radio stations should be allowed to carry advertising was a key point of the controversy. However, the Community Radio Order had already sought to reassure commercial broadcasters by imposing, first, restrictions on the amount of commercial funding that community radio stations could generate if their audience overlapped by more than 50 per cent with a commercial radio station; second, by specifying that a station could only generate up to 50 per cent of its income from spot advertising and commercial sponsorship; and third, that a single source of income should not exceed 50 per cent of a community radio station's income. These were general guidelines and it remained within Ofcom's power to impose tougher restrictions if there was an existing local radio station in the area of operation proposed for a community radio station. Stoller (2010) argued that these aspects of the Community Radio Order were late concessions to active lobbying by commercial radio stations, leaving community radio dependent on public funds that, as Gordon (2005) argues, were then used to justify regulatory intervention.

Significantly, DCMS had already specified the regulatory framework in its Community Radio Order, including that all rather than just some of the four mandatory commitments to provide social gain must be in place (namely, serving the relevant community; facilitating the public sphere; providing training and education; and fostering community links; Ofcom, 2004e: para. 28). By comparison with the IBA's earlier experiments in this area,[3] this approach simultaneously widened the scope of expectations about social gain on community radio while making it harder to achieve. That this was implemented has also been made clear from Ofcom's audit of annual reports from licensed stations.[4]

Evaluating Ofcom's regulation of community radio

Feedback from consultation and Everett's (2003) report to the Radio Authority argued that community radio stations were unlikely to meet all the criteria all of the time. Unsurprisingly, then, Hallett and Wilson (2009) suggest that Ofcom was expecting around 50 licences to be issued in the first round of licences between 2004 and 2006. But in the event, 107 licences were issued during that period, a number that has continued to rise, enabled in part by Ofcom's sustained practice of consulting the sector as it has developed, providing advice and support, attending community radio events, and holding regular meetings with representatives of the CMA and other civil society stakeholders. Indeed, the Community Media Association proved to be a key stakeholder, engaging with Ofcom's consultation and holding meetings with officials during the framing of Ofcom's regulatory approach. For example, as Hallett and Wilson (2009) document, Ofcom initially preferred to call these stations 'access radio stations', but the CMA preferred 'community radio stations' (see also Stoller, 2010), a robust argument that fed into Ofcom's approach to the licensing of community radio stations within the confines of the Community Radio Order.

The notable growth in licensing has brought praise to Ofcom in so far as it realised the vision of the New Labour government (specifically, the Radio Authority and then the DCMS) that there should be a vibrant community radio sector in the UK. There are now over 200 licensed community radio stations in the UK (although 169 of these were actively broadcasting by the end of 2009), which are testament to what can happen when there is political will and support, a proactive and capable regulator working with a vibrant user community, and a relatively small amount of public funding. Hallett and Wilson (2009) praise the effective collaboration between the CMA and first the Radio Authority, then Ofcom. Nevertheless, they ask three important questions. Is community radio too heavily regulated? Is the funding adequate? And is the sector sustainable?

On the question of the amount of regulation, Hallet and Wilson (2009) note that community radio is heavily regulated compared with commercial and public service local radio in the UK. Although this goes against the deregulatory trend that characterises Ofcom's broader remit and approach, Ofcom justifies it in the case of community radio by pointing to concerns expressed in the consultation phase about market impact. Responding to the Myers Review, Ed Richards outlines the paradox that local radio retains strong public support but experiences difficulty in generating revenue. In response to financial pressures the tendency is for stations to merge or for local stations to become regional in scope, thereby diminishing the key feature of local radio (its localness). It is in this context that Ofcom has sought to liberalise rules on the co-location of local commercial stations, to encourage the digital migration of such channels and review content rules to determine if these could be relaxed for local commercial radio (Richards, 2009).

But there remains a sense of historical accident here. For example, in countries where community radio has existed for decades, developing alongside other forms of radio (e.g. Australia), there is not the same imbalance of regulation. Perhaps it is due to the UK's strong public service broadcasting tradition, since it seems almost a ritual response of the commercial sector to call for restrictions on the use of public funds in broadcasting, however limited. Moreover, public service broadcasting is strongly identified with national and regional level services so that extending the social gain associated with public service broadcasting to community media has not gained widespread support. Consequently, community media seem to attract opposition from both commercial and public service media, as evidenced in Ofcom's consultation.

The differentiation of community radio from commercial and public service radio has been strategically useful, but is problematic in some respects. Community radio is hybrid; it extends the meaning of public service broadcasting in ways that are positive, but it is also varied in terms of how commercially valued its services are. Rather than being clearly differentiated from commercial and public service media, community media blur the boundaries between these and bring these diverse forms of media into contact with communities and everyday life. An alternative approach to regulation might take advantage of this overlap rather than seeking a clearer differentiation. Ofcom's approach works best for an ideal typical example of community radio – fixed in a location, serving a generic audience who live in the same area, and complementing the content of existing radio services. But in the digital future, the ideal of community radio – media made by and for people – is likely to be more dispersed in its audiences and delivered using different platforms.

Funding also remains an important concern. Since it was based on a considerable underestimate of the appeal of this form of media and the number of successful licence applications, the Community Radio Fund has been stretched too far and applicants may fail financial sustainability tests precisely because of the lack of available public funds. Thus Ofcom has informed the DCMS that the Community Radio Fund is too overstretched for Ofcom to fulfil its remit in granting licences to stations that in all other respects satisfy the conditions for licensing (Hallett and Wilson, 2009). However, no additional funds have been forthcoming from the DCMS and, as Hallett and Wilson (2009: 145) see it, 'Ofcom has not been particularly vocal in its support for an expanded Community Radio Fund'. However, Ofcom has changed its policy on allowing voluntary contributions to be included in the income lines of community radio budgets, thereby affording the potential to generate greater income from commercial sources. This demonstrates sensitivity to the needs of the sector, given the comparatively small levels of public funding available from a fund that is not only insufficient for the greater number of applicants than anticipated, but which is also dwindling in real value due to inflation and cuts by the Coalition government in 2010. But Ofcom has no power to change the conditions established in the Community Radio Order or the level of funding available to it. The community radio sector, for different reasons, also lacks the power to change these conditions. For example, audience research is very patchy in this sector, even though the terms of licences require statements of the value of the services to audiences, since community radio stations simply do not have the resources to commission RAJAR (the Radio Joint Audience Research Ltd) to do research on their audience (Hallett and Wilson, 2009). Thus audience research evidence of reach and impact that might, if available, strengthen the case for increased funding is sparse, indeed perhaps even absent.

Historically, the UK's community media sector has had to campaign against the odds for official recognition and financial support – including an extended period of campaigning and law-breaking by pirate stations and jammers attacking local radio stations. The attempt to bring these representatives of alternative, campaigning cultures under the wing of media regulation raises some important issues. The comparison with the case of popular music pirate stations and the BBC in the 1960s is instructive, because, as Lewis and Booth (1989) demonstrate, in that case it was the BBC that changed to accommodate popular music and engage a new and younger audience. Ofcom regards the take-up of licences as a measure of the success of its policy as a whole, but how could the community sector not take this opportunity given its history of marginalisation and lack of official support? Licensing was an offer the community sector could not refuse, but questions remain regarding the potential for regulatory capture and its consequences for the anti-establishment and diverse nature of community media projects. Arguably, Ofcom's close regulation of this section has resulted in a narrowing of scope and definition regarding community radio, while the promise of licences may defuse the debate over community radio's potential and even quieten opposition through the enrolment of bodies that were previously 'alternative' into the mainstreaming of a regulated community radio sector.

It remains difficult for community radio to form strategic alliances with commercial and public service local radio, partly because of the dearth of public funding and a lack of clarity on partnership proposals with the BBC. Although underlying Ofcom's proposals was an expectation that partnerships might develop between community radio stations and the BBC especially, these remain difficult issues for community radio. In one border skirmish, Hallett and Wilson (2009) discuss the conflict between BBC Radio Lincoln and Siren FM, a community radio station based at the University of Lincoln on the occasion of a Christmas Fair. The BBC manager expressed concern when the community radio station gave local travel news for this special event which it saw as complementing the BBC content but which the BBC interpreted as insufficiently distinctive in meeting the needs of a community and thus, in practice, competing with the BBC. This story appears to be a trivial example but it demonstrates the sensitivities that surround community media which might limit the potential for partnerships with local radio. It may seem that, in a contrary movement, the BBC is increasingly providing opportunities for audience feedback and participation in its own programmes and services; nonetheless, this falls short of the levels of engagement, production and co-production imagined by the community media project.

So what would be a reasonable expectation for community radio in the UK? Gordon (2005) contrasts the UK experience to that of Australia, a country of one-third the population but with twice as many stations serving diverse communities as part of a flourishing community radio sector. She argues that the top-down requirement in the UK to prove the delivery of social gain has been overly restrictive. While community radio in Australia undoubtedly benefits communities, these benefits are often hard to define and measure, especially in relation to the politics of recognition, engagement through practice and the extension of communication rights, all of which are critical to community building. The focus on social gain even contradicts the alternative, non-institutionalised ethos of community radio at its best, she suggests, while the strength of community radio in Australia lies precisely in the diversity of content, funding and approach. Nor is Australia's radio sector undermined by permitting sponsorship for community radio, since this is generally so low as to constitute little serious competition to any co-present commercial broadcaster. In the UK, by contrast, it seems that innovation outside the BBC model finds it hard to attract support for stable public funding even in an area for which the BBC does not provide. Her comparative study leads Gordon (2005) to recommend a less uniform approach to regulation in the UK, so as to 'let a thousand flowers bloom', adding that the organically-arising social needs of specific local communities should replace a standardised conception of social gain as the primary objective of community radio – and these, she suggests, would be revealed by rectifying the chronic absence of research on the audiences for community radio.

Conclusion

Community media in different parts of the world have different priorities (Rennie, 2006). In Europe, community media encourage alternative definitions of public interest and seek to break down public service monopolies (Carpentier, 2010; Stoller, 2010). In the USA, legal protests in the name of free speech have hindered the efforts of civil society groups to establish community media. In Australia, the focus is on multiculturalism at the cost of marginalising the somewhat unpredictable community media to the fringes. In the industrialising world, community media are promoted as a means of economic and social development. For regulators, the challenge should be to facilitate rather than curb the resultant creativity, the diversity of forms and purposes, the symbiotic relation between community media and the culture of everyday life, and the agonistic relationship between community and mainstream media. In this context, the lack of opportunities to develop community media in the UK, long a source of concern, frustration and resistance, was redressed by Ofcom's regulatory efforts.

Ofcom's achievement in granting over 200 licences to community radio stations since 2004 has been substantial. It has established the first long-term licensing system, overseen a radical expansion of the sector, consulted widely, produced transparent policies on the regulation of community radio and administered the Community Radio Fund as financed by the DCMS. This case study thus illustrates the regulator's capacity to promote innovation and to work in partnership with civil society in order to implement significant regulatory change. Yet as we have seen, for the most part the regulator has worked within rules established by government, and these tended to overstate the potential risk to both commercial and public service radio. Thus Ofcom has pointed to competition issues as a justification for what is arguably a heavy-handed approach to regulation, in contrast with its usual avowed preference for a 'lighter touch'. Greater recognition of the unique and valuable benefits to be offered by a strong community radio (or community media) sector, possibly in partnership with the BBC and commercial services, would surely be desirable.

However, funding remains a problem for community radio stations, as do the regulatory burden, the restrictions on financial arrangements and the insistence on the separation of community radio from commercial and public service radio. In its annual report on the community radio sector for 2009/10, Ofcom stated that almost 50 per cent of community radio stations had reported a deficit. These deficits are often covered by the parent organisations but raise concerns about the future viability of the sector (Ofcom, 2010f). Ofcom's role regarding both funding and approach was substantially determined by the DCMS, but there is still scope for some to ask whether community radio has paid too high a price for its licences, given the level and type of regulation to which it is subjected (e.g. Gordon, 2005; Hallett and Wilson, 2009). This regulation has focused on two key points – the specification of financial restraints and the imposition of social gain as licensing criteria. For each, as is often also argued of the BBC, the expectation of accountability in terms of public value would seem appropriate in return for public funding, if only that public funding were itself sufficient. While increased funding would ease current constraints, scaling up a vision for community radio remains problematic. How can a sector be regulated that, by its nature, depends on the enthusiastic, voluntary efforts of local communities? As popular interests and concerns are increasingly drawn into the scope of regulation, something is lost from the diversity, campaigning spirit and alternative cultural and political ethos that are central to community media (Cunningham and Flew, 2002), extending the sphere of governance in a way that may become more disabling than empowering (Lewis and Miller, 2003).

Despite Ofcom's efforts, it seems that the opportunity was missed to ask big questions about the role of community media in the UK, including in relation to public service broadcasting. Such questions remain pressing – in the age of networks of public connection typical of new forms of social order in 'the network society' (Castells, 1996), community media gain a revitalised contemporary relevance. Potentially, community radio can encompass both local embeddedness and global connectedness. It can represent the marginalised, it is grounded in the everyday, and it contributes to the public sphere. One might say, however, does not the BBC do this already, with its popular network of local radio stations? But for community radio advocates, radical or communitarian (Etzioni, 1993), the point is to develop a voice that emerges bottom up, networked horizontally, to complement that already well established which speaks on behalf of the public (Rennie, 2006). How this will develop in the emerging digital age remains unclear. As Rennie (2006) goes on to ask, can a role be found for community media that goes beyond self-consciously resistant or campaigning aims? Can they become more broadly based, overcoming opposition from mainstream media, while retaining their alternative and amateur aesthetic so as to sustain the input of enthusiastic volunteers (Atton, 2002)? We can also ask the question the other way around – what will the digital and convergent media future mean for community radio, already a rather fragile media form? Is there potential for community radio to connect the local to the global, to be part of global networks of interest in the digital age?[5]

Notes

1 For example, Gordon (2005) reviewed the 359 stations (plus 40 stations on temporary licences) that existed in Australia in 2005, including rural stations covering large geographical areas, stations based in cities catering for particular locations and stations that were vehicles for communities of interest.

2 The licences were used for a wide variety of purposes, including universities, hospitals, the Edinburgh International Science Festival, Royal Air Force (RAF) station open days and religious stations such as Fast FM established in Bradford for Ramadhan.

3 From 1989, the IBA issued a few experimental community radio licences to small-scale services in areas that already had local commercial or public service stations, as long as the content of community radio complemented existing services (Hallett and Wilson, 2009). Thus its focus was on encouraging complementary operation and content so that competition did not become an issue and a locale could end up with a diversity of radio services (national, local and community), rather than

on clearly differentiating local from community radio, as was the basis of Ofcom's approach. However, as Hallett and Wilson (2009) point out, the problem with the IBA's approach was that it did not develop a regulatory approach that was suited to community radio, instead extending its approach to commercial radio to a number of new radio stations of small scale (21), of which only some were what might be recognised as community radio. Undoubtedly Ofcom's approach has been successful in affording the expansion of the community radio sector.

4 Annual reports were to be published and stations expected to keep a record of the evidence behind their claims. In addition to these specific demands on community radio, the licensed stations were also expected to meet the conditions of the standard broadcasting codes in the production of news and current affairs and in the fairness of advertising and privacy rules. Ofcom reserved the right to sanction community radio stations that failed to meet either the requirements for licensing or the codes.

5 For example, Carpentier (2011) discusses strategies developed by six Belgian community radio stations to exploit file-sharing technology to link together a number of stations and connect them to other stations across the globe.

9

CONCLUSIONS

A change of direction

> By assigning quangos strictly administrative functions, we are removing them as actors in democratic politics and public debate. (Cameron, 2009)

In July 2009, nearly a year before the Conservatives formed a Coalition government with the Liberal Democrats in the UK, Conservative leader David Cameron gave a high-profile speech entitled 'People power – reforming quangos' (Cameron, 2009). Ofcom, surprising to many since it was neither very prominent nor funded by the tax payer, was first on his list of regulators in need of reform. Proposing no minor or procedural changes, Cameron called for a fundamental political reform of the governance strategy of the New Labour government, a radical redistribution of power 'from the state to citizens; from government to parliament; from Whitehall to communities; from Brussels to Britain; from judges to the people; from bureaucracy to democracy'. By way of justification, he identified a problem of responsibility, accountability, freedom and control affecting all levels of governance – local, national and regional. Citizens, he said, were losing out, and his proposals were designed to give control to people over the things that mattered to them and that affected their lives – local policing or schools policy, for example, as well as transparency for national government processes. Over the years, he argued, the quangos had assumed ever more power, not only in the procedural management of specific industries or sectors of society, but also in relation to decision making and policy. Halting the proliferation of these unelected non-government organisations was therefore a priority, and Cameron promised to return key policy-making functions to elected politicians.

Specifically, Cameron announced that his government would reform quangos substantially, reducing the number of bodies as well as their budgets, size, scope and influence, and only retaining those that fulfilled a necessary or useful purpose that either could not or should not be performed by government. Here he identified 'three particular areas where the public would want reassurance that actions, decisions, or the provision of services are insulated from political influence' – those requiring complex technical expertise (e.g. the Nuclear Installations Inspectorate or Ofwat, the water regulator), those requiring impartiality or independence from political preferences (e.g. the Research Councils), and those requiring transparency in the production and interpretation of evidence (e.g. the Office for National Statistics). But quangos would not need communications departments nor would they need a 'strategy' (let alone Ofcom's aspirations to having a 'philosophy'). And, Cameron insisted, ministers should retain control, holding these public bodies to account, preventing 'regulatory creep' or engagement in contested debates, and ensuring a resolute focus on cost-effectiveness so as to reduce the regulatory burden on industry and the indirect cost to consumers of the services that they regulated.

For New Labour, the converged regulatory agencies had offered a means for increasing public engagement, transparency and accountability in important policy areas so as to produce consensus and to balance the interests of government, commerce and the public. But for the incoming Coalition government, these same agencies had created problems of democratic governance and accountability – positioning themselves as intermediaries between government and the people and, therefore, actively getting in the way of democratic decision making. Cameron's (2009) rationale harks back to Margaret Thatcher's neoliberal policies to reform the welfare state, privatise public monopolies and deregulate markets. Taken together, this reflects an ideology of a small but strong state working with a 'big society' in which government intervention in markets or society is seen as the last resort rather than the preferred mode of governance. The assumption is that if government retreats as much as possible from areas of private life, then people, communities, local authorities and companies will find solutions that have more public legitimation and that will be more effective than proposals from national quasi-government agencies. As Lord Wei, government adviser on the Big Society, said on his appointment in 2010: 'I am excited to be working with this government on building the Big Society ... [though] I am determined to remain anchored in the daily reality of life as a citizen, standing with other citizens to build a stronger society from the bottom up.'[1]

Democratic as this sounds, it is important to remember the fundamental disagreements about what constitutes democracy in complex pluralistic societies, as revealed by our discussion in Chapter 2 of how liberal and republican positions frame the public interest in regulation. The Conservative approach, grounded in the traditions of liberal governance, seeks to protect society from government interference so that a plurality of interests can be freely expressed. In between elections, the public is encouraged to engage in local activism and volunteerism and then, at elections, the public gives its verdict on the national government via the ballot box. Crucially, while supporting self-regulation (by firms and individuals) backed by a small but powerful state, this approach rejects the dispersal of state power through the diversification of soft or cooperative modes of governance involving partnerships with hybrid or quasi-independent organisations. This contrasts with New Labour's preference for a more participatory democracy which, as we argued in this book, draws on the tradition of civic republicanism to develop a reformist rather than a radical agenda that works with rather than against the market. This includes constitutional reform – making the state more transparent, building links with Europe, embedding principles of human rights in all state activities – and, crucial to our argument, engaging the public between as well as at elections in a range of political and civic processes at all levels of society, including in the activities of regulatory agencies as institutions in the public sphere.

In practice, of course, the differences between these political positions are rather more nuanced, motivated in part by competition for the middle ground of electoral appeal. Nonetheless, it seems that the emerging regulatory regime of the present Coalition government, as signalled by Cameron's 2009 speech, is shifting away from the expectation that independent, quasi-governmental bodies such as Ofcom would or should play a role in framing policy and facilitating civic engagement. Rather, as is indeed now coming to pass as Ofcom adjusts to substantial cuts in its budget and activities, the normative expectation is for a technically expert body focused on evidence gathering, consumer protection, and the bread-and-butter job of enabling the operation of an effective market. One consequence is a retrenchment of its activities as regards engagement and consultation, though interestingly its research function is being strongly defended if more narrowly focused.

The power to make policy

In Cameron's pre-election (2009) speech, as we saw above, his central point was that the power to make policy should rest with government. Invoking public antipathy towards 'red tape' and the 'nanny state' (or, as he put it, the 'quango state'), he painted a picture of unaccountable bodies insidiously and excessively influencing the way people live:

> They determine what we can watch on TV and online. They control what our children are taught in school. They tell us what medicine we can take and what treatments we can receive. The growth in the number of quangos, and in the scope of their influence, raises important questions for our democracy and politics.

However, notwithstanding such populist rhetoric, the case studies of media and communications regulation that we have examined in this book speak to a subtler mode of governance through engagement and self-regulation rather than determination through command and control. Further, the hand of government has often been evident in the regulator's actions, through both the requirements imposed on it by a strongly framed Communications Act 2003 and the guiding influence thereafter from ministers and their departments. Nonetheless, Ofcom was clearly in the firing line of the Conservative Party in opposition leading up to the 2010 General Election. After all, Ofcom was a highly visible New Labour project, a convergent, principled regulator which encouraged public involvement beyond the ballot box so as to draw stakeholders into processes of engagement and deliberation. Moreover, its research might support but might also challenge aspects of government policy.

Before coming to office in 2010, the Conservative Shadow Cabinet reviewed the array of quangos (whose numbers were estimated to be between 790 and 1,100 in the UK) to ask which were really needed and if they were, whether some of their functions could be moved into the relevant government department. The resultant Public Bodies Bill was announced immediately the Coalition government came to power, entering the parliamentary process during 2010–11. In a so-called 'bonfire of the quangos', the Bill proposed the closure of 177 quangos and a reduction in the function and budget of many others, including Ofcom. Taking Ofcom as the first example of a regulatory agency in need of reform in his 2009 speech, Cameron accepted that a media and communications regulator was necessary to monitor the plurality of media, to deal with licensing and spectrum allocation issues and to enforce fair pricing in media and communications – the technical, impartiality and research functions noted above – but criticised its strategic role in policy making, saying:

Jeremy Hunt has concluded that Ofcom currently has many other responsibilities that are matters of public policy, in areas that should be part of a national debate, for example the future of regional news or Channel 4. These should not be determined by an unaccountable bureaucracy, but by ministers responsible to Parliament.

Setting aside the problematic implication throughout Cameron's 2009 speech that Ofcom had been – contrary to much of what we have demonstrated in this book – unaccountable, bureaucratic and undemocratic, especially by comparison with government departments, what really matters is the proposed 'return' of regulatory decision making and strategy to government. Specifically, key areas of Ofcom's activities are to be transferred to the Secretary of State for Culture, Olympics, Media and Sport (see Tambini, 2010). These include the review of public service broadcasting (discussed in

Chapter 5), ITV's networking arrangements (where, instead of being reviewed annually by Ofcom, these would be reviewed as and when requested by the minister), and Ofcom's duty to review public ownership rules (discussed in Chapter 4). The government signalled clearly that quangos should not contribute to policy or take an independent position on policy issues, they should no longer be engaged in public debate, and they should act under much tighter ministerial control compared with the relative independence that they enjoyed under the governance arrangements of New Labour. Interestingly, in a speech in January 2011, Hunt recognised that one reason Ofcom had undertaken so significant a policy role was that it had served under four Secretaries of State in its seven years, three of them between 2007 and 2010, and thus it had – for reasons of historical accident perhaps – found itself more often in the position of briefing government than of being briefed by it.[2]

These broader concerns regarding the locus of policy making that lie behind Cameron's polemic speech have, in various ways, been shared by governments of different complexions since the 1970s, reflecting a long-standing tension between lack of electoral accountability and the advantages of non-departmental public bodies (as quangos are officially known) delivering expert decisions, providing advice, regulating at arm's length from government and allowing important areas of social, cultural and economic life to be de-politicised. Indeed, the New Labour governments from 1997 to 2010, while supporting the development of new regulatory agencies with a range of powers such as the Financial Services Authority and Ofcom, themselves reduced the number of quangos by 10 per cent and supported the incremental reduction of the regulatory burden as a principle of better regulation (a point on which Ofcom regularly holds itself accountable in its Annual Reports). Provocatively perhaps, Schlesinger (2011) identifies a series of ways in which the Coalition government's policies, much mooted as radical change, in fact continue certain strands of New Labour policy. Diverting part of the BBC licence fee from core funding for the BBC is one such continuity (begun by Labour in funding for the digital switchover and continued by the Coalition government since), and another is the priority given to community media and local television (this latter being favoured by Hunt but with a longer precedent in Labour's support for the idea of independently funded news consortia). Nonetheless, the transformation in Ofcom proposed by the Public Bodies Bill seems, we would contend, a significant change, restricting the role of the regulator in its role as an institution in the public sphere and thus, as we have argued, in its ability to further the public interest, especially the citizen interest.

It should be noted that the proposal to cut the long list of quangos identified in the Public Bodies Bill remains controversial. A cross-bench committee of lawyers has argued that the Bill is potentially unconstitutional since many of the bodies affected (including Ofcom) were established by primary legislation which can only be superseded by further legislation. Indeed, it is ironic that a Bill drawn up on the pretext of increasing account-ability was itself seen to sidestep parliamentary debate and consultation with the bodies concerned and with the public. Further criticism came from Members of Parliament on the Public Administration Committee who also argued that the Bill had been rushed through without sufficient consultation, that the Cabinet Office had failed to set out a proper proce-dure for ministers to follow in deciding which bodies to eradicate or reform, and that the result was based on an insufficient analysis of the func-tions and powers of the bodies affected and an inconsistency of approach across ministries (Public Administration Committee, 2010). In addition, the committee argued, had adequate value for money tests been conducted, neither in relation to the bodies scrutinised nor regarding the cost implica-tions of proposed changes.

Focusing on the likely consequences of these reductions in Ofcom's areas of responsibility, Tambini (2010) warns of a significant adverse impact on media freedom. Media ownership decisions, he argues, should be made by an arm's length body acting in the public interest, independent of political and commercial interests, if media plurality is to be protected. Similarly, the removal of Ofcom's duty to review public service broadcasting grants the Secretary of State increased control over public service broadcasters, poten-tially constraining the latter's freedom to criticise government. Although reducing the cost of regulation might be argued to benefit industry and ulti-mately the consumer, the public finances are unlikely to save money by reducing the duties and responsibilities of Ofcom since, although its funds have been cut by 19 per cent, most of this is paid for by a levy on industry. Tambini therefore interprets these moves as an attempt to give more power to government over important areas of media policy that, whether for reasons of technical expertise or impartiality, are better served by an independent regulator. The Chairman of Channel 4, Lord Burns, expressed similar con-cerns (in *The Guardian*, 24/11/2010), namely that the Bill opens the door for the Secretary of State to influence Channel 4 and the BBC, since they are included in the Bill as publicly funded statutory bodies. Whether public service broadcasters are indeed subject to increased political pressure, thereby constraining editorial freedom, will be judged by future commentators.

On the value of an independent regulator

A critical decision facing government is whether institutions of public administration should retain the potential for independence, a principled basis for action, rational decision making and acting in the public interest or whether they should focus on delivering government policy (Du Gay, 2000). As we have seen throughout this book, many of these features characterised Ofcom precisely because, as Tambini (2010) argues, of its combination of statutory obligations, distance from government, bureaucratic principles, the requirements of producing evidence and engagement with stakeholders, which creates a context for regulatory decision making that stands apart from, if not totally immune to, such interests, helping to protect the independence and freedom of the media in the public interest. Yet the Coalition government that came to power in 2010 asserted that having political control over policy and clearer accountability for ministers is preferable to having matters of public policy influenced by an (electorally) unaccountable body. In addition, Ofcom was committed to applying public interest tests as well as market impact tests in both guidelines and judgements on media ownership, whereas it is not clear how important public interest tests will be for the DCMS, and the reasoning behind such decisions will potentially be less publicly visible than it has been under Ofcom. In relation to public service broadcasting, where Ofcom conducted reviews on behalf of, but at arm's length from, government and was relatively immune to industry pressure, aiming to balance the needs of the market with the broader public interest, it remains to be seen what will follow now that these review are to be at the discretion of the Secretary of State. The risk in all these changes is that political interests will have a more direct and stronger impact on policies regarding media ownership, public service broadcasting, the obligations of commercial broadcasters and more. And nor is it proven that, between elections, politicians will be more or even as transparent, consultative and accountable.

In our review of Ofcom's work on public service broadcasting in Chapter 5, we expressed concern that Ofcom's position affected the neutrality of its review, and we criticised the scope, methods and interpretation of findings in both Ofcom's reviews. Nonetheless, its work was transparent and publicly accountable and it encompassed extensive collaboration with stakeholders, research and public consultation in a manner that may not be the case for ministerial review. The notion that government control of public service broadcasting will increase is supported by the government's intervention duing the 2010 Spending Review. In his letter to the chair of the BBC Governors, the Secretary of State affirmed the government's view that the BBC was a world-class national asset which played an important role in UK culture and its democracy. But the letter came after a tough renegotiation between the government and the BBC, resulting in a change to the BBC's financial settlement under its charter, which had been set for a 10-year period in 2006, justifying this on the grounds that all other public services were now subject to additional spending cuts and the BBC could hardly be exempt.[3] The Secretary of State was satisfied with the agreement:

I believe the agreement we have reached provides certainty and security for the BBC over the settlement period. The requirement on the BBC to take on important new funding obligations and efficiencies provides the value to licence fee payers necessary in the current economic climate. (Hunt, 2010)

But there are a number of legitimate causes for concern in these events. First, the talks between the government and the BBC took place very rapidly and behind closed doors. Second, the renegotiation of the terms established under charter review undermined the principle of financial stability, itself aimed at giving the BBC independence from commercial pressures and political control, granted by that agreement. In short, if this negotiation was indicative of the way the DCMS is to regulate the media henceforth, the claim that government is more accountable and democratic than an independent regulator must surely refer to a system of accountability based predominantly on a representative government legitimated by the power of the vote (since the public cedes power to government between elections). This contrasts with the approach illustrated by Ofcom and other independent regulators during the past decade, namely of (at least some) public engagement in the ongoing process deliberation and decision making. It may be claimed that much of Ofcom's work, particularly on protecting consumer interests, may still be managed under the new regime as it promotes competition, ensures a plurality of media ownership, protects consumers from harm and offence, and reduces the regulatory burden (Ofcom, 2010d). However, it has been our contention that the citizen interest is best served by an independent regulatory agency using a variety of proactive methods to engage a wide range of stakeholders. We have argued that, in principle, such an approach legitimates media and communications policy in a dynamic and fast-moving environment. At the same time, we have acknowledged the practical and procedural difficulties involved in facilitating and managing public deliberation as part of regulatory processes.

Conclusions

In the opening chapters of this book, we conjoined academic theories of regulation with governmental responses to the growing challenges of globalisation and the network society in order to invoke the idea – perhaps the ideal – of a regulatory agency playing the role of an institution in the public sphere in addition to its instrumental and administrative tasks. Through our analysis of Ofcom's public-facing activities, we identified the issues and concerns that arose from a regulatory agency coming to play a prominent role in public life, especially at a time when the economic, social and cultural consequences for the interests of citizens and consumers are being greatly contested. Thus we have observed Ofcom's work in generating independent, publicly available research, encouraging public debate on communications policy, enhancing public deliberation through consultation and supporting the work of civil society bodies to represent public opinion on media and communications matters alongside enhanced stakeholder relations with industry bodies.

In these and related ways, Ofcom has, perhaps uniquely as a regulatory agency, played out its role as an institution in the public sphere with originality, energy and expertise. It exemplifies the advantages of arm's length, expert, public-facing regulatory agencies, for as an integrated and converged regulator, Ofcom has developed considerable capacity and expertise to deal with complex technical and market issues facing both firms and consumers in the media and communications sector. As a quasi-independent body, it has often proved itself flexible in its approach to adjudication and regulation – for example in its proposals for public service broadcasting or in the regulation of community radio. However, as we have also recognised, Ofcom has encountered a range of difficulties in terms of formulating a distinct policy and determining a consistent regulatory stance – consider its work on media literacy or the regulation of children's television advertising. In the case of the former, the difficulties of educating the general public, and in the case of the latter, the greater power of the health lobby, proved to be too great a challenge for the regulator to manage. Furthermore, many of the risks associated with the activities of regulatory agencies, as identified by Baldwin and Cave (1999), have also been in evidence throughout our analysis – the tendency of the regulator to reinterpret the agenda, often giving greater prominence to the market over social and cultural issues, grounds for concern over the effectiveness of public engagement and consultation, especially as regards civil society bodies and the wider public, and issues regarding the provenance and significance of research evidence in decision making. Thus our case studies have illustrated the difficulties of combining effectiveness as a regulator with promoting public engagement with media policy.

This conclusion is echoed in a review of Ofcom conducted by the National Audit Office (NAO, 2010). This focused on Ofcom's efforts to deliver efficiency savings and to measure the impact of its activities in outcomes and benefits to citizens and consumers. In order to evaluate these, the NAO (2010: 4) collated indicators of Ofcom's use of resources, outcomes for citizens and consumers, market indicators and stakeholder views. On efficiency savings, Ofcom was found to have made overall savings of £23 million at an average of 3 per cent per year. However, the NAO was unconvinced that Ofcom had fully realised the potential savings from the convergence of its five legacy regulators, and it was particularly critical of Ofcom for not doing enough to set targets for and analyse the financial impact of its activities.[4] In spectrum management also, Ofcom was criticised for lacking a strategic and structured approach to realising the value of spectrum allocation. It had done better, according to the NAO review, in realising positive outcomes for citizens and consumers, with increased satisfaction and confidence in the media and communications market resulting from increased competition and more service providers.[5]

Interestingly, the NAO's survey of respondents to Ofcom's consultations found that stakeholders were positive about the consultation process, but also concerned about the speed of Ofcom's delivery on the outcomes of consultation. This suggests that concerns about the speed of delivery reflect a perceived lack of transparency in the link between Ofcom's consultation process (which stakeholders value) and how consultation is taken account of and influences Ofcom's decision making, policies and practices. While the NAO points to the mitigating effects of the time and money that Ofcom is bound to spend on appeals against its regulatory decisions, this reflects responses from those directly affected by decisions rather than the ways in which citizens and their representatives are concerned to influence regulation. The NAO report itself demonstrates a central theme of this book; that it is often easier and more straightforward to define, measure and take account of consumer interests than citizenship interests. The focus of the NAO report – which was on relations between the regulator and industry – reflects the widespread tendency, criticised in this book, of neglecting the consumer and, especially, the citizen aspects of the public interest in regulation.

More broadly, the shift of government from a reformist social democratic to a Conservative-led coalition had the immediate effect of changing the terms of reference by focusing the regulator on its technical administrative functions and reducing its public-facing role. This shift demonstrates the vulnerability of regulatory agencies as a means of establishing consensus and continuity in the delivery of media and communications policy, and it also demonstrates the vulnerability of civil society bodies with, it seems likely, even less purchase in the future than hitherto on processes of policy deliberation. Regulatory agencies, being creatures of statute, are always dependent on government to provide a stable context within which public consensus can be built and through which important areas of media and communications policy can be managed at arm's length from party political disputes and commercial pressures. As we have seen periodically during Ofcom's past decade (witness several of our case studies) and as we are likely to see more in the future, governments determine the powers, responsibilities and functions of regulators and, more importantly, they determine the nature of regulation itself. As noted above, any government must decide whether or not to use regulatory agencies as an extension of public administration so as to bolster the power of central government or whether to create public institutions that will disperse power, bolster civil society and enhance public discussion and debate (relatively) independent of government.

Such choices are, inevitably, positioned within their particular historical context. Of considerable significance today are the challenges posed by a globalising, networked society to public engagement, democratic governance and political culture. In Chapter 1, we identified a set of public sphere-related criteria by which to evaluate Ofcom's claims to go beyond the technical implementation of government policy, and in Chapter 2, we grounded these criteria in an account of changes in governance that point up the potential advantages of regulatory agencies in determining policy over central government departments. But, as we also argued in Chapter 2, the models by which governance may be conducted by regulators are complex and diverse; two in particular – the liberal pluralist and the civic republican – have proved influential in shaping the bifurcation in both Ofcom and New Labour more widely between the consumer and citizen interests.

Consistent with the long-dominant liberal pluralist tradition in the UK, Ofcom has met its statutory duties regarding the citizen and consumer interests primarily by balancing competition policy and consumer protection. In terms of its claims for regulatory effectiveness (or power), this has prioritised the consumer dimension of the public interest (although, since Ofcom declares that citizen and consumer interests overlap, and in highlighting the domains in which, indeed, they do intersect, this point tends to be obscured). Accordingly, the regulator grounds its claims for legitimation in the evidence of public opinion research, which aggregates individual views and the views of competing stakeholders in terms of preferences and needs rather than, as a civic vision would have it, in terms of arguments for social justice and self-actualisation. However, recognition of the public's expressed preferences and needs does not, as we and many other critics have argued, exhaust the concept of the public interest. As revealed in our case studies, Ofcom has at times also represented the public interest in terms of the citizen interest as conceived by a civic republican ethos. Here its effectiveness, in so far as it has been effective, is evidenced through such specific actions as its support for public service broadcasting and media pluralism, its restrictions on advertising junk food to children, and in promoting media literacy. Such activities have been legitimated, significantly, in so far as Ofcom has worked as an institution in the public sphere, supporting the foregoing actions through public engagement, consultation, research and debate.

But as Habermas (1976) argues the combination of capitalism and liberal democracy creates a more fundamental crisis of legitimation than any single regulator can resolve – markets create inequality, and this undermines the claims of liberal democracy to treat citizens as equals. Consequently, Ofcom has faced tensions regarding its principal duties of serving the interests of citizens and consumers ever since those initial debates over its formation as a converged and principled regulator during the passage of the Communications Act 2003. Clearly, there is no easy solution to the legitimation crisis that lies at the heart of liberal capitalism and so, unsurprisingly, there remains a tension at the heart of media and communications policy and regulation. The welfare state uses public ownership and high levels of public services to moderate the impact of market volatility on citizens. The recent shift towards neoliberalism removes many of these protections, exposing the public to increased risks as well as opportunities in increasingly dynamic global markets. And thus there are real grounds for concern that the reforms of Ofcom in 2011, by reining in the regulator and prioritising its technocratic over its public sphere functions, will be to the detriment of informed public debate about media and communications regulation and policy. They may therefore, more significantly, also be to the detriment of media and communications policy itself – from the perspective of its citizens and consumers (or, to use other well-established terms, its audiences and publics).

So what of the achievements of the Ofcom as an institution in the public sphere? In Chapter 1 we drew on Habermas's (1996) normative criteria for evaluating whether Ofcom as a public institution has supported deliberation as a means of ensuring it furthers the interests of citizens and consumers, over and above its role in enabling economic competitiveness. Deliberative democracy theory comprises a relatively recent cluster of ideas and writings focused on resolving problems in liberal democracy arising from crises of authority and the legitimacy of the state (Held, 2006). It recognises that the mere fact of providing opportunities for participation or extending the state in relation to social and economic affairs may not necessarily result in effective and legitimate government. Those who advocate deliberative democracy are thus concerned to find ways of improving the quality of democratic participation in decision making so as to enable issues of public concern to be addressed in an inclusive way that has a regard for evidence, the broader public interest, and the diversity of views and interests in society. To be sure, this places a significant burden on the management of public engagement: efforts to enhance deliberation in the public interest must demonstrate that the public interest is not better served by elite or expert decision making and that it will not get lost in a cacophony of competing expressions of interest.

Habermas (1996) argues that the effective and legitimate use of public reason will enable participants with divergent interests to engage as equals in an impartial, considered deliberative process and will also, in turn, sustain the effectiveness and legitimacy of governing institutions. From the point of view of the liberal democratic state, enhancing deliberation requires 'constitutional designs which help build in to the process of politics itself the opportunity to learn and test publicly citizens' views' (Held, 2006: 233-4). Going beyond the mere aggregation and collation of individual citizens' views via opinion polling, deliberation aims to enhance the public under-standing of complex social problems, expose the vested interests of particu-lar positions, allow public opinion to form through an open, fluid and dynamic process and replace expressions of interest with reason (Coleman and Blumler, 2009; Fishkin, 1991; Held, 2006).

Public institutions can play a key role in creating the conditions by which people can deliberate freely and equally. How then do Ofcom's varied forms of public engagement, as documented in the case studies in this book, meet Habermas's four criteria - of articulating the public interest, balancing con-straints, combining effectiveness and legitimation, and ensuring reflexivity regarding the consequences of regulation? Ofcom has employed a range of methods to enable public expression in relation to media policy questions. It has placed most reliance, as observed in our case studies, on the combina-tion of public consultation and audience research to represent public opin-ion on such matters as the value of public service broadcasting, advertising to children, media literacy and community radio.

However, Ofcom's processes of engagement have not entirely met the criteria required for public reason to reach a collective understanding in the public interest. First, processes of consultation are vulnerable to substantial inequalities in the resources to participate and, in consequence, can silence a number of constituencies; meanwhile the use of social research methods – supposedly to represent those who do not speak for themselves in public consultations – frequently underestimates the complexity of collective public opinion (as opposed to merely aggregated expressions of individual self-interest). In terms of the second criterion, namely that as a public institution the regulator should enhance deliberation among a wide range of stakehold-ers representing established power, civil society bodies and the public, we have indeed noted many instances of proactive engagement, but it remains less clear that diverse views are deliberated in a public and accountable manner, directly informing the decision-making process and, ultimately, rais-ing the quality of any decisions made. Third, the balance between effective-ness and legitimation thus remains in some doubt – common criticisms from civil society are that Ofcom weighs the consumer interest over the citizen interest and that it often puts the business interest ahead of both. The fourth criterion covers institutional reflexivity concerning the effects of the regula-tor's own actions. Here Ofcom has been criticised by the National Audit Office (NAO, 2010) for not being as clear as it might have been about the consequences of its own actions and, as our case studies have also shown, there are several ways in which Ofcom could be more explicit and reflexive about its role in structuring public opinion and the consumer experience.

Habermas's approach to deliberation insists on impartiality as a guarantee of reasonable public deliberation. However, not all theorists of deliberation would agree, arguing instead that the political sphere should pro-actively seek out expressions of diverse, even agonistic ways of thinking, reasoning and expression in order to support a range of modes of public deliberation (Mouffe, 1992, 2000; Young, 2000). On this alternative view of deliberation, it is not to be expected that deliberation will resolve conflict, enable participants to transcend their own interests or reach a consensual resolution. Compatible with both approaches, we have seen Ofcom over and again approach its task of public engagement in a serious and effortful manner. But it is unclear whether it conceives its goal in terms of reasoned consensus among the views that come before it, proactive and agonistic deliberation among the views that exist in society, or merely the public expression of interests in advance of an expert process of decision making undertaken in private. We have identified elements of each approach on different occasions but, beyond an occasional mention of Ofcom's 'philosophy', there has been little reflexive explication of the regulator's approach to the public's involvement in decision making.

So much for process. What, in terms of outcomes, do our case studies reveal regarding whether Ofcom has furthered the interests of citizens and consumers? In relation to public service broadcasting, at first Ofcom appeared more concerned about the financial sustainability of public service broadcasters and about their market impact; this only added to the concerns of critics that public service was being threatened by the application of a market or business logic to a cultural enterprise acting in the public interest. Yet Ofcom's first public service review also sought to explicate the public value delivered by public service broadcasting, and this informed the government's review of the BBC Charter, complementing the BBC's own analysis of its public value. Ofcom's second review marked a shift, in which it emphasised the value of public service broadcasting in general and the BBC in particular, encouraging public service broadcasters to lead the way in innovations and developments in digitisation and new media services, while still scrutinising these for their potential market impact. In this case, a balance was thus struck between consumer and citizen interests such that the public value of public service broadcasting became more explicit, a more transparent governance structure was advocated, and a greater focus was placed on audience/user participation in public service media.

In the case of media literacy, our discursive method proved peculiarly apt since many policy statements begin with a disclaimer regarding the definition of media literacy. The term attracts considerable societal expectations regarding the potential of audiences to engage with a converged media and communications environment. Yet it is also so open that it can accommodate opposed political agendas, from the social democratic (or civic republican) to the liberal pluralist or even the neoliberal. In the UK, media literacy policy builds on a long tradition of media education, despite rather sporadic intervention from government, mild support from industry and, since the 2010 General Election, a significant cut in budget. It seems that Europe is now taking the lead, with international initiatives from UNESCO and others following suit, in seeking to raise national levels of media literacy, undoubtedly a valiant if difficult task (European Association for Viewers' Interests, 2009). As regards citizens' and consumers' interests, Ofcom's work in researching and promoting media literacy has been worthy, but overly focused on increasing access to and instrumental use of media platforms and services, with too little grasp of how media literacy might more ambitiously serve the citizen interest. Still, we see the definitional debates as having been both lively and important, opening the door to the public expression of ambition regarding media literacy to a degree that cannot, it seems, be easily reversed. Thus these ambitions remain in circulation, providing some demanding criteria by which media literacy policy will continue to be judged.

While the public service case study revealed the importance of multistakeholder consultation, and the media literacy case study revealed the discursive power of terminological debates, our third case study – on the advertising of junk food to children – revealed on the one hand, how an evidence-based regulator was forced to rethink when the evidence challenged its initial views, but also, in a manner typical of older rather than new regimes of regulation, how the state will still intervene if the regulator is heading in a direction that contravenes its interests. In this case, the state had itself conflicting interests – to reduce the burden of regulation on advertising and yet, at the same time, to reduce the problem of childhood obesity which not only costs the health service an increasing amount but which has been linked, consistently (over studies) though not greatly (in terms of explanatory value), to their exposure to advertising. Generally speaking, children like advertising, and they like junk food, so on one reading, the decision to restrict such advertising prioritised the citizen interest (or, the long-term, collective interest of society) over the immediate preferences of individual children. However, it must be said that contributing to children's health, especially in such a relatively modest manner, and only when made to do so by government, is not the citizen interest that critics generally have in mind in advocating for its importance or when evaluating the actions of the regulator.

Our final case study of community radio also demonstrates the complex interplay between consumer and citizen interest. On the one hand, the regulator's work has supported the development of a viable sector that facilitates audience participation and mediated public deliberation, thereby contributing to meeting the needs of (or delivering 'social gain' to) particular communities or groups in society. Yet while this has furthered the citizen interest, at the same time Ofcom has placed a high regulatory burden on community radio stations, to limit their impact on the market for local commercial radio. Moreover, for some critics the effect of regulation has produced a mainstreaming of formats and content that has undermined the sector's 'alternative' or campaigning spirit. The requirements of business accountability, care in market positioning, even the requirement to deliver social gain have all contributed to a situation in which, although the main thrust of the regulation was to promote the citizen interest, the outcome has been significantly shaped and constrained by the logic of the market and, by implication, of the consumer interest.

In practice, the distinction between competition policy, consumer interests and market liberalism on the one hand, and social and cultural policy, citizen interest and civic republicanism (or social democracy) on the other hand, is often blurred and each shapes regulation and policy making. Yet only occasionally is this process conflictual. On many occasions, the process of developing policy is more pragmatic than oppositional, perhaps reflecting the twin statutory obligations that define Ofcom's primary duties. Humphreys (2008) makes a parallel observation at the European level, seeing media and communications policy as precisely emergent as a compromise between the values of market-oriented and public service approaches (see also Feintuck and Varney, 2006). Rarely, if ever, does Ofcom give absolute priority to either the citizen or the consumer interest, and just as rarely, if ever, does it significantly neglect the promotion of markets, the protection of consumers or the citizen issues in media and communications. Over and again in this book, we have observed Ofcom striking a complex, sometimes clever, sometimes unsatisfactory, but never disastrous balance between competing priorities. We have noted, too, that it has proved easier to find occasion for praise in Ofcom's operation as an independent, principled regulator, and as a neutral but not disinterested party providing a bridge between government, commerce, civil society and individuals, than it has been easy to praise the particular decisions it has made or to evaluate their long-term effects on the media and communications environment. However, since Ofcom has generally acted as an institution in the public sphere, arguably the liability for its decisions may be at least partially spread among the stakeholders who participated in its policy making and, even, among those who for various reasons did not.

Our analysis of Ofcom as a regulatory agency has, we hope, illuminated the pressing choices facing many governments regarding where the balance should lie between protecting consumer interests, facilitating citizen interests and creating the conditions for competitive markets. As markets become ever more international, and while the citizens and consumers to whom government is accountable remain predominantly national, this tension is exacerbated. We suggest that, as these and other tensions become more not less contested, a sphere for reflexive, participatory deliberation will become ever more vital if the widely trusted, relatively inclusive and generally impartial media system Britain has long valued is to survive much further into the twenty-first century. If the public, through a diversity of means, is not included in these debates, and if their visibility is further marginalised by the inexorable rise of the neoliberal creed that consumer choice and the vote are the only legitimate forms of public expression, then the interests of citizens and consumers in the media and communications environment, and consequently in all those spheres mediated by today's media and communications technologies and services, will be undermined.

Notes

1 As announced on the Cabinet Office website, 18 May 2010, http://www.cabinet-office.gov.uk/news/nat-wei-appointed-big-society-adviser.
2 Hunt, Jeremy, speech delivered at LSE, 12/1/11. Secretaries of State for Culture, Media and Sport during Ofcom's history have included Tessa Jowell (8/6/01–27/6/07), James Purnell (28/6/07–24/1/08), Andy Burnham (24/1/08–5/6/09) and Ben Bradshaw (5/6/09–11/5/10).
3 The renegotiation froze the licence fee for six years and moved some activities that had been funded by government to the BBC so that they would be funded by the licence fee (notably, the World Service, the Welsh language broadcaster S4C and BBC Monitoring). Adding some new responsibilities that, arguably, further confused the role of the licence fee and the relation between the audience and the BBC (a contribution to the rollout of superfast broadband, the digital radio network and Hunt's particular project, local television), the outcome was effectively to cut BBC funding by 16 per cent over a six-year period.
4 Overall, the NAO (2010) was unconvinced that Ofcom had done enough to ensure that all its practices delivered value for money, suggesting that Ofcom's overall strategy was to spend available funds on its statutory and core activities rather than bearing down on costs in all cases, and thus it made three recommendations. First, Ofcom should demonstrate value for money by linking its activities more clearly and explicitly to outcomes in the market; second, that Ofcom should review its performance on spectrum management (where income of £200 million a year costs £70 million in grant aid from government to Ofcom); and third, that Ofcom should report efficiency savings more routinely to the government departments from which it received funding.
5 Further, Ofcom's efforts to regulate the mobile phone market resulted in significant reductions in the cost of a basket of mobile phone services, although efforts continued to reduce contractual constraints in relation to switching, enhancing broadband speeds and regulating silent calls.

AFTERWORD

It has been a challenge to stop revising this manuscript in mid 2011, knowing that the situation is about to change. On 7 January, Ofcom published its Draft Annual Plan, announcing that following a major review of expenditure, it would cut spending by 28 per cent over four years, with most of the savings delivered during 2011/12. Then on 19 January, the Secretary of State Jeremy Hunt (2011a) announced 'a radical rethink', moving key responsibilities from the Department of Business, Innovation and Skills (BIS) to his own ministry, the DCMS, and announcing a Green Paper for the end of 2011, leading to a Bill in 2012 and a new Communications Act by 2015:

It is now seven years since the last Act — a long time in today's fast-paced environment. Now is the moment to make sure we have the most modern, innovation- and investment-friendly legal structure in place ... I am prepared to radically rethink the way we do things ... This is not about tweaking the current system, but redesigning it — from scratch if necessary — to make it fit for purpose.

In May, he issued an 'open letter' inviting consultation responses on the requirements for communications regulation in the digital age, a letter almost entirely focused on a deregulatory approach designed to stimulate economic growth (Hunt, 2011b).[1] We could comment further, but we have decided to stop now, having charted the history of Ofcom under New Labour, from its prehistory before its establishment by the Communications Act 2003 through to the transition to a new government in 2010. We have documented how Ofcom has addressed its responsibilities during this period across a range of domains – the review of public service broadcasting, community radio, the promotion of media literacy, developing co-regulatory arrangements in advertising and, most generally, furthering the interests of citizens and consumers. The next decade – for Ofcom, for UK citizens, for the media and communications landscape – cannot yet be clearly discerned. But we hope that our analysis offers a context, a point of comparison, and some clear criteria against which further changes in the governance and regulation of media and communications in the UK and elsewhere may be judged.

Notes

1 The three themes highlighted in the letter were 'Growth, innovation and deregulation; A communications infrastructure that provides the foundations for growth; Creating the right environment for the content industry to thrive.'

REFERENCES

Abercrombie, N. and Longhurst, B. (1998) *Audiences: A Sociological Theory of Performance and Imagination*. Thousand Oaks, CA: Sage.

ACMA (Australian Communications and Media Authority) (2009) 'What is digital media literacy and why is it important?' (www.acma.gov.au/WEB/STANDARD/pc=PC_311470).

Alexander, J. C., and Jacobs, R. N. (1998) 'Mass communication, ritual and civil society', in T. Liebes and J. Curran (eds), *Media, Ritual and Identity*. London: Routledge, pp. 3–22.

America Online (AOL) (2002). Evidence to the Joint Select Committee, House of Commons Research Paper, 26 November, Westminster.

Anderson, J. (2007) 'Public service television for children', *Early Day Motion*, 585 (http://edmi.parliament.uk/EDMi/EDMDetails.aspx?EDMID=34730).

Appadurai, A. (1996) *Modernity at Large: Cultural Dimensions of Globalization*. Minneapolis, MN: University of Minnesota Press.

Ashley, J., Wintour, P. and Oliver, M. (2003) 'Curb on junk food adverts to combat obesity', *The Guardian*, 1 December.

Atton, C. (2002) *Alternative Media*. London: Sage.

Aufderheide, P. (1993) *Media Literacy: A Report of the National Leadership Conference on Media Literacy*. Aspen, CO: Aspen Institute.

Bachmair, B. and Bazalgette, C. (2007) 'The European Charter for Media Literacy: meaning and potential', *Research in Comparative and International Education*, 2(1): 80–7.

Bailey, O., Cammaerts, B. and Carpentier, N. (2007) *Understanding Alternative Media*. Buckingham: Open University Press.

Bailey, R. (2011). *Letting Children be Children: Report of an Independent Review of the Commercialisation and Sexualisation of Childhood*. London: Department for Education.

Baldwin, R. and Cave, M. (1999) *Understanding Regulation: Theory, Strategy and Practice*. Oxford: Oxford University Press.

Baldwin, R., Scott, C. and Hood, C. (eds) (1998) *A Reader on Regulation*. Oxford and New York: Oxford University Press.

Barnett, S. (2010) *What's Wrong with Media Monopolies? A Lesson from History and a New Approach to Media Ownership Policy*. Media@LSE Electronic Working Paper Series No. 18. London: LSE.

Barnett, S. and Seaton, J. (2010) 'Why the BBC matters: memo to the New Parliament about a unique British institution', *The Political Quarterly*, 81(3).

Barry, A., Osbourne, T. and Rose, N. (eds) (1996) *Foucault and Political Reason*. London: UCL Press.

Bazalgette, C. (2001) 'An agenda for the second phase of media literacy development', in R. Kubey (ed.), *Media Literacy in the Information Age: Current Perspectives*. New Brunswick, NJ, and London: Transaction Publishers, pp. 69–78.

BBC (2004) *Building Public Value: Renewing the BBC for a Digital World* (http://downloads.bbc.co.uk/aboutthebbc/policies/pdf/bpv.pdf).

BBC (2007) *Memorandum of Understanding between the Office of Communications (Ofcom) and the BBC Trust* (http://www.bbc.co.uk/bbctrust/assets/files/pdf/about/ofcom_trust_mou.pdf).

Beck, U. (1986/2005) *Risk Society: Towards a New Modernity*. London: Sage.

Berlin, I. (1969) 'Two concepts of liberty', in *Four Essays on Liberty*. London: Oxford University Press.

BIS (Business, Innovation and Skills) and DCMS (Department for Culture, Media and Sport) (2009) *Digital Britain*. London: BIS and DCMS (http://webarchive.nationalarchives.gov.uk/20100511084737/ and www.culture.gov.uk/images/publications/digitalbritain-finalreport-jun09.pdf).

BIS and DCMS (2010) *National Plan for Digital Participation*. London: BIS and DCMS (www.digitalparticipation.com/sites/default/files/national-plan/National-Plan-Digital-Participation-Final.pdf).

Black, J. (2002) *Critical Reflections on Regulation*. Discussion Paper. London: London School of Economics and Political Science, Centre for the Analysis of Risk and Regulation.

Black, J., Lodge, L., and Thatcher, M. (2005) (Eds.) *Regulatory Innovation: A Comparative Analysis*. Cheltenham: Edward Elgar.

Blumler, J. G. (ed.) (1992) *Television and the Public Interest: Vulnerable Values in West European Broadcasting*. London: Sage.

Boaz, A., Fitzpatrick, S. and Shaw, B. (2009) 'Assessing the impact of research on policy: a literature review', *Science and Public Policy*, 36(4): 255–70.

Bohman, J. (1996) *Public Deliberation: Pluralism, Complexity, and Democracy*. Cambridge, MA: MIT Press.

Born, G. (2004) *Uncertain Vision: Birt, Dyke and the Reinvention of the BBC*. London: Secker and Warburg.

Braman, S. (ed.) (2003) *Communication Researchers and Policy-Making*. Cambridge, MA: MIT Press.

Buckingham, D. (1998) 'Media education in the UK: moving beyond protectionism', *Journal of Communication*, 48(1): 33–42.

Buckingham, D. (2005) *The Media Literacy of Children and Young People*. London: Ofcom.

Buckingham, D. (2007) 'Digital media literacies: rethinking media education in the age of the internet', *Research in Comparative and International Education*, 2(1): 43–55.

Buckingham, D. (2009a) *The Impact of the Commercial World on Children's Wellbeing. Report of an Independent Assessment*. London: Department for Children, Schools and Families and the Department for Culture, Media and Sport. [Includes a *Technical Appendix: Children, Commerce, and Obesity: What Role Does Marketing Play?*].

Buckingham, D. (2009b) 'The appliance of science: the role of evidence in the making of regulatory policy on children and food advertising in the UK', *International Journal of Cultural Policy*, 15(2): 201–15.

Buckingham, D. (2009c) 'Beyond the competent consumer: the role of media literacy in the making of regulatory policy on children and food advertising in the UK', *International Journal of Cultural Policy*, 15(2): 217–30.

Bustamante, E. (2008) 'Public service in the digital age: opportunities and threats in a diverse Europe', in I. Fernández Alonso and M. d. Moragas i Spa (eds), *Communication and Cultural Policies in Europe*. Barcelona: Government of Catalonia, Department of the President.

Cabinet Office (2010) 'Deputy Prime Minister highlights the government's commitment to children and families' (www.cabinetoffice.gov.uk/newsroom/news_releases/2010/100617-children.aspx).

Calhoun, C. (1993) *Habermas and the Public Sphere*. Cambridge, MA: MIT Press.

Cameron, D. (2009) Speech: People Power – Reforming Quangos, 6 July (www.conservatives.com/News/Speeches/2009/07/David_Cameron_People_Power_-_Reforming_Quangos.aspx).

Carpentier, N (2011) *Media and Participation: A Site of Ideological-Democratic Struggle*. Bristol: Intellect.

Carpentier, N., Lie, R. and Servaes, J. (2001) *Community Media – Muting the Democratic Media Discourse? Social Theory and Discourse*. Brighton: Centre for Critical Studies in Communication and Culture: The International Social Theory Consortium, pp. 1–24.

Carter, S. (2003a) Speech: *The Communications Act: Myths and Realities*, 9 September (http://www.ofcom.org.uk/media/speeches/2003/10/carter_20031009

Carter, S. (2003b) Ofcom speech: Royal Television Society Cambridge Convention, 19 September (http://media.ofcom.org.uk/2003/09/19/royal-television-society-cambridge-convention-friday-19-september-2003/

Carter, S. (2004) Speech to the Voice of the Listener and Viewer Spring Conference, 29 February (www.ofcom.org.uk/media/speeches/2004/04/carter_voice_20040429.

Castells, M. (1996) *The Rise of the Network Society. The Information Age: Economy, Society and Culture Vol. I*. Cambridge, MA, and Oxford: Blackwell.

Castells, M. (2003) 'Global information capitalism', in D. Held and A. McGrew (eds), *The Global Transformations Reader* (2nd edition). Cambridge: Polity Press.

Cave, M. (2005) *Independent Audit of Spectrum Holdings*. London: HMSO (http://www.spectrumaudit.org.uk/pdf/caveaudit.pdf).

Chalaby, J. (2009) *Transnational Television in Europe: Reconfiguring Global Communications Networks*. London: I.B. Tauris.

Charles, H. (2010) *UK Community Radio: Policy Frames and Outcomes*. Media@LSE Electronic Working Paper Series. London: LSE (http://www.lse.ac.uk/collections/media@lse/mediaWorkingPapers/MEDIA@LSE Electronic MSc Dissertation Series).

Christians, C. G., Glasser, T. L., McQuail, D., Nordenstreng, K. and White, R. A. (2009) *Normative Theories of the Media: Journalism in democratic societies*. Urbana, Ill: University of Illinois Press.

Christou, G. and Simpson, S. (2006) 'The internet and public-private governance in the European Union', *Journal of Public Policy*, 26(1): 43–61.

Clarke, J., Newman, J. and Smith, N. (2007) *Creating Citizen-Consumers: Changing Publics and Changing Public Services*. London: Sage.

Clyburn, M. L. (2010) Remarks of Commissioner Mignon L. Clyburn 'A national Digital Literacy Corps to meet the adoption challenge'. Speech delivered at the Digital Inclusion Summit, 9 March (http://hraunfoss.fcc.gov/edocs_public/attachmatch/DOC-296738A1.pdf).

Coleman, S. and Blumler, J. G. (2009) *The Internet and Democratic Citizenship: Theory, Practice and Policy*. Cambridge: Cambridge University Press.

Cohen, J. L. and Arato, A. (1992) *Civil Society and Political Theory*. Cambridge, MA: MIT Press.

Collins, R. (1994) *Broadcasting and Audio-Visual Policy in the European Single Market*. London: John Libby.

Collins, R. (2007) 'The BBC and public value', *Medien und Kommunikationswissenschaft*, 65(2): 164–84.

Collins, R. (2009) 'Paradigm found: the Peacock Report and the genesis of a new model UK broadcasting policy', in T. O'Malley and J. Jones (eds), *The Peacock Committee and UK Broadcasting Policy*. Basingstoke: Palgrave Macmillan, pp. 146–64.

Collins, R. and Murroni, C. (1996) *New Media, New Policies: Media and Communications Strategies for the Future*. Cambridge: Polity Press.

Collins, R. and Sujon, Z. (2007) 'UK broadcasting policy: the "long wave" shift in conceptions of accountability', in P. Baldi and U. Hasebrink (eds), *Broadcasters and Citizens in Europe: Trends in Media Accountability and Viewer Participation*. Bristol: Intellect, pp. 33–52.

Commission of the European Communities (1984) *Television without Frontiers: Green Paper on the Establishment of the Common Market for Broadcasting Especially by Satellite and Cable*. COM 9840 300 final. Brussels: Commission of the European Communities.

Commission of the European Communities (1999) *Principles and Guidelines for the Community's Audiovisual Policy in the Digital Age*. COM 657 final, Brussels.

Commission of the European Communities (2009) *Europe's Digital Competitiveness Report: Main Achievements of the i2010 Strategy 2005–2009*. Brussels: Commission of the European Communities.

Committee of Advertising Practice (n.d.) 'The codes' (www.cap.org.uk/The-Codes.aspx).

Communications Consumer Panel (2010) *Putting the Consumer First: The Work of the Communications Consumer Panel*. London: Communications Consumer Panel.

Corner, J. (2004) 'Freedom, rights and regulations', *Media, Culture & Society*, 26(6): 893–9.

Couldry, N., Livingstone, S., and Markham, T. (2010) *Public Connection? Media Consumption and the Presumption of Attention*. Houndmills: Palgrave.

Council of the European Communities (1989) *Directive on the Coordination of Certain Provisions Laid Down by Law, Regulation or Administrative Action in Member States Governing the Pursuit of Television Broadcasting Activities*, (Television without Frontiers Directive) 89/552/EEC. *Official Journal of the European Communities*, I: 298/23.

Cowie, C. and Marsden, C. (1998) 'Convergence, competition and regulation', *International Journal of Communications Law & Policy*, Summer(1). Available online at: http://www.ijclp.net/ijclp_web-doc_6-1-1998.html

Crisell, A. (2002) *An Introductory History of British Broadcasting* (2nd edition). London: Routledge.

Cunningham, S. and Flew, T. (2002) 'Policy', in Cunningham, S. and Turner, G. (eds), *The Media and Communications in Australia* 3rd ed (St Leonards: Allen & Unwin, 2002), pp. 48–61.

Curran, J. (2002) *Media and Power*. London: Routledge.

Curran, J. and Seaton, J. (2010) *Power without Responsibility: Press, Broadcasting and the Internet in Britain* (7th edition). London: Routledge.

Currie, D. (2003) Speech to the English National Forum Seminar, 7 July (www.ofcom.org.uk/media/speeches/2003/07/currie_20030707).

Currie, D. (2005) Speech to the ISPA Parliamentary Advisory Forum, 26 January (www.ofcom.org.uk/media/speeches/2005/01/ispa).

D'Haenens, L. (2007) 'Media governance: new ways to regulate the media', *Communications*, 32: 323–5.

Dahlgren, P. (2009) *Media and Political Engagement*. Cambridge: Cambridge University Press.

Danby, G. and Hart, I. (2010) *BBC Governance and Financial Accountability*. London@ House of Commons Library (http://www.parliament.uk/briefingpapers/commons/lib/research/briefings/snha-05332.pdf).

Darlington, R. (2008) *An Introduction to the Communications Consumer Panel* (http://www.rogerdarlington.co.uk/OCP.html).

DCMS (Department for Culture, Media and Sport) (n.d.) 'Media literacy' (http://webarchive.nationalarchives.gov.uk/+/http://www.culture.gov.uk/what_we_do/broadcasting/3179.aspx).

DCMS (2004) *The Community Radio Order* (http://www.legislation.gov.uk/uksi/2004/1944/contents/made).

DCMS (2006) *A Public Service for All: The BBC in the Digital Age*. White Paper. London: The Stationery Office.

DCMS and BERR (Department for Business Enterprise and Regulatory Reform) (2009) *Digital Britain: The Interim Report*. London: DCMS and BERR (www.culture.gov.uk/images/publications/digital_britain_interimreportjan09.pdf).

de Bens, E. (ed.) (2007) *Media Between Culture and Commerce*. Bristol: Intellect.

Denzin, N. K. and Lincoln, Y. S. (1994). (Eds.), *Handbook of Qualitative Research*. London: Sage.

DH (Department of Health) (2004) *Choosing Health: Making Healthy Choices Easier*. White Paper. London: The Stationery Office.

DH (2008) *Changes in Food and Drink Advertising and Promotion to Children*. London: Department of Health.

Donges, P. (2007) 'The new institutionalism as a theoretical foundation of media governance', *Communications: The European Journal of Communication Research*, 32(3): 325–9.

Dorr, A. (1986) *Television and Children: A Special Medium for a Special Audience*. Beverley Hills, CA: Sage.

Doyle, G. and Vick, D. W. (2005) 'The Communications Act 2003: A new regulatory framework in the UK', *Convergence: The International Journal of Research into New Media Technologies*, 11(3): 75–94.

Driver, S. and Martell, L. (1998) *New Labour: Politics after Thatcherism*. Cambridge: Polity Press.

Driver, S. and Martell, L. (2002) *Blair's Britain*. Cambridge: Polity Press.

DTI (Department of Trade and Industry)/DCMS (Department for Culture, Media and Sport) (1998) *Regulating Communications: Approaching Convergence in the Information Age*. London: DTI (www.dti.gov.uk/converg/).

DTI/DCMS (2000) *A New Future for Communications*. The Communications White Paper. London: DTI (www.communicationswhitepaper.gov.uk/).

DTI/DCMS (2002, June) 'Note on the meaning of "customer", "consumer" and "citizen"', to the Joint Select Committee, Department of Trade and Industry and the Department for Culture, Media and Sport (www.parliament.the-stationery-office.co.uk/pa/jt200102/jtselect/jtcom/169/2070808.htm).

Du Gay, P. (2000) *In Praise of Bureaucracy*. London: Sage.

Eagle, B. and Ambler, T. (2002) 'The influence of advertising on the demand for chocolate confectionery', *International Journal of Advertising*, 21: 437–54.

Etzioni, A. (1993) *The Spirit of Community: Rights, Responsibilities and the Communitarian Agenda*. New York: Crown Publishers, Inc.

Europa (2009a) 'Media literacy in the digital environment' (http://europa.eu/legislation_summaries/audiovisual_and_media/am0004_en.htm).

Europa (2009b) 'Commission sets new information society challenge: Becoming literate in new media' (http://europa.eu/rapid/pressReleasesAction.do?reference=IP/09/1244&format=HTML&aged=0&language=EN&guiLanguage=en).

European Association for Viewers' Interests (2009) *Study on Assessment Criteria for Media Literacy Levels*. Brussels: European Commission, Directorate General, Information Society and Media, Media Literacy Unit.

European Commission (n.d.) 'High level expert group (HLEG) 2006–2009' (http://ec. europa.eu/information_society/activities/digital_libraries/other_expert_groups/ hleg/index_en.htm).

European Commission (1989) *Council Directive of 3 October 1989*. Brussels: European Commission.

European Commission (2007) *Report on the Results of the Public Consultation on Media Literacy*. Brussels: European Commission.

European Commission (2009) 'Commission sets new information society challenge: becoming literate in new media' (http://europa.eu/rapid/pressReleases Action.do?reference=IP/09/1244&format=HTML&aged=0&language=EN&guiL anguage=en).

European Commission (2010) *A Digital Agenda for Europe*. Brussels: European Commission.

European Parliament (2008) *Report on Community Media in Europe*. A6-0263/2008, 24/06, Brussels: European Parliament.

European Parliament (2010) *Opinion of the Committee on the Internal Market and Consumer Protection (25.3.2010)*. Brussels: European Parliament (www.europarl. europa.eu/sides/getDoc.do?pubRef=-//EP//NONSGML+REPORT+A7-2010- 0066+0+DOC+PDF+V0//EN).

European Parliament and the Council (2007) 'Directive 2007/65/EC of the European Parliament and of the Council', *Official Journal of the European Union* (332): 27–45 (http://eurlex.europa.eu/LexUriServ/LexUriServ.do?uri=OJ:L:2007:332:0027:0045: EN:PDF).

European Parliament and the Council (2010) *Directive of the European Parliament and of the Council on the Coordination of Certain Provisions Laid Down by Law, Regulation or Administrative Action in Member States Concerning the Provision of Audiovisual Media Services (Audiovisual Media Services Directive)*. Brussels: European Parliament and the Council (http://register.consilium.europa.eu/pdf/ en/09/st03/st03683.en09.pdf).

Everett (2003) *New Voices – An Evaluation of 15 Access Radio Projects* (http://stake-holders.ofcom.org.uk/binaries/broadcast/radio-ops/new_voices.pdf).

Fairclough, N. (2002) 'Language in new capitalism', *Discourse & Society*, 13(2): 163–6.

Feintuck, M. and Varney, M (2006) *Media Regulation, Public Interest and the Law*. Edinburgh: Edinburgh University Press.

Fielder, A., Gardner, W., Nairn, A. and Pitt, J. (2007) *Fair Game? Assessing Commercial Activity on Children's Favourite Websites and Online Environments*. London: National Consumer Council and Childnet International.

Fischer, A. (2008) 'Swiss telecommunications policy: from state monopoly to intense regulation', *Flux*, 11(4): 78–91.

Fishkin, J.S. (1991) *Democracy and Deliberation: New directions for democratic reform*. London: Yale University Press.

Foster, R. (2005) *Competition and the Public Interest: A More Transparent Approach*. A Paper for the OECD/Ofcom Roundtable on Communications Convergence (http:// media.ofcom.org.uk/2005/06/07/competition-and-the-public-interest-a-more-transparent-approach-a-paper-for-the-oecdofcom-roundtable-on-communications-convergence-2-june-2005/).

Foucault, M. (1991) 'Governmentality', in G. Burchell, C. Gordon and P. Miller (eds), *The Foucault Effect: Studies in Governmentality*. Hemel Hempstead: Harvester Wheatsheaf.

Fraser, N. (1990) *Unruly Practices: Power, Discourse and Gender in Contemporary Social Theory*. Cambridge: Polity Press.

Frau-Meigs, D. (ed.) (2007) *Media Education: A Kit for Teachers, Students, Parents and Professionals*. Paris: UNESCO Communication and Information Sector.

Frau-Meigs, D. and Torrent, J. (eds) (2009) *Mapping Media Education Policies in the World: Visions, Programmes and Challenges*. New York: United Nations Alliance of Civilizations and Grupo Comunicar.

Freedman, D. (2008) *The Politics of Media Policy*. Cambridge: Polity Press.

Freepress (2009) *2009 Media and Tech Priorities: A Public Interest Agenda*. Washington, DC: Freepress (www.freepress.net/files/2009techpolicy.pdf).

Gangadharan, S. P. (2009) 'Public participation and agency discretion in rulemaking at the Federal Communications Commission', *Journal of Communication Inquiry*, 35(4): 337–53.

Garnham, N. (1999) 'Amartya Sen's "capabilities" approach to the evaluation of welfare: its application to communications', in A. Calabrase and J.-C. Burgelman (eds), *Communication, Citizenship and Social Policy*. Boulder, CO: Rowman & Littlefield, pp. 113–24.

Gee, J. P. (2003) *What Video Games Have To Teach Us About Learning and Literacy*. New York: Palgrave Macmillan.

Gibbons, T. (2005) 'Competition policy and regulatory style – issues for OFCOM', *Info*, 7(5): 42–51.

Gibbons, T. (2009) 'The future of public service content in the United Kingdom', *Journal of Media Law*, 1: 1–13.

Giddens, A. (1998) *The Third Way: The Renewal of Social Democracy*. Cambridge: Polity Press.

Gordon, J. (2005) 'A comparison of new British community radio stations with established Australian community radio stations', *3CMedia Journal of Community, Citizen's and Third Sector Media and Communication*, 2: 15–29.

Government Office for Science (2007) 'Tackling obesities: future choices', *Foresight Report*, October.

Graf, P. (2008) Speech to the Voice of the Listener and Viewer, 2/10/08 'Public Service Broadcasting – Putting the People First'. http://www.ofcom.org.uk/media/speeches/2008/09/vlv_psb

Graham, A and Davies, G (1997) *Broadcasting, Society and Policy in the Multimedia Age*. Luton: University of Luton Press.

Gripsrud, J. and Weibull, L. (eds) (2010) *Media, Markets & Public Spheres*. Bristol: Intellect.

Habermas, J. (1962, trans 1989) *The Structural Transformation of the Public Sphere: An Inquiry into a Category of Bourgeois Society*. Cambridge: Polity Press.

Habermas, J. (1976) *Legitimation Crisis*. Translation and introduction by Thomas McCarthy. London: Heinemann Educational Books.

Habermas, J. (1996) *Between Facts and Norms: Contributions to a Discourse Theory of Law and Democracy*. Cambridge: Polity Press.

Habermas, J. (2006) 'Political communication in media society: does democracy still enjoy an epistemic dimension? The impact of normative theory on empirical research', *Communication Theory*, 16: 411–26.

Hallett, L. and Wilson, D. (2009) *Community Radio: Collaboration and Regulation*. (http://www2.lse.ac.uk/media@lse/events/MeCCSA/MeCCSA_Conference_Papers.aspx).

Hallin, D. C. and Mancini, P. (2004) *Comparing Media Systems: Three Models of Media and Politics*. Cambridge: Cambridge University Press.

Hamelink, C. (2002) 'The civil society challenge to global media policy', in M. Raboy (ed.), *Global Media Policy in the New Millennium*. Luton: Luton University Press, pp. 251–60.

Hamelink, C. (2003) 'Statement on communication rights', Paper presented at the World Forum on Communication Rights, Geneva, Switzerland (www.globalizacija.com/doc_en/e0030ict.htm).

Hansard (2002) Written answer from the Secretary of State for Culture, Media and Sport, 16 December (http://hansard.millbanksystems.com/written_answers/2002/dec/16/television-services#S6CV0396P0_20021216_CWA_156)

Hansard (2003) *Report stage of the passage of the Bill, House of Lords, 23 June 2003*, (www.publications.parliament.uk/pa/ld200203/ldhansrd/vo030623/text/3062304.htm)

Hansard (2007) Parliamentary business, 2 May. (www.publications.parliament.uk/pa/cm200607/cmhansrd/cm070502/text/70502w0011.htm)

Hardy, J. (2008) 'Ofcom, regulation and reform', *Soundings*, 39(1): 87–97.

Hargittai, E. (2010) 'Digital na(t)ives? Variation in internet skills and uses among members of the "Net Generation"', *Sociological Inquiry*, 80(1): 92–113.

Harrison, K., Bost, K. K., McBride, B. A., Donovan, S. M., Grigsby-Tussaint, D. S., Kim, J., Liechty, J. M., Wiley, A., Teran-Garcia, M. and Jacobsohn, G. C. (2011) 'Towards a developmental conceptualisation of contributors to overweight and obesity in childhood: the six-C's model', *Child Development Perspectives*, 5(1): 50–58.

Harvey, S. (2006) 'Ofcom's first year and neo-liberalism's blind spot: attacking the culture of production', *Screen*, 47(1): 91–105.

Harvey, S. (forthcoming) 'Ofcom: the reluctant regulator', in J. Petley and G. Williams (eds), *The Media in Contemporary Britain*. Basingstoke: Palgrave MacMillan.

Hasebrink, U. (2009) 'Quality assessments and patterns of use. Conceptual and empirical approaches to the audiences of public service media', in G. F. Lowe (ed.), *The Public in Public Service Media*. Göteborg: Nordicom, pp. 135–49.

Hastings, G., Stead, M., McDermott, L., Alasdair, F., MacKintosh, A. M., Rayner, M. et al. (2003) *Review of the Research on the Effects of Food Promotion to Children (Final report)*. London: Food Standards Agency.

Hawkes, C. (2005) Self-regulation of food advertising: what it can, could and cannot do to discourage unhealthy eating habits among children. *Nutrition Bulletin*, 30(4): 374–382.

Hawkes, C. (2007) *Marketing Food to Children: Changes in the Global Regulatory Environment 2004–2006*. Geneva: World Health Organization.

Hay, J. (2002) Speech, Westminster Media Forum, 5 December, *The Communications Bill and the Citizen*. (www.vlv.org.uk/combill291202issues.html).

Held, D. (1995) *Democracy and the Global Order: From the Modern State to Cosmopolitan Governance*. Cambridge: Polity Press.

Held, D. (2006) *Models of Democracy* (3rd edition). Cambridge: Polity Press.

Held, D. (2007) 'Co-regulation in European Union member states', *Communications*, 32: 415–22.

Held, D. and McGrew, A. (eds) (2003) *The Global Transformations Reader: An Introduction to the Globalization Debate* (2nd edition). Oxford: Polity Press.

Helsper, E. J. (2005) *R18 Material: Its Potential Impact on People Under 18: An Overview of the Available Literature*. London: Office of Communications.

Helsper, E. J. and Eynon, R. (2010) 'Digital natives: where is the evidence?', *British Educational Research Journal*, 36(3): 503–20.

Hesmondhalgh, D. (2005) 'Media and cultural policy as public policy: the case of the British Labour Party', *International Journal of Cultural Policy*, 11(1): 1–13.

High Level Expert Group (2008) *Digital Literacy: High Level Expert Group Recommendations*. Brussels: European Commission High Level Expert Group.

Hobbs, R. (1998) 'The seven great debates in the media literacy movement', *Journal of Communication*, 48(1): 6–32.

Hobbs, R. (2008) 'Debates and challenges facing new literacies in the 21st century', in K. Drotner and S. Livingstone (eds), *International Handbook of Children, Media and Culture*. London: Sage, pp. 431–47.

Holden, R. (2002) *The Making of New Labour's European Policy*. London: Palgrave.

Horrigan, J. B. (2010) *Broadband Adoption and Use in America*. Washington, DC: Federal Communications Commission.

Hood, C. (1994) *Explaining Economic Policy Reversals*. Buckingham: Open University Press.

House of Commons (2002) Research Paper 02/6, 26 November (www.parliament.uk/commons/lib/research/rp2002/rp02-067.pdf).

House of Lords (2010) *Public Bodies Bill*. London: The Stationery Office.

Humphreys, P. (2008) 'The principal axes of the European Union's audiovisual policy', in I. Fernández Alonso and M. d. Moragas i. Spa (eds), *Communication and Cultural Policies in Europe*. Barcelona: Government of Catalonia, Department of the President, pp. 151–82.

Hunt, J. (2010) 'Letter to Sir Michael Lyons'. London: DCMS (http://www.culture.gov.uk/images/publications/Lyons_BBC.pdf).

Hunt, J. (2011a) 'Speech to the Oxford Media Convention.' 19 January 2011. (http://www.culture.gov.uk/news/ministers_speeches/7726.aspx)

Hunt, J. (2011b) 'A Communications Review for the Digital Age. An open letter, 16 May 2011.' London: DCMS. Available at: http://www.culture.gov.uk/images/publications/commsreview-open-letter_160511.pdf

Institute of Medicine of the National Academies (2005) *Preventing Childhood Obesity: Health in the Balance*. Washington, DC: The National Academies Press.

Iosifidis, P. (ed.) (2010) *Reinventing Public Service Communication: European Broadcasters and Beyond*. Basingstoke: Palgrave Macmillan.

Jakubovitz, K. (2007) *Rude Awakening: Social and Media Change in Central and Eastern Europe*. Cresskill, NJ: Hampton Press Inc.

Jakubovitz, K. (2010) 'PSB 3.0: reinventing European PSB', in P. Iosifidis (ed.), *Reinventing Public Service Communication: European Broadcasters and Beyond*. London: Palgrave Macmillan.

Janssen, I., Katzmarzyk, P. T., Boyce, W. F., Vereecken, C., Mulvihill, C., Roberts, C. et al. (2005) 'Comparison of overweight and obesity prevalence in school-aged youth from 34 countries and their relationships with physical activity and dietary patterns', *Obesity Reviews*, 6(2): 123–32.

Jenkins, H. (2006) *An Occasional Paper on Digital Media and Learning. Confronting the Challenges of Participatory Culture: Media Education for the 21st Century*. Chicago, IL: The John D and Catherine T. Macarthur Foundation.

Jessop, B. (2000) 'The state and the contradictions of the knowledge-driven economy', in J. R. Bryson, P. W. Daniels, N. D. Henry and J. Pollard (eds), *Knowledge, Space, Economy*. London: Routledge.

Just, N. (2009) 'Measuring media concentration and diversity: new approaches and instruments in Europe and the US', *Media, Culture & Society*, 31(1): 97–117.

Keane, J. (1991) *The Media and Democracy*. Cambridge: Polity Press.

Kelly, G., Mulgan, G. and Muers, S. (2002) *Creating Public Value: An Analytical Framework for Public Service Reform*. London: Strategy Unit, Cabinet Office (http://www.cabinetoffice.gov.uk/strategy/downloads/files/public_value2.pdf).

Klinke, A. and Renn, O. (2001) 'Precautionary principle and discursive strategies: classifying and managing risks', *Journal of Risk Research*, 4(2): 159–74.

Kress, G. (2003) *Literacy in the New Media Age*. London: Routledge.

Kroes, N. (2010) Speech: 'The digital agenda: challenges for Europe and the mobile industry', the Mobile World Congress 2010, Barcelona, 15 February.

Kunkel, D. (1990) 'The role of research in the regulation of US children's television advertising', *Science Communication*, 12(1): 101–19.

Kunkel, D. (2001) 'Children and television advertising', in D. Singer and J. Singer (eds), *Handbook of Children and Media*. Thousand Oaks, CA: Sage, pp. 375–93.

Kunkel, D. (2010) 'Commentary: mismeasurement of children's understanding of the persuasive intent of advertising', *Journal of Children and Media*, 4(1): 109–17.

Kunkel, D., Wilcox, B., Cantor, J., Palmer, E., Linn, S. and Dowrick, P. (2004) *Report of the APA Task Force on Advertising and Children: Psychological Issues in the Increasing Commercialization of Childhood*. Washington, DC: American Psychological Association.

Lazarsfeld, P. F. (1941) 'Remarks on administrative and critical communication research', *Studies in Philosophical and Social Sciences*, 9: 2–16.

Lessig, L. (1999) *Code and Other Laws of Cyberspace*. New York: Basic Books.

Lewis, P. M. (ed.) (1993) *Alternative Media: Linking Global and Local*. UNESCO Reports and Papers in Mass Communication No. 107. Paris: UNESCO.

Lewis, P. M. and Booth, J. (1989) *The Invisible Medium: Public, Commercial and Community Radio*. London: Macmillan.

Lewis, J. and Miller, T. (eds) (2003) *Critical Cultural Policy Studies: A Reader*. Oxford: Blackwell.

Livingstone, S. (1998) 'Audience research at the crossroads: the "implied audience" in media and cultural theory', *European Journal of Cultural Studies*, 1(2): 193–217.

Livingstone, S. (2002) *Young People and New Media: Childhood and the Changing Media Environment*. London: Sage.

Livingstone, S. (2003) *The Changing Nature and Uses of Media Literacy*. Media@LSE Electronic Working Paper No. 4. London: London School of Economics and Political Science.

Livingstone, S. (2004) *A Commentary on the Research Evidence Regarding the Effects of Food Promotion on Children. Report Prepared for the Market Research Department of the Office of Communications*. London: Office of Communications (http://eprints.lse.ac.uk/21756/).

Livingstone, S. (2005) 'On the relation between audiences and publics', in S. Livingstone (ed.), *Audiences and Publics: When Cultural Engagement Matters for the Public Sphere*. Bristol: Intellect, pp. 17–41.

Livingstone, S. (2006) *New Research on Advertising Foods to Children: An Updated Review of the Literature* [published as Annex 9 to the report, *Television Advertising of Food and Drink Products to Children*. London: Ofcom, March] (http://eprints.lse.ac.uk/21758/).

Livingstone, S. (2008a) 'Engaging with media – a matter of literacy?', *Communication, Culture & Critique*, 1(1): 51–62.

Livingstone, S. (2008b) 'Internet literacy: young people's negotiation of new online opportunities', in T. McPherson (ed.), *Unexpected Outcomes and Innovative Uses of Digital Media by Youth*. Cambridge, MA: MIT Press, pp. 101–21.

Livingstone, S. (2009a) 'On the mediation of everything. ICA Presidential address', *Journal of Communication*, 59(1): 1–18.

Livingstone, S. (2009b) *Children and the Internet: Great Expectations, Challenging Realities*. Cambridge: Polity Press.

Livingstone, S. (2010) 'Media literacy and media policy' [in German], in B. Bachmair (ed.), *Medienbildung in Riskanten Erlebniswelten*. Stuttgart: Kohlhammer Verlag, pp. 33–44.

Livingstone, S. (2011) 'Regulating the internet in the interests of children: emerging European and international approaches', in R. Mansell and M. Raboy (eds), *The Handbook on Global Media and Communication Policy* (505–524). Oxford: Blackwell.

Livingstone, S. and Helsper, E. J. (2004) *Advertising 'Unhealthy' Foods to Children: Understanding Promotion in the Context of Children's Daily Lives. A Review of the Literature for the Market Research Department of the Office of Communications.* London: Office of Communications.

Livingstone, S. and Helsper, E. J. (2006) 'Does advertising literacy mediate the effects of advertising on children? A critical examination of two linked research literatures in relation to obesity and food choice', *Journal of Communication*, 56: 560–84.

Livingstone, S. and Lunt, P. (1994) *Talk on Television*. London: Routledge.

Livingstone, S. and Lunt, P. (2007) 'Representing citizens and consumers in media and communications regulation', in *The Politics of Consumption/The Consumption of Politics, The Annals of the American Academy of Political and Social Science*, 611: 51–65.

Livingstone, S. and Lunt, P. (2011) 'The implied audience of communications policy making: regulating media in the interests of citizens and consumers', in V. Nightingale (ed.), *Handbook of Media Audiences*. Oxford: Blackwell, pp. 169–89.

Livingstone, S., Lunt, P. and Miller, L. (2007a) 'Citizens and consumers: discursive debates during and after the Communications Act 2003', *Media, Culture & Society*, 29(4): 613–38.

Livingstone, S., Lunt, P. and Miller, L. (2007b) 'Citizens, consumers and the citizen-consumer: articulating the interests at stake in media and communications regulation', *Discourse and Communication*, 1(1): 85–111.

Livingstone, S., van Couvering, E. J. and Thumim, N. (2005) *Adult Media Literacy: A Review of the Literature*. London: Ofcom.

Livingstone, S., and Wang, Y. (2011) 'Media Literacy and the Communications Act: What has been achieved and what should be done?' *LSE Media Policy Project Brief 2* (http://www.scribd.com/doc/57742814/Policy-Brief-Progress-in-digital-skills-has-stalled).

Lunt, P. and Livingstone, S. (2007) 'Consumers, citizens and regulation: case studies in financial services and communications regulation', in M. Bevir and F. Trentmann (eds), *Governance, Citizens, and Consumers: Agency and Resistance in Contemporary Politics*. London: Palgrave. pp. 139–62.

Lunt, P., Livingstone, S., and Malik, S. (2008) 'Public understanding of regimes of risk regulation: a report on focus group discussions with citizens and consumers', *Social Contexts and Responses to Risk Network (SCARR) Working Paper series (WP26)* (http://eprints.lse.ac.uk/21445).

McChesney, R. W. (1996) 'The internet and US communication policy-making in historical and critical perspective', *Journal of Communication*, 46(1): 98–124.

McChesney, R. W. (1999) *Rich Media Poor Democracy*. New York: The New Press.

McGinnis, J. M., Gootman, J. A. and Kraak, V. I. (2005) *Food Marketing to Children and Youth: Threat or Opportunity?* Washington, DC: Institute of Medicine of the National Academies.

McQuail, D. (1992) *Media Performance: Mass Communication and the Public Interest*. London: Sage.

Majone, (1998) 'The rise of the regulatory state in Europe', in R. Baldwin, C. Scott and C. Hood (eds), *A Reader on Regulation*. Oxford and New York: Oxford University Press.

Mansell, R. (2002) 'From digital divides to digital entitlements in knowledge societies', *Current Sociology*, 50(3): 407–26.

Mansell, R. (2007) 'Crossing boundaries with new media: introductory remarks for the panel on "the responsibility of the media"', *United Nations General Assembly Third Informal Thematic Debate on 'Civilizations and the Challenge for Peace: Obstacles and Opportunities'*, New York, 10–11 May.

Mansell, R. (2011) 'New visions, old practices: policy and regulation in the internet era', *Continuum: Journal of Media and Cultural Studies*, 25(1): 19–32.

Media Awareness Network (2010) *Digital Literacy in Canada: From Inclusion to Transformation*. Ottawa: Media Awareness Network.

Michalis, M. (2007) *Governing European Communications: From Unification to Coordination*. Lanham, MD and Plymouth, MA: Lexington Books.

Millwood Hargrave, A. and Livingstone, S. (2009) *Harm and Offence in Media Content: A Review of the Empirical Literature* (2nd edition). Bristol: Intellect.

Millwood Hargrave, A. and Shaw, C. (2009) *Accountability and the Public Interest in Broadcasting*. London: Palgrave Macmillan.

Moe, H. (2010) 'Governing public service broadcasting: "public value tests" in different national contexts', *Communication, Culture & Critique*, 3(2): 207–23.

Montgomery, K. C. and Chester, J. (2009) 'Interactive food and beverage marketing: targeting adolescents in the digital age', *Journal of Adolescent Health*, 45(3): S18–S29.

Morley, D. (2006) 'Unanswered questions in audience research', *The Communication Review*, 9: 101–21.

Mouffe, C. (1992) 'Democratic citizenship and the political community', in C. Mouffe (ed.), *Dimensions of Radical Democracy*. London: Verso, pp. 225–39.

Mouffe, C. (2000) *The Democratic Paradox*. London: Verso.

Mulgan, G. (1997) *Connexity: How to Live in a Connected World*. London: Chatto & Windus.

Murdock, G. (2005) 'Public broadcasting and democratic culture: consumers, citizens, and communards', in J. Wasko (ed.), *A Companion to Television*. Malden, MA: Blackwell, pp. 174–98.

Nairn, A. and Fine, C. (2008) '"Who's messing with my mind?" The implications of dual-process models for the ethics of advertising to children', *International Journal of Advertising. Special Issue on Brain Sciences*, 27(3): 447–70.

NAO (National Audit Office) (2010) *Ofcom: The Effectiveness of Converged Regulation*. London: The Stationary Office.

Needham, C. (2003) *Citizen-Consumers: New Labour's Marketplace Democracy*. A Catalyst Working Paper. London: The Catalyst Forum.

Newman, J. (ed.) (2005) *Remaking Governance: Peoples, Politics and the Public Sphere*. Bristol: Policy Press.

NHS (2008) *Statistics on Obesity, Physical Activity and Diet: England, January 2008*. London: The NHS Information Centre.

NHS (2010) *Statistics on Obesity, Physical Activity and Diet: England, 2010*. London: The NHS Information Centre.

Nutley, S. M., Walter, I. and Davies, H. T. O. (2007) *Using Evidence: How Research Can Inform Public Services*. Bristol: Policy Press.

Ofcom (n.d.-a) *How Will Ofcom Consult? Ofcom Consultation Guidelines*. (http://stakeholders.ofcom.org.uk/consultations/how-will-ofcom-consult.)

Ofcom (n.d.–b) *Statutory Duties and Regulatory Principles*. (http://www.ofcom.org.uk/about/what-is-ofcom/statutory-duties-and-regulatory-principles/)

Ofcom (n.d.-c) *A case study on public sector mergers and regulatory structures.* (www.ofcom.org.uk/about/what-is-ofcom/a-case-study-on-public-sector-mergers-and-regulatory-structures/)

Ofcom (n.d.-d) *Spectrum Strategy.* (http://stakeholders.ofcom.org.uk/spectrum/spectrum-strategy/.)

Ofcom (n.d.-e) *Report to the Secretary of State (Culture, Media and Sport) on the Media Ownership Rules.* (http://stakeholders.ofcom.org.uk/consultations/morr/statement/)

Ofcom (Office of Communications) (2004a) *Annual Report, 2003/4.* London: Ofcom.

Ofcom (2004b) *Ofcom's Strategy and Priorities for the Promotion of Media Literacy: Consultation Document.* London: Ofcom (http://stakeholders.ofcom.org.uk/binaries/consultations/strategymedialit/summary/medialit.pdf).

Ofcom (2004c) *Ofcom's Strategy and Priorities for the Promotion of Media Literacy: A Statement.* London: Ofcom (http://stakeholders.ofcom.org.uk/binaries/consultations/strategymedialit/summary/strat_prior_statement.pdf).

Ofcom (2004d) *Child Obesity – Food Advertising in Context: Children's Food Choices, Parents' Understanding and Influence, and the Role of Food Promotions.* July, London: Ofcom.

Ofcom (2004e) *Licensing Community Radio.* London: Ofcom.

Ofcom (2005a) *Annual Plan, 2005/6.* London: Ofcom.

Ofcom (2005b) *Ofcom Review of Public Service Television Broadcasting, Phase 3: Competition for Quality.* London: Ofcom (http://stakeholders.ofcom.org.uk/binaries/consultations/psb3/psb3.pdf).

Ofcom (2005c) *The Broadcasting Code.* London: Ofcom.

Ofcom (2006a) *Ofcom's Consumer Policy Statement.* London: Ofcom (http://stakeholders.ofcom.org.uk/binaries/consultations/ocp/statement/statement.pdf).

Ofcom (2006b) *Media Literacy Audit: Report on Adult Media Literacy.* London: Ofcom (http://stakeholders.ofcom.org.uk/market-data-research/media-literacy/medlitpub/medlitpubrss/medialit_audit/).

Ofcom (2006c) *Ofcom Response to European Commission Consultation on Media Literacy.* London: Ofcom.

Ofcom (2006d) *Television Advertising of Food and Drink Products to Children: Options for New Restrictions.* London: Ofcom.

Ofcom (2007a) *Taking Account of Consumer and Citizen Interest. Progress and Evaluation – 12 Months On.* London: Ofcom.

Ofcom (2007b) *The Future of Children's Television Programming: Research Report.* London: Ofcom.

Ofcom (2008a) *Citizens, Communications and Convergence.* London: Ofcom (http://stakeholders.ofcom.org.uk/consultations/citizens/).

Ofcom (2008b) *The Digital Opportunity.* London: Ofcom.

Ofcom (2008c) *Public Service Broadcasting Review Phase 1: Summary of Consultation Responses.* London: Ofcom.

Ofcom (2008d) *Media Literacy Audit: Report on UK Adults' Media Literacy.* London: Ofcom (http://stakeholders.ofcom.org.uk/market-data-research/media-literacy/medlitpub/medlitpubrss/ml_adult08/).

Ofcom (2009a) *Citizens' Digital Participation: Research Report.* London: Ofcom.

Ofcom (2009b) *UK Adults' Media Literacy: 2009 Interim Report.* London: Ofcom (http://stakeholders.ofcom.org.uk/market-data-research/media-literacy/medlitpub/medlitpubrss/uk_adults_ml/).

Ofcom (2009c) *Community Radio: Annual Report on the Sector 2008/2009*. London: Ofcom (http://stakeholders.ofcom.org.uk/binaries/broadcast/radio-ops/cr_annualrpt 0809.pdf).

Ofcom (2010a) *Citizens, Communications and Convergence: A Summary of Stakeholder Responses, and Our Next Steps*. London: Ofcom (http://stakeholders.ofcom.org.uk/binaries/consultations/citizens/statement/Citizen_Statement.pdf).

Ofcom (2010b) *HFSS Advertising Restrictions: Final Review*. London: Ofcom.

Ofcom (2010c) *The Communication Markets Report*. London: Ofcom.

Ofcom (2010d) *Annual Report 2009/10*. London: Ofcom/The Stationary Office.

Ofcom (2010e) *Report on Public Interest Test on the Proposed Acquisition of British Sky Broadcasting Group Plc by News Corporation*. London: Ofcom.

Ofcom (2010f) *Community Radio: Annual Report on the Sector 2009/2010*. London: Ofcom (http://stakeholders.ofcom.org.uk/broadcasting/radio/community/annual reports/09-10/).

Ofcom (2011) *Draft Annual Plan 2011/12*. London: Ofcom (http://stakeholders.ofcom.org.uk/consultations/draftap1112/).

O'Malley, T. and Jones, J. (eds) (2009) *The Peacock Committee and UK Broadcasting Policy*. London: Palgrave Macmillan.

Ouellette, L. and Hay, J. (2008) *Better Living Through Reality TV: Television and Post-Welfare Citizenship*. Oxford: Blackwell.

Outhwaite, W. (Ed.). (1996). *The Habermas Reader*. Cambridge: Polity.

Paliwoda, S. and Crawford, I. (2003) *An Analysis of the Hastings Review*. London: Food Advertising Unit.

Papadopoulos, L. (2010) *Sexualisation of Young People Review*. London: Home Office Publication.

Pitt, J. (2010) *A Tangled Web*. London: Consumer Focus.

Public Administration Committee (2010) *Public Administration Committee – Fifth Report Smaller Government: Shrinking the Quango State*. Westminster: House of Commons (http://www.publications.parliament.uk/pa/cm201011/cmselect/cmpubadm/537/53702.htm).

Puppis, M. (2010) 'Media governance: a new concept for the analysis of media policy and regulation', *Communication, Culture & Critique*, 3(2): 134–49.

Puttnam, D. (2002) *The Report of the Joint Committee on the Draft Communications Bill (25 July 2002)*. House of Commons and House of Lords. London: The Stationery Office. (www.parliament.the-stationery-office.co.uk/pa/jt200102/jtselect/jtcom/169/169.pdf)

Puttnam, D. (2006) 'The continuing need to advance the public interest', in Ofcom (ed.), *Communications: The Next Decade*. London: Ofcom, pp. 125–138.

Raboy, M. (2007) 'Global media policy – defining the field', *Global Media and Communication*, 3(3): 343–61.

Raboy, M. (2008) 'Dreaming in Technicolor: the future of PSB in a world beyond broadcasting', *Convergence*, 14(3): 361–5.

Raboy, M., Abramson, R. D., Proulx, S. and Welters, R. (2001) 'Media policy, audiences, and social demand: research at the interface of policy studies and audience studies', *Television & New Media*, 2(2): 95–115.

Raboy, M., Proulx, S. and Dahlgren, P. (2003) 'The dilemma of social demand: shaping media policy in new civic contexts', *Gazette*, 65(4–5): 323–9.

Rantanen, T. (2005) *The Media and Globalization*. London: Sage.

Redding, D. (2005) 'Our.info', in J. Lloyd and J. Seaton (eds), *What Can be Done? Making the media and politics better*. Oxford: Blackwell. Pp. 146–158.

Rennie, E. (2006) *Community Media: A Global Introduction*. Oxford: Rowman and Littlefield.

Richards, E. (2003) Speech to the Royal Television Society Dinner, 4 December (www.ofcom.org.uk/media/speeches/2003/12/richards_20031204).

Richards, E. (2004). Speech to the Westminster Media Forum, 25 May, *Ofcom Review of Public Service Broadcasting*. http://www.ofcom.org.uk/media_office/speeches_presentations/richards_20040525

Richards, E. (2009) Speech at Radio 3.0, 21 May (http://media.ofcom.org.uk/2009/05/22/radio-a-vital-part-of-the-media-landscape-extract-from-ed-richards-speech-at-radio-3-0-21-may-2009/).

Richards, E. and Giles, C. (2005) 'The future of public service broadcasting and the BBC', in A. Peacock (ed.), *Public Service Broadcasting without the BBC?* London: IEA.

Richards, D. and Smith, M. J. (2004) 'The "Hybrid State": New Labour's response to the problem of governance', in S. Ludlam and M. J. Smith (eds), *Governing as New Labour*. London: Palgrave.

Robinson, C. (ed.) (2007) *Utility Regulation in Competitive Markets: Pproblems and Progress*. Cheltenham: Edward Elgar.

Roedder, D. L. (1981) 'Age difference in children's responses to television advertising: an information processing approach', *Journal of Consumer Research*, 8: 144–53.

Rose, N. (1990) *Governing the Soul: Technologies of Human Subjectivity*. New York: Routledge.

Rose, N. (1999) *Powers of Freedom*. Cambridge: Cambridge University Press.

Sarikakis, K. (ed.) (2007) *Media and Cultural Policy in the European Union*. Amsterdam: Rodopi.

Scannell, P. (1989) 'Public service broadcasting and modern public life', *Media Culture & Society*, 11: 135–66.

Scannell, P. and Cardiff, D. (1991) *A Social History of British Broadcasting: 1922–1939, Serving the Nation*. Oxford: Blackwell.

Schlesinger, P. (2009) *The Politics of Media and Cultural Policy*. Media@LSE Electronic Working Paper Series No. 17. London: London School of Economics.

Schlesinger, P. (2011) *Smoke and Mirrors? Media and Cultural Policy under the Coalition*. Seminar presented at LSE, 12 January.

Scott, C. (2001) *Analysing Regulatory Space: Fragmented Resources and Institutional Design*. London: Sweet & Maxwell.

Seaton, J. and McNicholas, A. (2009) 'It was the BBC wot won it', in T. O'Malley and J. Jones (eds), *The Peacock Committee and UK Broadcasting Policy*. London: Palgrave Macmillan.

Seiter, E. (2005) *The Internet Playground: Children's Access, Entertainment, and Mis-education*. New York: Peter Lang.

Select Committee on Culture, Media and Sport (2001) Second Report. Westminster: House of Commons (www.publications.parliament.uk/pa/cm200001/cmselect/cmcumeds/161/16103.htm#n13)

Seymour-Ure, C. (1987) 'Media policy in Britain: Now you see it, now you don't.' *European Journal of Communication,* 2: 269–288.

Simpson, S. (2004) 'Universal service issues in converging communications environments: the case of the UK', *Telecommunications Policy*, 28(3–4): 233–48.

Smith, P. (2006) 'The politics of UK television policy: the making of Ofcom', *Media, Culture & Society*, 28(6): 929–40.

Smythe, D. W. (1984) 'New directions for critical communications research', *Media, Culture & Society*, 6: 205–17.

Snyder, I. (2007) 'Literacy, learning and technology studies', in R. Andrews and C. Haythornthwaite (eds), *The SAGE Handbook of E-Learning Research*. London: Sage, pp. 394–415.

Spyrelli, C. (2003) 'Regulating the regulators? An assessment of institutional structures and procedural rules of national regulatory authorities', *International Journal of Communications Law & Policy*, Winter (8). Available online at: http://www.ijclp.net/files/ijclp_web-doc_1-8-2004.pdf.

Stevenson, N. (2003) *Cultural Citizenship: Cosmopolitan Questions*. Maidenhead: Open University Press.

Stoller, T. (2010) *Sounds of Your Life: The History of Independent Radio in the UK*. New Barnet, Herts: John Libby.

Story, M., Neumark-Sztainer, D. and French, S. (2002) 'Individual and environmental influences on adolescent eating behaviors', *Journal of the American Dietetic Association*, 102(3): S40–S51.

Street, B. V. (1984) *Literacy in Theory and Practice*. Cambridge: Cambridge University Press.

Street, B. V. (2003) 'What's new in new literacy studies? Critical approaches to literacy in theory and practice', *Current Issues in Comparative Education*, 5(2): 77–91.

Syvertsen, T. (2004) 'Citizens, audiences, customers and players', *European Journal of Cultural Studies*, 7(3): 363–80.

Tambini, D. (2006) 'What citizens need to know: digital exclusion, information inequality and rights', in Ofcom (ed.), *Communications: The Next Decade*. London: Ofcom, pp. 112–24.

Tambini, D. (2010) 'Ofcom cuts are grave assault on freedom', *The Guardian*, 18 October.

Tambini, D., Leonardi, D. and Marsden, C. (2008) *Codifying Cyberspace: Communications Self-regulation in the Age of Internet Convergence*. London: Routledge.

Thompson, G. (2003) *Between Hierarchies and Market: The Logic and Limits of Network Forms of Organization*. Oxford. Oxford University Press.

Thompson, J. (1995) *The Media and Modernity*. Cambridge: Polity Press.

Tomlinson, J. (1999) *Globalisation and Culture*. Cambridge: Polity Press.

Tongue, C. and Harvey, S. (2004) *Citizenship, Culture and Public Service Broadcasting*. Submission to Ofcom's Review of Public Service Television Broadcasting, Phase 1 'Is Television Special?' 14 June, 2004.(http://www.bftv.ac.uk/policy/ofcom040614.htm).

Trentmann, F. (2006) 'Knowing consumers – histories, identities, practices: an introduction', in F. Trentmann (ed.), *The Making of the Consumer: Knowledge, Power and Identity in the Modern World*. Oxford: Berg, pp. pp. 1–27.

UNESCO (n.d.) *Media and Information Literacy* (http://portal.unesco.org/ci/en/ev.php-URL_ID=15886&URL_DO=DO_PRINTPAGE&URL_SECTION=201.html).

Uricchio, W. (2009) 'Contextualizing the broadcast era: nation, commerce and constraint', *Annals of the American Academy of Political and Social Science*, 625: 60–73.

Van Cuilenburg, J. and McQuail, D. (2003) 'Media policy paradigm shifts: towards a new communications policy paradigm', *European Journal of Communication*, 18(2): 181–207.

Van Cuilenberg, J. and McQuail, D. (2008) 'Towards a new communication policy paradigm', in I. Fernández Alonso and M. d. Moragas i Spa (eds), *Communication and Cultural Policies in Europe*. Barcelona: Government of Catalonia, Department of the President.

Watkins, S. C. (2009) *The Young and the Digital: What the Migration to Social Networking Sites, Games, and Anytime, Anywhere Media Means for Our Future*. Boston, MA: Beacon Press.

211

Webster, J. G. and Phalen, P. F. (1994) 'Victim, consumer, or commodity? Audience models in communication policy', in J. S. Ettema and D. C. Whitney (eds), *Audiencemaking: How the Media Create the Audience*. London: Sage, pp. 19–37.

Wenger, E. (1998) *Communities of Practice: Learning, Meaning and Identity*. Cambridge: Cambridge University Press.

WHO (World Health Organization) (2000) *Obesity: Preventing and Managing the Global Epidemic* (No. 894). Geneva: WHO.

WHO (2002) *World Health Report*. Geneva: WHO.

Wilson, W. (1887) 'The study of administration', cited in Du Gay, P. (2000) *In Praise of Bureaucracy*. London: Sage.

Woolgar, S. (1996) 'Technologies as cultural artefacts', in W. H. Dutton (ed.), *Information and Communication Technologies: Visions and Realities*. Oxford: Oxford University Press, pp. 87–102.

Wyplosz, C. (2010) *The Failure of the Lisbon Strategy* (http://www.voxeu.org/index. php?q=node/4478).

Young, I. (2000) *Inclusion and Democracy*. New York: Oxford University Press.

Zürn, M. and Koenig-Archibugi, M. (2006) 'Conclusion II: the modes and dynamics of global governance', in M. Koenig-Archibugi and M. Zürn (eds), *New Modes of Governance in the Global System: Exploring Publicness, Delegation and Inclusiveness*. Basingstoke: Palgrave Macmillan, pp. 236–55.

INDEX

Institute of Medicine of the National
    Academies (US), 151
Institute for Public Policy Research, 75
International Chamber of Commerce, 146
Internet access, 99, 105, 131, 133
Internet Governance Forum, 123
Iosifidis, P., 113
ITV, 97–8, 155, 181
    children's programming, 155
    and Ofcom, 103–4, 108, 112

Jacobs, R.N., 7
Jessop, B., 5–6
Jowell, Tessa, 127, 150
'junk food' advertising, 144, 146, 149–56,
    158–9, 187, 191
    and childhood obesity, 144, 146, 149–54,
    156, 158–9
    and Ofcom, 144–6, 148–59

'knowledge society' concept, 5–6, 10, 13,
    19, 132
Kroes, Neelie, 131
Kunkel, D., 156–7

Labour Government *see* New Labour
    Government
Lammy, David, 128
Lazarsfeld, P.F., 130
Lewis, P.M., 97, 164, 172
liberal democracy, 2, 10, 18, 187–8
liberal pluralism, 19, 37–40, 187, 191
Livingstone, S., 149, 151
local media, 73

Maastricht Treaty (1992), 32
McChesney, R.W., 96, 130
McIntosh, Andrew, 48
McNally, Tom, 47
McQuail, D., 14, 36, 41
Majone, G., 18, 35
Mansell, R., 60
market competition, 19, 36, 105
market harmonisation, 3, 27, 30–3, 41, 96
Martell, L., 27–8
media convergence, 2–3, 65–6, 70
media literacy, 60, 117–20, 129–36, 138–40
    and the Communications Act, 120–1, 128
    and the European Union, 123–8, 135,
        137, 139
    and neoliberalism, 118, 127–9
    and Ofcom, 16, 120–9, 134–5, 138–9, 190
    and UNESCO, 123, 125
media markets, 2, 13, 70, 118, 128, 143
media ownership and pluralism, 2, 14–15, 31,
    36, 72–3, 75, 182
    and Ofcom, 60, 65–6, 69, 72–4, 100,
        182–3, 187
media policy, 13–15, 29, 31, 34, 89, 104, 113,
    137, 139, 182, 185, 189
Media Reform Movement, 130
Media Watch UK, 80

Meek, Kip, 51, 83
Michalis, M., 31
Milne, Claire, 53
Murdoch, Rupert, 57, 73–4
Murroni, C., 34, 74–5
Myers, John, 170
Myers, Julie, 56, 85

National Audit Office, 185–6, 189
National Health Service (NHS), 147
National Leadership Conference on Media
    Literacy, 122
Needham, C., 51
neoliberalism, 4, 15, 19, 27, 188, 191, 193
    and media literacy, 118, 127–9
'network society' concept, 1, 70, 123, 175, 184
New Labour Government (1997–2010), 3–4,
    11–12, 21, 29, 43, 74, 179
    and the European Union, 30–3
    and Ofcom, 3, 11, 20, 35, 180, 187
    and regulatory reform, 6, 23, 26–30,
        177, 181
Newman, J., 21–2
News Corporation, 73–4
News International, 74
Normoyle, Helen, 56
Nutley, S.M., 157–9

Ofcom (Office of Communications), 3, 6, 17,
    29, 35, 179–82, 185, 194
    accountability of, 67, 85, 183
    approaches to regulation, 28, 30, 69–70
    and the BBC, 95, 100–9, 111–15, 183
    Broadcasting Code, 39, 82, 144, 146
    and children's media, 143–4, 155
    and citizen/consumer interests, 31, 39–62,
        66, 69, 75–6, 82–5, 184–7
    and the Coalition Government, 3, 73,
        180–2, 186
    and the Communications Act, 11, 16,
        33, 36, 46–8, 64–5, 67, 77, 90, 100,
        120, 188
    and community radio, 163, 167–72,
        174–5 192
    Consumer Panel, 44–5, 50, 53–6, 58, 62, 67,
        75–6, 79–84
    Content Board, 45, 50, 55, 57, 68, 79, 81–4,
        95, 100
    duties and obligations of, 17, 39, 42–5,
        48–9, 64–7, 86, 89, 183, 192
    evidence-based policy of, 11, 79, 145,
        147–51, 156–8, 160
    and 'junk food' advertising, 144–6, 148–59
    and media literacy, 16, 120–9, 134–5,
        138–9, 190
    media ownership and pluralism, 60, 65–6,
        69, 72–4, 100, 182–3, 187
    National Audit Office review (2010),
        185–6, 189
    and New Labour, 3, 11, 20, 35, 180, 187
    and public engagement, 17, 77–81, 102,
        108, 184–5, 187–9

Ofcom (Office of Communications) *cont.*
  and public service broadcasting, 69–70, 94,
    99–115, 183, 187, 190
  as a regulatory body, 4, 26, 33, 42, 64–5,
    68–9, 89
  structure and organization of, 68–70
  and telecommunications, 35, 49, 53, 55,
    65–6, 69–70, 78, 83–4
  wireless spectrum management by, 3, 65,
    69–72, 168
  working practices of, 67–9
Oftel (Office of Telecommunications),
    53, 66, 70
online media services, 43, 104–5, 109

Peacock, Alan, 98–9
Peacock, Matt, 51, 120
Peyton, John, 47
Phalen, P.F., 41–2
PhonepayPlus, 66, 82
pirate radio stations, 164–6
Press Complaints Commission, 66
privacy, protection of, 44, 65–6, 81, 88, 127
public administration, 9–11, 21–2, 29, 38–9,
    182, 186–9
Public Bodies Bill (2010), 180–2
public engagement, 7–9, 16, 35, 38, 64, 104,
    120, 178
  and Ofcom, 17, 77–81, 102, 108, 184–5,
    187–9
public service broadcasting, 2, 12, 16,
    36, 94–9
  and the BBC, 94–5, 97–9
  and the European Union, 31–2, 96
  and Ofcom, 70, 94, 99–115, 183, 187, 190
  in the US, 96
public service media, 16, 69
public sphere, 7–12
Public Voice, 48–50, 79
Puttnam, David, 45–8

Raboy, M., 19, 61
Radio Authority, 165–7, 169–70
Radio Joint Audience Research, 172
Redding, Don, 49
regulation, 2, 4–5, 14, 19,
  of advertising, 145–6, 148, 152–6, 159
  of community radio, 168–74
  Ofcom role in, 4, 26, 28, 30, 33, 42, 64–5,
    68–70, 89
  public perception of, 86–8
  reform of, 5–6, 23, 26–30, 33, 88,
    177–8, 181
  strategies for, 23–6
  of telecommunications, 32, 53, 66, 70
  theory of, 21–3

regulation *cont.*
  'Westminster model' of, 21
  see also co-regulation; deregulation;
    self-regulation
Reith, John, 94, 97
Rennie, E., 175
Richards, Ed, 53–5, 95, 100, 170

Satellite and Cable Broadcasting Group, 111
Scannell, P., 97
Schlesinger, P., 181
Scott, C., 23
Seaton, J., 97
Seiter, E., 137
self-regulation, 24–5, 28, 66, 69,
    117, 145
Seymour-Ure, C., 34
social and cultural policy, 11, 18–20, 31,
    33, 61, 113, 192
Spyrelli, C., 64, 77
'stakeholder economy', 28–9, 77
Stoller, T., 163–6, 169
Street, B.V., 136–7
Sujon, Z., 8

Tambini, D., 182–3
telecommunications, 2–3, 12, 26
  and Ofcom, 35, 49, 53, 55, 65–6, 69–70,
    78, 83–4
  ownership of infrastructure, 2, 12, 31, 98
  regulation of, 32, 53, 66, 70
Thatcher, Margaret, 22–3, 97–8, 178
Timms, Stephen, 133
Tomlinson, J., 1

United Nations Educational, Scientific and
    Cultural Organization (UNESCO),
    123, 125, 191
United Nations General Assembly, 60

Van Cuilenberg, J., 14, 41
Vick, D.W., 33
Voice of the Listener and Viewer (VLV),
    47, 52, 57, 79, 111

Watkins, S.C., 137
Webster, J.G., 41–2
Wei, Nat, 178
Whittle, Stephen, 52, 84
Williams, Allan, 52–3
Williams, Rhodri, 85
Wilson, D., 169–72
Wilson, Woodrow, 21–2
wireless spectrum, 3, 65, 69–72, 168
Woolgar, S., 135
World Health Organisation, 145, 147